SECOND EDITION

200+ ACTIVE
Learning Strategies
and Projects
for Engaging Students'
Multiple Intelligences

*To all teachers who are striving to make learning an active,
rewarding experience for their students.*

SECOND EDITION

200+ ACTIVE
Learning Strategies
and Projects

for Engaging Students' Multiple Intelligences

JAMES BELLANCA

CORWIN PRESS

A SAGE Company

For information:

Corwin Press
A SAGE Company
2455 Teller Road
Thousand Oaks, California 91320
www.corwinpress.com

SAGE India Pvt. Ltd.
B 1/I 1 Mohan Cooperative
   Industrial Area
Mathura Road, New Delhi
India 110 044

SAGE Ltd.
1 Oliver's Yard
55 City Road
London, EC1Y 1SP
United Kingdom

SAGE Asia-Pacific Pte. Ltd.
33 Pekin Street 02-01
Far East Square
Singapore 048763

Printed in the United States of America.

Library of Congress Cataloging-in-Publication Data

Bellanca, James A., 1937-
200+ active learning strategies and projects for engaging students' multiple intelligences /
James Bellanca.—2nd ed.
      p. cm.
Includes bibliographical references and index.
ISBN 978-1-4129-6884-3 (cloth)
ISBN 978-1-4129-6885-0 (pbk.)
   1. Active learning. 2. Activity programs in education. 3. Project method in teaching. 4. Multiple intelligences. I. Title. II. Title: Two hundred plus active learning strategies and projects for engaging students' multiple intelligences.

LB1027.23.B448 2009
371.39—dc22   2008038228

This book is printed on acid-free paper.

08   09   10   11   12   10 9 8 7 6 5 4 3 2 1

Acquisitions Editor:	Cathy Hernandez
Associate Editor:	Desirée A. Bartlett
Editorial Assistant:	Sarah Bartlett
Production Editor:	Eric Garner
Copy Editor:	Alison Hope
Typesetter:	C&M Digitals (P) Ltd.
Proofreader:	Susan Schon
Indexer:	Ellen Slavitz
Cover Designer:	Karine Hovsepian

Contents

Preface to the Second Edition

If you ever had the chance to go hiking or canoeing into the backcountry, you will remember those freeze-dried meals. Light to carry, fast to prepare, high in nutrition, but short on taste and tough on the senses. Remember how you couldn't wait to have real food as soon as you returned home? And remember the days you sat in classroom lessons that were just as dry, tasteless, and oh so unappealing to look at? Even when the lesson was packed with meaty material, remember how you couldn't wait for the bell to ring?

When I did my student teaching, my critic teacher and first mentor made me think hard and deep about my responsibility to interest and challenge my students. Her method to engage and enrich students was to ask over and over four simple questions: "What were you expected to do?," "What did you do well?," "What do you need to do differently the next time?," and "How can I help you?" No day passed when she didn't ask her students to respond to those questions. After she had observed me teach my lessons, she would ask me these same questions. And believe me she had her antennas extended to discern any waffling. I have never forgotten her favorite admonition: "When you prepare a lesson, don't give them a freeze-dried meal. If you do, the only thing you can expect in return is a classroom of freeze-dried brains."

I quickly learned from Mrs. Potter that sumptuous meals were much more effective than the freeze-dried type. Since I was preparing to teach language arts, I had abundant opportunity to have students write, speak, and read about their own reactions to the literature prescribed in the curriculum. This was my start with active learning. "When your students leave the classroom," my critic teacher said over and over, "*they* should be taking the Tums, not you. Make them think until their stomachs hurt and you will know they are eating up what you want them to learn."

I took her mentoring to heart. Over the years, I saved those tactics and strategies that helped me to mentally engage my students. What worked best to activate their learning? I also added ideas that I picked up from colleagues, from advanced coursework, and from other mentors. Selections from that collection comprised the first edition of this book.

I am now at the second edition. In addition to gathering feedback from teachers who used these ideas, I have measured the many tactics, strategies, and projects against the emerging research studies for much of the material. What I had learned in my student teaching and in the following years about active learning was often the result of intuition about what would most help students engage. There were no scientific studies on thinking skills or on group projects for many of the other approaches I used. Since then, the research field has grown and researchers have measured what works best in raising student achievement and enriching student thinking. These studies have helped refine what approaches are most worth the time and effort to enrich student learning.

In this second edition, I have made changes that many who already used its principal contents have suggested will make the book's use simpler and better.

The first change is the book's title. I wanted the new title to signal more about what active learning, the original title, will do for you and your students. "Active learning" describes only the surface. You will get your students active by using your selection of the tactics, strategies, and projects described here. Just to do the cooperative learning activities collected under the "interpersonal intelligence" means they have to move their bodies. The activity, however, is not just about moving bodies so that their limbs don't atrophy. It is about engaging their minds in the content of your curriculum so that their brains don't atrophy. Along with cooperative learning tactics, they will find that you have selected multiple ways to activate their many intelligences. As the various strategies you select pump energy into the brain cells and encourage the dendrites to grow, you see before your eyes how your students are learning faster and smarter—not just for that moment, but for a lifetime of greater academic success as they learn by and from their doing.

FORMAT CHANGES

Let me start by identifying the changes in each guide's format. These changes should make the guides simpler to use.

1. To increase the variety and to align and update the teaching guides with the ever-evolving literature on proven practice, I replaced close to two dozen of the original two hundred activities.

2. To enrich the remaining guides and to better align them with literature that has emerged since the first edition, especially the research on learning tactics, I have modified the substance of another 170 teaching guides. In addition, I have cross-referenced the strategies and projects with numbered tactics. These cross-references are designed for use by those of you who are selecting a lesson or project that incorporates one or more of the research-backed tactics.

3. In each teaching guide, I have added a recommendation about the most appropriate grade levels for using the guide. In many cases, such as if you are teaching in grades that the activity does not target, you may wish to adjust the guide by making your own age-adjusted variations. In many cases, age-appropriate adjustments are suggested in the *variation* section at the end of each guide.

4. At the recommendation of teachers who have drawn from the first edition, I have changed the "What-to-Do" outline in several ways. First, I changed it from a list of numbered instructions to a checklist of important procedures. This will allow you to copy the list of procedures or place them on a computer screen so that you can have them as a quick reference guide when you are first using the guide. After you become competent and confident in using a tactic or policy, you can readily set aside the guide. The guide also allows you to discuss each step and plan modifications with a colleague who will observe and give feedback on the learning experience. This may be especially helpful when you are first learning to use a tactic or project.

5. At the end of each guide, I have added a list of other intelligences that are activated in the guide. These speak to the intent of Gardner's theory that it is important for students to develop multiple intelligences.

6. I have added a resource section at the back of the book that guides you in the design of your own active learning experiences or helps you modify your favorites.

CONTENT CHANGES

Second, I have made changes that are more subtle. These changes are designed to increase the impact of the activity on the students' active learning experiences.

1. I have more closely aligned the teaching guides with what the research says about increasing student achievement. This starts with the understanding that when teachers activate students' brains, they not only help students recall information in the short term, but also help students physically change the structure of the brain so that the students become more-efficient learners. (Feuerstein, Feuerstein, & Rand, 2007). This change happens because of the students' change from being passive receptacles of information to active makers of learning. The more actively students engage their minds in a learning task, the faster and smarter they are able to learn.

2. The emerging, validated brain research reinforces much of the best research on student achievement. As reflected in Marzano, Pickering, and Pollack (2001) such instructional strategies as comparing, summarizing, hypothesizing, and asking questions not only induce achievement, but also—when used well and regularly—develop students with well-refined learning skills that strengthen their cognitive functioning and mental operations (Feuerstein et al., 2007). For this reason, I have replaced those first edition teaching guides that were less aligned with these principles of brain and achievement research with guides that incorporate one or more of the best practices. If you are targeting one or more of these high-effect strategies as a pathway to higher achievement for your students, I recommend you keep your own journal of the different tactics related to each of these strategies. For instance, if you are trying to build a learning community, you will want to keep a list of all the tactics and projects you use from this book on cooperative learning and the interpersonal intelligence. Star those that you found work especially well with your students. Do the same with other strategies such as summarizing and hypothesizing that are interspersed among several intelligences.

3. I have rewritten the introduction to reflect best uses of the "learning smarter" approach. The introduction now includes a discussion of the theories of learning transfer and mediated learning experiences as each applies to transforming students into more efficient learners. Included in this discussion is a more explicit description of the importance of creating the classroom as a learning community and the role of cooperative learning not only to make group work more efficient, but also to make the classroom learning environment more supportive of students' transfer of learning.

WHAT HAS NOT CHANGED IN THIS EDITION?

This new edition reinforces the belief that active learning more strongly engages students' minds and better prepares them for a lifetime of learning. This engagement enriches the immediate learning by increasing students' will to learn. The increased will to learn, the essence of intrinsic motivation, attracts students to the tasks they are asked to do as they "eat up" the curriculum.

When properly structured and infused with instructional tactics and strategies, active learning helps the students gather, make sense of, and understand the key concepts outlined in the **standards** in a more efficient manner. As students learn from these experiences and apply their new "how-to-learn" strategies to their next set of learning challenges, they establish themselves as efficient learners. Like a racecar driver who not only learns how to maneuver a car, but also learns how to win races, these students learn the basics and become better and better each time they get behind the wheel of learning. Like the racecar drivers, the more the students learn from each experience about how to learn, the more their potential grows. In this context, we can say with confidence that the benefits of active learning extend to all students, in all situations, as the best option not only for raising their test scores, but also for transforming them into more effective learners for a lifetime and for expanding their learning potential.

Acknowledgments

I offer my deepest appreciation to the many mentors and collaborators who made the content of this book possible. From Peggy Pink, my department chairperson at New Trier High School, who encouraged me as a young teacher to attend my first active participation workshop, to my SkyLight colleagues Robin Fogarty and Kay Burke, who invented new practices at a frenetic pace, my life thoughts and teaching have been enriched by an endless number of master teachers. These include Merrill Harman, Howie Kirschenbaum, and Sidney Simon, the three teachers who conducted that first workshop. Through Howie and the Sagamore Institute, I add Joel Goodman and Margie Ingram, Eliott Masie, Rod Napier, Roger Johnson, David Johnson, and Jack Canfield. Through Roger and David, I can chart what I learned from Bob Slavin, Elizabeth Cohen, Richard Schmuck, and Shlomo and Yael Sharan. Searching for answers to questions about active learning led me to Art Costa, John Barell, and others who focused me on the active engagement of the mind.

Beyond the classroom, I owe Larry Chase, Phil Harris, Mary Kay Kickles, Marie Meyers, Bill Peters, and a long, long list of classroom teachers for encouraging the application of active learning practices to our teacher-training programs. Foremost among the teachers were my inspired and inspiring colleagues at New Trier's Center for Self-Directed Learning—Bob Applebaum, Bill Gregory, Vernoy Johnson, and Arlene Paul—who demonstrated and proved "way back when" the power and the benefit of classrooms where students were the core of active engagement in authentic learning experiences.

Finally, I want to honor the thinking of Reuven Feuerstein. I also want to thank my colleagues Shannon Almquist, Kate Bellanca, and Meir Ben Hur. Their understanding and deep, practical knowledge of Feuerstein's Theory of Structural Cognitive Modifiability, and their passion for stretching every student beyond imposed limits of learning with the theory and practices of Mediated Learning Experiences has deepened my own understanding of how to help all students become more engaged and successful learners.

To each and every one, I say, "Thank you."

PUBLISHER'S ACKNOWLEDGMENTS

Corwin Press gratefully acknowledges the contributions of the following individuals:

Debbie Christian
Third-Grade Teacher
Anderson Elementary School
Reno, NV

Ken Garwick
Retired Elementary School Teacher
Manhattan, KS

Pam Jackson
Alternative Seventh-Grade Teacher
Elkhorn Middle School
Frankfort, KY

Rebecca Joseph
Assistant Professor of Curriculum & Instruction
California State University, Los Angeles
Los Angeles, CA

Judy Steinel
Teacher
Eleanor Roosevelt High School
Greenbelt, MD

About the Author

James Bellanca. After twelve years as an award-winning teacher, Jim's career shifted. He was asked to lead teams of teachers in finding better ways to enrich students' learning experiences. In the following ten years, he developed two innovative alternative school programs, a Regional Special Education Professional Development Program and a Regional Service Center for Professional Development. In 1982, he founded SkyLight Publishing and Professional Development, Inc. Through that company, he championed the introduction of best instructional practices including cooperative learning, the asking of questions, multiple intelligences, and cognitive instruction. Collaborating with Ron Brandt, Carolyn Chapman, Art Costa, Reuven Feuerstein, Robin Fogarty, Howard Gardner, Madeline Hunter, Roger and David Johnson, and other leaders in the professional development arena, Jim developed pioneering publications and programs to provide teachers with the most practical ways to use these strategies. At the same time, he authored and coauthored more than two dozen books that introduced the intensive use of instructional strategies for improving achievement. Among his publications are *What Is It About Me That You Can't Teach?*, *Graphic Organizers*, *Multiple Assessments for Multiple Intelligences*, *BluePrints for Achievement in the Cooperative Classroom*, and *Professional Development for Change*.

Introduction

Mr. Ali frowned. "Rosita, I don't understand," he said. "You spent the entire period sketching me talking to the class. You didn't take a single note. What were you thinking?"

Rosita shrugged, "I don't know. When you're talking to us it's like I don't hear a word."

"You didn't hear a word I said?" asked the teacher.

"No, but what I *saw* made a lot of sense to me."

All the time Mr. Ali was delivering his well-organized lecture on the principles of culture, Rosita had paid close attention, but she didn't hear a word he said. Instead, her fingers squeezed her thick lead pencil and sketched the details of her teacher's face. Over and over, she caught his many expressions from different angles until she had a collage of heads. Now, it was difficult for him to comprehend what was going on in the head of this articulate student who drew so well.

This is one example of an intelligence clash. A lecturing teacher is an example of an individual with a strong verbal/linguistic preference. As learning psychologist Howard Gardner (1983) has characterized, individuals with this intelligence, which is the type that dominates curriculum and instruction in most schools, are bound to be successful when the ability to use the written and spoken word is dominant. A daydreaming, doodling student, on the other hand, has a dominant visual/spatial intelligence. That student doesn't focus on words. He focuses on the images, processes the pictures, and ends the class period not with notes but with sketches.

This clash of intelligences may seem extreme. Following Gardner's theory to its logical conclusion, though, it is easier to understand why the way many students learn and understand doesn't seem to fit the dominant intelligences implicit in most teaching that happens in classrooms. Students in contemporary classrooms are most likely to be taught by teachers who have a well-developed verbal/linguistic (words) or logical/mathematical (numbers) intelligence. On the one hand, if a student's intelligence aligns with one or both of these intelligences, that student has a better chance of understanding the assigned schoolwork, earning higher grades, and testing well on the standardized tests that measure in terms of those two intelligences. On the other hand, if the student is strong in one of the other intelligences identified by Gardner, she may not do as well in the school setting as her counterpart who identifies with the verbal/linguistic or logical/mathematical intelligence.

GARDNER'S MULTIPLE INTELLIGENCES

Verbal/linguistic intelligence is the intelligence of words, or the ability to use the core operations of language with clarity. The significant components of this intelligence are employed by communicating through reading, writing, listening, or speaking. More important, the use of this intelligence helps link prior knowledge and understanding to new information and explains how the linkage occurs. The verbal/linguistic intelligence enables personal perceptions to be communicated and is highly valued in schools.

Verbal/linguistic intelligence helps students produce and refine language use in many formats. The ability to form and recognize words and their patterns by sight, sound, and—for some—touch is a start. The techniques of language, such as metaphor, hyperbole, symbol, and grammar, are next. These are enriched with meaning by abstract reasoning, conceptual patterns, feeling, tone, structure, and an expanding vocabulary across the curriculum. Ultimately, the peaks of language development are reached by those who combine sound and sense in unique patterns to express themselves.

The value of the verbal/linguistic intelligence is emphasized through testing reading and language arts and comprehension in other content areas. How well a student performs in mathematics, for instance, is interwoven with his ability to comprehend the test questions.

Logical/mathematical intelligence is the intelligence of numbers and reasoning, or the ability to use inductive and deductive reasoning, solve abstract problems, and understand the complex relationships of interrelated concepts, ideas, and things.

This intelligence includes the skills of classifying, predicting, prioritizing, formulating scientific hypotheses, and understanding cause-and-effect relationships. Reasoning skills apply to a broad array of areas and include using logical thinking in science, social studies, literature, and other areas such as word processing, creating and reading spreadsheets, learning a foreign language, building a model, using the Internet, and "reading" music (learning to interpret musical notation).

Young children develop this intelligence as they work with concrete manipulatives and grasp the concept of one-to-one relationships and numeration. They advance from concrete to representational ideas in the form of symbolic language, working equations, and formulas they learn about abstraction through the world of logic. The critical thinking skills of sequencing, analyzing, and estimating are taught in most school curricula, but need to be emphasized through active learning activities.

Visual/spatial intelligence is the intelligence of pictures and images, or the capacity to perceive the visual world accurately and to recreate visual experiences. It involves the ability to see form, color, shape, and texture in the "mind's eye" and to transfer these to concrete representation in art forms.

This intelligence begins with the sharpening of sensorimotor perceptions. The eye discriminates color, shape, form, texture, spatial depth, dimension, and relationships. As the intelligence develops, hand-eye coordination and small-muscle control enable the individual to reproduce the perceived shapes and colors in a variety of media. The painter, sculptor, architect, gardener, cartographer, drafter, and graphic designer all transfer images in their minds to the new object they are creating or improving. In this way, visual perceptions are mixed with prior knowledge, experience, emotions, and images to create a new vision for others to experience.

Bodily/kinesthetic intelligence is the intelligence of the whole body,. This intelligence enables us to control and interpret body motions, manipulate physical objects, and establish harmony between the mind and the body. The Spartans of ancient Greece built their culture around the importance of the body, its looks, and its performance. The modern Olympic Games carry on this tradition.

It is a mistake, however, to think that the development of this intelligence is limited to athletics. A surgeon's fine small-motor control when performing an intricate operation or an airplane navigator's ability to fine-tune the instruments also are developments of this intelligence.

Musical/rhythmic intelligence is the intelligence of tone, rhythm, and timbre. It starts with the degree of sensitivity one has to a pattern of sounds and the ability to respond emotionally. As students develop their musical awareness, they develop the fundamentals of this intelligence.

This intelligence grows as students increase their sophistication when listening to music. It further develops as students create more complex and subtler variations of musical patterns, develop talent on musical instruments, and advance to complex compositions.

Interpersonal intelligence is the intelligence of social understanding, or the ability to understand and relate to others. Those exhibiting this intelligence notice and distinguish moods, temperaments, motivations, and intentions. For example, at a simple level this intelligence is seen in children who notice and are sensitive to the moods of the adults around them. A more complex interpersonal skill is an adult's ability to read and interpret the hidden intentions of others.

This intelligence includes the capacity to understand and interact with other people with a win-win result. Interpersonal intelligence involves verbal and nonverbal communication skills, collaborative skills, conflict management, consensus-building skills, and the ability to trust, respect, lead, and motivate others to the achievement of a mutually beneficial goal. Empathy for feelings, fears, anticipations, and beliefs of others, the willingness to listen without judging, and the desire to help others raise their level of performance to its highest are all critical traits of those with a strong interpersonal intelligence.

Intrapersonal intelligence is the intelligence of self-knowledge, or the ability to know oneself and assume responsibility for one's life and learning. The individual with a strong intrapersonal intelligence is able to understand his or her range of emotions and draw on them to direct her behavior. This individual thrives on time to think, to reflect, and to complete **self-assessments**. The need for such introspection makes this intelligence the most private. In Gardner's words, "the intrapersonal intelligence amounts to little more than the capacity to distinguish a feeling of pleasure from one of pain and, on the basis of such discrimination, to become more involved in or to withdraw from a situation" (1983, 239).

This intelligence enables learners to take greater responsibility for their lives and learning. Too few students, Gardner suggests, realize they can take responsibility for their learning, especially when they attend schools that base recognition of achievements on external motivations.

Naturalist intelligence, which Gardner added to his original seven in 1995, is the intelligence of nature and springs from an individual's ability to recognize species of plants and animals in the environment and to create taxonomies that classify the many different subspecies. Individuals such as John Audubon, Rachel Carson, Charles Darwin, and Jane Goodall are well-known naturalists. Young children who can pick out different types of flowers, name different types of animals, or even arrange such items as shoes, cars, or designer clothes into common categories are budding naturalists.

The connection to naturalistic learning is obvious in botany and zoology; individuals who work in organic chemistry, entomology, medicine, photography, civil engineering, and a host of other fields also must develop their naturalist skills.

MINIMALIST APPROACH REJECTED

In the past decade, the conflict between teachers' and schools' dominant intelligences and the divergent intelligences of many students has become more evident. No Child Left

Behind's compulsive emphasis on measurement of the logical/mathematical and verbal/linguistic intelligences, the intelligences most aligned with traditional school, has played an enormous role in dousing interest in developing students' many other intelligences. As a result, the visual and musical arts, sciences, and other curricula that traditionally encouraged students to learn in their own ways are being threatened. Schools are responding to declining funding and increasing student populations by taking a minimalist approach, demanding programs that teach with the fastest reading and arithmetic results and the least fuss.

What is this minimalist approach? In the past several decades, textbook publishers, influenced by social forces, have perfected product lines that align curriculum, instruction, and assessment while attaining minimal content standards. The publishers, some owned by conglomerates that also own the test-making companies, have led the way in making it necessary for schools and teachers to show results by the measurement of the lowest common denominator skills and competencies. What is measurable? So far, the testing companies can measure isolated bits and pieces of verbal and numerical information. Test makers have yet to find a valid or reliable way to measure how well students understand information or how well they transfer what they have learned. As a result of the importance placed on measurable standards, teacher-proof classrooms have been created that require teachers to follow a strict curriculum and that allow little flexibility for the teacher to be creative or to tailor teaching style to the needs of the students. The emphasis, especially in the early grades, is on the accumulation of memorized minutia in the verbal and numerical arenas.

Among those who oppose the minimalist approach are Richard Murnane, a Harvard economist, and Frank Levy, an MIT economist, who together wrote *Teaching the New Basic Skills: Principles for Educating Children to Thrive in a Changing Economy* (1996). They argue that, despite a changing economic structure, schools have retained a nineteenth-century minimalist curriculum. Murnane and Levy show the mismatch between the knowledge and skills needed to survive in a modern, high-performing workplace and those that are being taught in today's schools.

Murnane and Levy do not deny the need for mathematics and literacy. They do question the low level of these skills that are expected as well as the nonemphasis given to working in teams (interpersonal intelligence), solving problems (intrapersonal intelligence), and the ability to organize information (logical/mathematical intelligence).

BEYOND LEARNING FOR RECALL

Other voices add hard facts that support the idea that teaching and learning are more than just the recall of facts and figures. Among these are Anne Brown and Anne Palincsar (1989), who have shown the powerful effects of metacognition. Their work with reciprocal teaching, a key active learning strategy, illustrates what can happen when teachers have the opportunity to focus students' attention on the process of reading by developing students' abilities to make predictions in their reading material.

Israeli cognitive psychologist Reuven Feuerstein also adds his voice and strong evidence that the minimalist measurement school is doing a great disservice to students, especially those who come to school unready. Feuerstein and colleagues (2007) has demonstrated how challenging cognitive approaches can lead to radical changes in learning performance, even by students labeled "unteachable." The success of his program,

Instrumental Enrichment, which changes cognitive performance, depends on a process called "mediation."

The double goal of Feuerstein's approach is (1) transforming students into more efficient learners and (2) teaching for potential. These goals enable a teacher who is prepared to help children discover their capacity to compare, ask questions, and hypothesize as they solve more and more complex problems and to do more than read from a script. Research studies show improved learning performance when teachers as mediators of thinking and **problem solving** have the time and support to help students learn how to be active generators of knowledge rather than passive receptors of factual information.

Gardner, Feuerstein, Brown, and Palincsar are but a few who have demonstrated through research the benefits of learning in ways that challenge students to go beyond what is measurable. When challenging students, they argue, educators need to realize that there are many more ways to teach than by rote alone. There is teaching for understanding, decision making, problem solving, and connecting a part to a whole, detail to concept, and concept to concept. There also is inference, prediction, analysis for bias, and learning for transfer. Each of these processes requires some form of critical thinking. If students are going to attain and exceed instructional standards, they must develop and learn to use skillfully the processes of thinking and learning the content in the standards-based curricula. The more efficiently students can compare, contrast, raise questions, prove hypotheses, and perform the other thinking operations inherent in the standards, the better they will do on their annual state-standards tests and the more successfully they will be in learning the more rigorous content to follow in the next years of schooling.

To deepen understanding, students must learn to gather and process information with precision and accuracy from multiple sources, and learn to transfer new concepts across the curriculum and forward into advanced studies. Unlike bygone days when information was selected and passed along through a teacher's lecture or a textbook, information in a high-tech world comes from a plethora of sources, of which only two are the teacher and the textbook. Television, the World Wide Web, CD-ROMs, and other research tools place students in the role of selective information gatherers. In order to choose wisely from a variety of sources, students who learn to analyze data for bias, make correct inferences, classify, and synthesize are better prepared to understand and use information from a multitude of sources. Students with these skills have the gates to the future open to them.

How well students understand and process data determines how well they perform in a variety of learning experiences and how well prepared they are for the world of work tasks. In the classroom, how students decipher the meaning of classic literature or complete a science project—not just how they memorize tables and formulas—prepares them to use these understandings and insights in life. It also better prepares students to pass more easily through the SAT or ACT test gates. How well students apply problem-solving processes to algebra or geometry helps them through trigonometry and calculus, and gives them the essential tools for advanced mathematical study. Younger students who learn only computation or how to memorize facts may test well in the short run, but they will have much less chance to develop the necessary skills for lifelong achievement in mathematics, science, law, or medicine. Whenever schools fail to develop students' cognitive functions, the schools destroy the students' opportunities for mastering the more rigorous upper-grade curriculum. When students leave the high school unready to think critically and creatively, the graduates are condemned to struggle in college. Without success in college, these students enter our high-tech work world unprepared.

TRANSFER-ORIENTED CURRICULUM

Any curriculum designed to promote students as critical thinkers must allow time for teachers to work on the development of the thinking processes to the point of transfer. This works best when the teaching of critical thinking is the foundation on which other teaching builds. In order for the content curriculum to develop students' understanding, teachers need to develop students' cognitive skills that are implicit in the content. For example, in the fourth-grade reading curriculum, the teacher will have to teach students how to draw inferences and make predictions. In the ninth-grade writing curriculum, the teacher needs to teach students how to connect specific arguments to general statements and apply those across many content areas.

Using a critical-thinking approach to curriculum challenges teachers to develop instructional techniques that will help students prepare for the world beyond the school walls. Critical-thinking approaches develop students' abilities to understand and transfer what they are learning to real-world situations. As Perkins and Salomon (1988) point out, teaching for transfer doesn't just happen: skilled teachers shepherd the transfer across the curriculum and beyond the school walls. In a *transfer-oriented instruction* mode, a critical-thinking curriculum opens the door to authentic assessments that can tell teachers what students know and what students can do. Authentic assessment techniques such as observation checklists and video demonstrations go well beyond short-answer tests. These tools not only tell what factual information the student recalls, but they also show how well the student can use knowledge and skills in novel situations. In a fact-based classroom, students may match chemical symbols with the proper element name, while in a transfer-based classroom, a teacher can check how well the student uses his or her knowledge of chemical elements to complete an experiment. By combining elements from both fact-based and transfer-oriented strategies, a language arts teacher can not only give a fill-in-the-blank quiz to check what punctuation the sixth grade students can identify, she can also set criteria for the use of punctuation in an essay and look to see that students can use the punctuation rules in their essays.

Opportunities for students to develop critical-thinking processes are not found in classrooms dominated by the regurgitation of short answers. They are found in classrooms where active engagement of the students' minds strengthens the ways their brains function and makes them more efficient learners, whichever intelligence they are using.

ACTIVE LEARNING

Active learning operates at many levels in any classroom that challenges students to learn smarter. At the first level, teachers make skilled and extensive use of instructional tactics that have proven their impact on student achievement. These tactics, most of which are included in the meta-studies of the most effective strategies (Marzano et al., 2001), give students an equitable chance to engage their minds regularly during every class period and throughout the school day. They must use their brains. The more students have to use their brains, the more complex the brain's wiring becomes. The more complex the wiring, the more data the brain is able to store for later recall. In this sense, the packed wiring enriches the students' storehouse of knowledge.

Instructional tactics such as the **graphic organizers** (**webs**, **concept maps**, **T-Charts**, and so on) or cooperative learning tools (**think-pair-share**, roles, guidelines, and so on), fall under the research categories labeled strategies (nonrepresentational figures, cooperative learning, asking questions, and so on). When carefully selected and integrated into content-strong lessons or projects, the tactics enrich Gardner's multiple intelligences (visual/spatial, interpersonal, verbal/linguistic, and so on) and Feuerstein's criteria for effective mediated learning experiences (meaning, regulation of behavior, and so on).

Using instructional tactics engages students' minds and enables them to transform how they learn from a passive state to an active state in which they are generators of knowledge. As they intertwine various tactics through the lessons, teachers heighten students' chances to increase their achievement and to develop lifelong learning habits.

With instructional tactics, teachers may plan sequences of tasks or whole lessons and projects that develop targeted intelligences and enrich others at the same time. For instance, teachers electing to appeal to the bodily/kinesthetic intelligence may select basic bodily/kinesthetic activities such as the **carousel**, **human graph**, or **four corners** that require physical movement as they complete a social studies lesson studying the Westward Movement. By using such tactics as **think-pair-share**, **round-robin responses**, **journals**, and the **question web**, teachers enrich instruction, increase engagement, and expose students to development of other intelligences such as verbal/linguistic and visual/spatial.

At a more complex level, the active learning teacher constructs learning experiences that require students to work hands on. First-grade students may discover patterns (visual/spatial) by building simple houses with colored blocks. Middle school students may study buoyancy (naturalistic) by floating pumpkins, oranges, and pine nuts in a sink. Eighth-graders may investigate the justice system by holding a mock trial (verbal/linguistic), and high school geometry students may study radius and circumference with tape measures and paper plates of many sizes (logical/mathematical) or use their visual/spatial intelligence to study the use of triangles in a modern skyscraper.

In each of these experiences, teachers will use tactics that compound the learning effects. For instance, in the geometry lesson teachers may use an advanced organizer such as the **KWL** graphic to help students ascertain their prior knowledge (see Activity 54), or may use formal **cooperative groups** (see Activity 128) to help students gather information and create a **matrix** to make sense of the information. Using lead-in statements (see Activity 9), teachers will prompt students to make daily journal entries (see Activity 153) that record what they are learning and lead to a final summary (see Activity 129). To promote transfer of the content they have learned about geometry, teachers will assign students to make a poster (see Activity 61) that communicates their deepened understandings.

At the highest level, active learning uses the active engagement of the students' thinking processes in gathering new information, making sense of new ideas, and applying new knowledge. There are five elements in an effective learning experience that especially engage students as mindful learners: the focus activity, cooperative structure, mediation, transfer, and self-assessment.

Three Phases of Learning

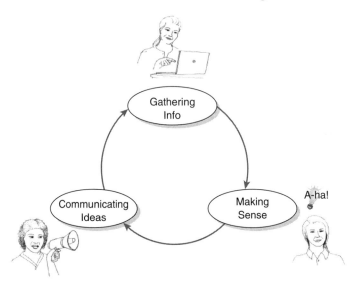

Focus Activity

In large group instruction, the active-engagement teacher designs the lesson or project to enable all students for gathering information through several intelligence-based strategies. These strategies focus reluctant learners on the lesson and invite them to reciprocate with their interest. There are many simple tactics and strategies with which a teacher can stimulate this focus. For example, the teacher may use **wraparounds**, **three-level questions**, **think-pair-shares**, or **random checks** to prompt student responses and promote the active gathering of information for the lesson.

Cooperative Structure

The active-engagement teacher designs learning experiences that involve all students in collaborative, hands-on tasks related to the curricular goal and to the targeted intelligence. The teacher assigns group roles, coaches active participation, checks for understanding, assesses contributions and knowledge gained, and posts performance **rubrics** (see Activity 8). Students learn content by working in a cooperative and interpersonal structure, performing assigned roles, assisting others in learning, and sharing responsibility for a group goal. Based on their intention to differentiate instruction, teachers may use different-sized groups (e.g., pairs, trios, or groups of five), formal or informal groups, and groups of mixed abilities or talents (see Activity 145). They may also use groups of similar abilities, interests, or talents (see Activity 128). Differentiated instruction allows teachers to use a variety of criteria to mix group make-up. Most commonly, these cooperative groups are mixed by academic ability. Other mixes by gender, special interests, intelligences, or learning style are possible.

Mediation

The teacher mediates each student's achievement of curricular goals in a variety of ways. These ways always include intention, reciprocity, meaning, and transcendence. Teachers may also mediate challenge, feelings of competence, and planning behaviors. At other times, the teacher challenges students to change, individuates instruction, promotes sharing behavior, and encourages self-regulation of behavior. As a result of the teachers' interventions, students set goals, develop control of their own behavior, make connections among ideas, explain reasons why something has happened when responding to questions, and develop their reflective thinking habits. In short, students learn how to be more efficient learners through teachers' mediation.

Transfer

The active-engagement teacher shows students how to understand a specific lesson but also how to transfer new understanding into other content areas and life situations. To promote transfer, the teacher identifies implicit thinking processes, labels and demonstrates the thinking, structures tasks requiring thinking processes, and teaches strategies that facilitate the bridging of ideas into other content areas. Students describe and plan thinking processes and monitor and assess their own thinking processes. Very often, the teacher may rely on graphic organizers that stimulate the visual/spatial intelligence as students attempt to build **bridges** that will transport an idea into a new topic, curricular area, or life situation (see Activity 47).

Self-Assessment

The active-engagement teacher evaluates student learning by using a variety of assessment approaches. These approaches include teacher-made tests that gauge recall, understanding, and application; rubrics for performance, products, and projects (see Activity 8); student self-assessments and reflections (see Activity 176); and a variety of evidences such as written and oral responses and videos. Students perform self-assessments, keep **portfolios** of their work, and reflect on standards of performance through journal writing and other guided activities that stimulate a variety of intelligences and build lifelong learning habits.

Structuring an Engaging Environment for Learning

By using Gardner's (1983) theory of multiple intelligences, a teacher who is increasing student engagement will highlight ways to structure an environment so that it also contributes to the principles and practices that best engage students more deeply in their academic work. On one level, Gardner's theory helps teachers select active and engaging instructional methods that enrich the varied intelligences. For students who learn best by seeing and touching, the teacher can include active learning strategies and materials that challenge their visual/spatial and bodily/kinesthetic intelligences. For students who learn better through reflection, the curriculum can include **paired think-alouds** and journal responses that spark the intrapersonal intelligence.

Since most current curricula are tailored to the verbal/linguistic and logical/ mathematical intelligences, it is especially important for the teacher to engage the many students who learn better through the other six intelligences by including a variety of intelligence-appropriate strategies, lessons, and projects. By using brain-enriching strategies that awaken and engage one or more of the eight intelligences, the teacher gives all students a more equitable chance to learn and remember even the most challenging material. In the elementary and middle grades, teachers have a special chance to create a modifying environment in which all students are more willing to accept their peers' different intelligences as well as to take greater risks in expanding their own multiple intelligences.

By designing brain-enriching tactics and strategies that engage each student's strongest learning tendencies, a teacher evens out the learning field. An equal learning field provides each student, regardless of wealth, race, natural origin, sex, or past success pattern in school, with a better chance to succeed academically. By using a variety of strategies representative of all the intelligences, the teacher can make great strides toward the goal of "equity," and provide each student with a fairer opportunity to learn in their naturally dominant intelligence as well as develop the others.

THE CHALLENGE PRINCIPLE

Reuven Feuerstein (2001), the Israeli cognitive psychologist whose lifework is dedicated to finding how to best help students develop their intelligence, has developed systems for mediating those students that others have labeled as "impossible to teach." These systems have proven successful around the world. The systems develop students' cognitive functions in a purposeful and systematic way so that students experience success step by step as they build their learning skills.

Called Instrumental Enrichment, the systems help students learn how to use their many intelligences more efficiently by increasing the level of challenge in each new task. When these systems are not available to students, Feuerstein's model provides teachers with a better understanding of what it takes to transform students into more-intelligent learners. Although he stresses the primacy of cognition, Feuerstein notes that no pathway should be closed to helping students develop their learning capabilities. If the theory of multiple intelligences can assist in this task by having teachers recognize students' different learning pathways, that theory is valuable for helping students become more efficient and effective learners.

Consider students in two different elementary classrooms. In one, the teacher hands out a worksheet with fifty fill-in-the-blank questions about a story they have just read. The students are instructed to fill in the blanks as the teacher monitors their work. One-half hour later the teacher tells the students to pass their worksheets forward. The worksheets are set aside for the teacher to grade at home. In the next half hour, students may complete true and false statements on another worksheet or do similar pencil-and-paper tasks. The pattern continues throughout the school day. Teachers reward those who complete enough pages and punish the slaggards, usually with more worksheets.

In another classroom, a teacher committed to creating a community of actively engaged learners divides the class into mixed-ability groups of three, giving each group the same three short stories. The teacher then reviews with the class the goals for the reading lesson, presents a rubric showing expectations, and invites the students in each group to share how they will help each other reach those goals. As the students work, the teacher walks among the groups to coach, provide information, and note progress. After a designated period, the teacher guides the students through a review of what they have learned and the problem-solving skills they used to compare the three stories. After the review, the teacher gives the students feedback on what they did well, and prepares them for the next, more difficult reading task.

When teachers follow a successful learning experience with a more difficult task in the same vein, Feuerstein teaches that they mediate challenge. This experience is similar to that of an advanced skater when she masters a difficult jump or spin, after which she moves to the next level of difficulty. Doing a single axel well is good, but it is not enough to keep the skater's interest. The skater needs to move on to the double, the triple, and, eventually, multiple combinations that are more challenging.

What are the specific responsibilities of the teachers who understand the motivational value of challenge in the engaged classroom? First, the teachers present an open and excited attitude about taking on a challenge. When students show concern, the teachers acknowledge the difficulty of the challenge, empathize, and provide support and encouragement. "Remember," the teachers say, "how you did on the last tough assignment. Together we can do this one, too."

Second, the teachers prepare a sequence of increasingly complex tasks and chart the pathway to success. Instead of boring, repetitive worksheets that just get done, the teachers provide engaging and enriching learning opportunities that are increasingly difficult.

Third, the teachers structure tasks that require students to take risks. They help students consider a variety of ways to overcome doubts and fears, and to finish the task.

Fourth, the teachers coach their students. While students are engaged in their active learning tasks, the active-learning teachers walk among their students like a coach at practice. During the walk, they observe, check for understanding, reinforce, provide suggestions, and prompt the students. When the students don't appear to need coaching, the teachers keep quiet.

Finally, the teachers teach strategies that students can use to handle their personal difficult challenges in a self-directed way. To do this, the teachers build in the time for students to apply new problem-solving strategies to an increasingly difficult curriculum. In the challenge classroom, there is no regression to easier tasks. Success breeds success in each more-difficult step.

The multiple intelligences prism allows teachers to design lessons that follow the challenge principle. In addition to allowing the teacher to teach students established and strong ways of learning, the teacher can design ways to introduce and improve other ways of learning. Thus in any lesson, unit, or project the teacher can integrate several intelligences. This is so even when the curriculum, such as mathematics, forces a primary focus on a specific intelligence.

Consider the following example. In the fourth grade, fractions are an important unit. In a typical workbook, the logical/mathematical approach stands alone. In order to challenge students who find mathematics boring, the teacher can integrate other intelligences into the instruction of fractions. First, the teacher can present a pie or cake and have students cut it into two, four, and eight parts (bodily/kinesthetic). She can pair students (interpersonal) and assign the pairs to cut pictures of houses or offices into equal parts (bodily/kinesthetic), to divide clothespins or toothpicks into equal piles (bodily/kinesthetic), or to draw trees with a set number in each group (visual/spatial). In addition, the teacher can ask students to write a letter explaining why fractions are important (verbal/linguistic) or sing a verse about the importance of fractions (musical/rhythmic).

FROM COMMON SENSE TO RESEARCH

In the early 1960s, teachers began to make extensive use of engaged learning tasks in their lessons. At first, there was an activity focus. Activities were hands on and highlighted learning by doing. Sometimes activities were used to teach a lesson such as counting blocks to teach numeracy or making a diorama for a history project. As researchers learned more about what works they began to identify tactics that not only were active, but also engaged the students' minds. These included such purposeful acts of engagement as wait time, checking for understanding, and asking "why" and other higher-order questions. Eventually researchers Roger and David Johnson, Robert Slavin, and others identified strategies such as cooperative learning and graphic organizers that had a strong impact on student achievement. By 1991, Robert Marzano had completed his meta-analysis of which strategies were most effective.

Most of the high-effect strategies that Marzano identified are found in this book as tactics. The tactics are the subactivities within a classification called strategy. For instance, the large-group cooperative learning is called a strategy. Within that strategy, tactics include think-pair-share, three questions, group roles, 2-4-8, and others. The strategy described as "asking questions" includes such tactics as wait time, equitable distribution, and complex questions.

In the past decade, a new form of research has emerged to validate the use of tactics and strategies for active learning. In the next decade, it is likely that research on the brain from neurologists and neurological psychologists will be able to follow the path of the effectiveness researchers. Hopefully, those researchers will be able to pinpoint which of the highly effective instructional strategies and tactics do the best job of engaging minds and developing intelligences. In the meantime, teachers will have to rely on the effectiveness research and their own intuitive common sense to decide what will most benefit their students.

TAKING TIME TO ENGAGE

A common concern expressed about an engaged learning lesson is, "It takes more time." This is true. Active learning lessons *can* take more time to plan, gather materials, complete, and assess. If, however, the teacher designs the lesson or unit with student understanding and learning transfer as the final objectives, the results in terms of achievement (as measured by teacher-made and standardized test scores) by students in their understanding and ability to transfer (as measured by diverse performance assessments) will more than compensate for the increased time and effort. Students will not only produce higher test scores, but they will also develop new habits of learning that will continue to influence their learning well beyond the test day. In short, students will learn how to learn smarter. Smarter students will make up any time lost when teachers were transforming them from passive, inefficient drinkers of information to active, efficient generators of knowledge (Feuerstein et al., 2007).

In actuality, the time issue may concern only the novice users of active learning strategies. As the novice teacher-designer moves toward expert status in creating and using mind engaging lessons, he is most likely to notice the following: (1) In-class time with multidimensional lessons and projects take less time than was previously spent in one-dimensional classroom work. (2) Preparation time for each use of a well-designed active learning unit eventually becomes reduced to small bits of time for making refinements that increase student engagement and learning results even more. (3) Assessment requires less and less after-class grading time as students' observable in-class performance provides more valid and reliable data. (4) Increased student engagement propelled by students' growing intrinsic motivation to learn leads to other useful active learning strategies that students learn faster, better, smarter.

DIFFERENTIATING INSTRUCTION IN THE ENGAGED LEARNING CLASSROOM

In order to easily differentiate instruction to meet individual needs, teachers can best rely on those tactics and strategies that engage the different intelligences. By using the intelligences as a design framework, teachers can make sure that they meet the learning needs of all children regardless of how they learn best, their speed of learning, or their current interest in school.

One practical model of differentiation begins with an all-class search for information. The teacher makes a well-illustrated slideware (computer programs for presentations, such as PowerPoint) presentation accompanied by background music to review prior knowledge of a topic. (Three intelligences in one presentation—musical, visual/spatial, verbal/linguistic!) She then pairs the students to make a web of the key ideas they found in the presentation to share with another pair. (Two more intelligences—interpersonal, visual/spatial!) She checks for understanding by asking students to draw, write, or speak a summary of the main points. She samples responses until she is sure that all the points are included before she introduces the students to a hands-on experiment in which they test an hypothesis. (Another intelligence—naturalist!) The students work in homogeneous groups with the experiment and prepare collages to show their results. (More intelligences engaged—visual/spatial and interpersonal!) Finally, she asks each students to reflect on a rubric by which they can assess how they did with this task. (A grand ending with a final intelligence—intrapersonal!)

HOW TO USE THE BOOK

I selected a wide variety of active learning tools to make it easier for you and other teachers to better enable students to learn smarter. The variety of choices will help you succeed in any classroom, even with those students who have been reticent to "sit and git" as passive learners. At the most, you will have only to make minor adjustments in the guides that make the procedures, questions, and content age appropriate.

There is, however, a danger in this approach. It is easy to use many of these strategies as "filler" activities. On Friday afternoon when a unit is finished, a teacher may fill in the blank space in the schedule with a random graphic organizer or the making of a mobile. There is no more intention in these activities than to keep the students' hands busy. Using active learning strategies as an occasional filler is appropriate when a teacher wants to lighten the moment or provide a welcome release from the day's stress. However, the benefits of regular and consist use of the tactics and strategies to help students develop their many intelligences and better master their curricula go far beyond single fun fillers. At the very least, teachers can use the time for an active tactic to review or introduce the next lesson.

Using active learning for fun alone fails to take advantage of the full potential of learning strategies that transform the different ways by which students learn. Since an active learning strategy is an activity used with a specific learning purpose it is best for teachers to select a tactic or strategy so that students have the best chance of attaining a lesson's goals.

Whenever teachers are designing lessons and units, they can incorporate the following active learning principles as their guide to best use. The following principles can even serve as a rubric for assessing the quality of their design in achieving the academic goals called for in the mandated standards:

- **Differentiate the most important concepts** students need to learn through the lesson or unit.
- **Identify** the most appropriate large-group, small-group, and individual instructional strategies that will enable all students to accomplish the lesson goals.
- **Establish challenging performance standards** for both lesson content and the learning process.
- **Identify what mediated learning interactions** are necessary to ensure each student's high achievement.
- **Use an instructional design that ensures** the incorporation of the most appropriate active learning strategies. Such a strong design will

  1. start the lesson, unit, or goal with a knowledge check or provide some sort of knowledge,
  2. clarify the performance expectations,
  3. provide adequate information resources,
  4. provide clear instructions for each task,
  5. incorporate a variety of strategies individuated to multiple ways of learning,
  6. bridge learning between tasks,
  7. mediate individual achievement,
  8. provide for multiple forms of assessment,
  9. maintain a balanced pace, and
  10. build time for many interactions.

Central to any lesson or project is the way that the teacher interacts with the students. There is no teacher's desk sitting in a classroom where the intention is to help students learn smarter. The primary goal in this approach to instruction directs teachers to mediate students' thinking for the full class period. As mediators, the teachers activate, reinforce, and extend student thinking so that students become more efficient and more effective learners.

There is no shortage of achievement-producing interactions that teachers can make with students as teachers guide students to deeper understanding of curricular content. As teachers develop their skills as facilitators and mediators of student learning, many of the following tactics will enable students to learn smarter, quicker, and deeper.

- **Remember wait time.** Provide at least three seconds of thinking time after each question and after each response.
- **Utilize think-pair-share.** Allow individual thinking time (wait time), discussion with a partner, and then open up for class discussion.
- **Ask follow-up questions.** "Why? Do you agree? Can you elaborate? Tell me more. Can you give an example?"
- **Withhold premature judgment.** Respond to student answers in a nonevaluative fashion.
- **Ask for a summary to promote active listening.** "Could you please summarize [John's] point?"
- **Survey the class.** "How many people agree with the author's point of view?"
- **Allow for student calling.** "[Richard], will you please call on someone else to respond?"
- **Play devil's advocate.** Require students to defend their reasoning against different points of view.
- **Ask students to unpack their thinking.** "Describe how you arrived at your answer."
- **Call on students randomly or using a round-robin questioning pattern.** Avoid the pattern of only calling on students who raise their hands.
- **Encourage student questioning.** Let the students develop their own questions.
- **Cue student responses.** "There is not a single correct answer for this question. I want to consider alternatives."

Source: Adapted from "Language and Learning Improvement Branch Division of Instruction", Maryland State Department of Education.

In addition to the interactions with students that thoughtful questions provoke, the type of questions that teachers ask is important when building a learning community. The adaptation of Bloom's taxonomy as a tool to guide thoughtful responses into the Three-Story Intellect is familiar to many teachers as an easy-to-use framework for effective questions. However, asking questions, one of the most prominent achievement-inducing strategies identified by researchers, is a waste of time if students are asked to recall only words. What is essential is that teachers use the higher-order or upper-story questions throughout every lesson. It is not essential that they start students at the bottom floor with recall questions before proceeding to analysis and prediction on the upper floors. From an active learning perspective, teachers most engage students with questions if they start with analysis and evaluation as open-ended prompts combined with the tactics such as response-in-turn (see Activity 24), lead-in statements (see Activity 9), and graphics (see Activity 47) that structure responses from all students, including the most reticent.

The Three-Story Intellect

There are one-story intellects, two-story intellects, and three-story intellects with skylights. All fact collectors, who have no aim above their facts, are one-story men. Two-story men compare, reason, generalize, using the labors of the fact collectors as well as their own. Three-story men idealize, imagine, predict–their best Illumination comes from above, through the skylight.

–Oliver Wendell Holmes

SOURCE: Bellanca, J., & Fogarty, R. (2003). *Blueprints for Achievement in the Cooperative Classroom*, (3rd ed.). Thousand Oaks, CA: Corwin Press.

The asking of questions does not have to remain in the domain of teachers. Students, too, can learn to ask complex and insightful questions. The more skilled they become in asking questions (see Activities 6 and 137) about what they are learning, the more they will engage with the teacher and each other. That students can frame questions becomes especially important when they are engaged in hypothetical thinking, information gathering, and the transfer of new ideas across the curriculum. Question asking is a key tool in helping students become more-efficient thinkers in every phase of the learning process, with every intelligence, and in every subject area.

CREATING A CLASSROOM LEARNING COMMUNITY

Every classroom has a distinctive climate. If the climate reinforces passive learning, students will accept the norms of behavior that reinforce student passivity. Conversely, if the climate reinforces active learning, students will more readily accept the norms of active engagement and the expectation of learning smarter. No research-based strategy makes it easier for teachers to establish the norms of active engagement than cooperative learning (Bellanca and Fogarty, 1991). In this edition, you will find that a predominant number of the activities are built on the use of informal and formal cooperative learning as a tool that enables teachers to build a strong learning community with shared values and expectations.

As they build a learning community in the classroom, teachers can use cooperative learning strategies and tactics for a variety of purposes:

- To capture student reciprocity at the start of a lesson or project by immediate, stimulating engagement with their peers in an informal cooperative task such as the draw-pair-share (see Activity 148), or a formal collaborative task in the making of a prior knowledge collage (see Activity 68)
- To build cohesion among diverse individuals by establishing base-groups that work together over time, establish trust, and teach the social skills of teamwork (see Activity 145)
- To use cooperative task groups (see Activity 128) with their guidelines, roles, shared goals, and other elements to have many-hands-make-short-work-of-learning experiences in lessons and projects
- To mix students in a class in a variety of learning experiences so that they begin to form a cohesive, inclusive community of learners (see Activity 145)

Community comes as a result of students having many opportunities to work with each other and to develop the interpersonal intelligence that will play such an integral part in their postschool experiences. In the development of the interpersonal processes, all the students in the class learn to work toward a shared goal of classroom collaboration. As the school year unfolds, all students work in a variety of grouping patterns—same ability, mixed ability, informal, formal, base, and functional—with all other students. This is their living lab where they safely develop the collaborative skills and work habits that make up the interpersonal intelligence. By way of daily collaborative experiences, the students create a classroom that meets the criteria established by Roger Johnson and David Johnson (1991) for a collaborative community. It is a classroom community with

- strong interpersonal connections,
- individual accountability,
- a shared goal,
- daily face-to-face, mind-to-mind interactions, and
- shared assessment of the learning process where outcomes guide daily work.

While the methods of cooperative learning provide the food for development of the interpersonal intelligence in all students, they also provide the healthiest food for development of the verbal/linguistic intelligence along with multiple opportunities for students to develop the other intelligences. As is evident in many of the lessons and projects in this book, cooperative learning tactics enrich the study of mathematics, science, language arts, art, and other content areas. These tactics teach students that many hands really do make lighter work; these tactics provide more students with time and support to think and learn. More students are engaged when six students in six groups have to respond to questions or solve problems than when the question is answered in a large-group discussion by the same two or three who dominate the teacher-student interaction.

IN CONCLUSION

A classroom that engages students and challenges them to learn smarter has many dimensions. Gardner's Theory of the Multiple Intelligences provides teachers with a strong framework for supporting teachers' intentional use of instructional tactics and strategies to design lessons and projects that enrich the intellectual development of all students. It encourages teachers to differentiate instruction by choosing tactics and strategies that most help in this enrichment for the most number of students. By enabling teachers to see more clearly how students' learning differences are much deeper than styles, whims, or talents, the theory better enables teachers to more easily differentiate instruction.

Moving instruction from a passive activity to the active engagement of students' minds is not something that happens with the wave of a magic wand. The active engagement starts with an intent to bring to all students, regardless of their preferred intelligence, the opportunity to benefit from rich instruction that will help each of them become a smarter learner. With the goal of teaching mindful learners who actively pursue knowledge, teachers become more actively engaged, smarter learners who make significant changes in how they teach the curriculum and how they develop each students' learning potential. They shy away from quick fixes and magic scripts. They mix and match a variety of research supported tactics to ensure that students not only learn more, better and faster, they also learn smarter.

When students leave your active learning classroom having been deeply engaged in making the maximum use of their thinking capabilities, they leave with minds that are full of sumptuous, enriching, nutritious food. This food provides the energy for their minds to continue learning long after they are out the door. And do they remember the meal?

How can they not?

PART I

Verbal/Linguistic Intelligence

ACTIVITY 1

Vocabulary Bank

Targeted Grades: Elementary, Middle, and Secondary

ACTIVITY AT A GLANCE

Purpose

- To build a bank of vocabulary words for a course of study, a project, or a topic
- To connect new concepts with prior knowledge by using vocabulary word banks

When to Use

- In sequenced lessons or a unit of study where each lesson's vocabulary forms a foundation for the next lesson
- In a project or in-depth study of a topic

What You'll Need

- Journals

WHAT-TO-DO CHECKLIST

- ❏ On the overhead or board, post four to seven key vocabulary words that students learned in previous lessons or units.
- ❏ Review definitions of the words and discuss their importance in the upcoming lesson or unit.
- ❏ Invite students to start a vocabulary section in their journals (see Activity 153).
- ❏ After reviewing the first set of words with the students, identify four to seven new key words and definitions to be studied in the upcoming lesson or unit.
- ❏ Ask students to visualize each word as a picture.
- ❏ Invite students to use their own words to record meanings in their journals.

VARIATIONS

1. Use three to five words per week for elementary students, four to seven for middle school students, and seven to ten for secondary students.

2. Use the classroom bulletin board to post the words of the week or the entire vocabulary word bank.

3. Pair students to share their definitions, sentences, and drawings. Encourage them to coach each other on spelling and definitions.

4. Hold a team competition to match definitions with words.

Other Intelligences

- Visual/spatial
- Intrapersonal

ACTIVITY 2

What's It All About?

Targeted Students: Middle School and Secondary

ACTIVITY AT A GLANCE

Purpose

- To preview textbook topics using predicting, scanning, and summarizing techniques

When to Use

- When preparing students to read new textbook chapters or articles

What You'll Need

- Journals

WHAT-TO-DO CHECKLIST

- ❒ Explain to students that they are going to learn some reading strategies that will help them study, and that will help them improve their comprehension.

- ❒ Select a chapter from the textbook. Have students read the chapter's title, look at the pictures or diagrams, and predict what they will learn in the chapter. Write students' predictions on the board or overhead using a web diagram.

- ❒ Invite students to read the chapter's major subheadings. Ask how these headings give more insight into the chapter's content. Add their responses to the list on the board or overhead with branches from each web entry.

- ❒ Have students read the paragraph under the first major heading and compare it to their predictions. Ask if this information adds to, clarifies, contradicts, or simply repeats what they predicted; have them explain their answers. Add any new ideas to the list.

❏ Have students read the paragraph under the last major heading in the chapter and repeat the process of comparing the new information to their predictions.

Title

The United States: The Early Years

Predictions

It's about the Pilgrims.

How we became a country.

George Washington.

The war we had with England.

The people who started this country.

❏ Show students how to construct a summary with a topic sentence and two or three detailed sentences. Present a sample for them to see.

❏ Ask students to write brief summaries in their journals (see Activity 153) describing, confirming, or correcting their predictions.

❏ When all have finished, ask for volunteers to read their summaries aloud. Discuss any missing information that should be added.

❏ Assign pairs of students to read the chapter's remaining sections, with each pair taking one section.

❏ After all have finished, ask for volunteers to compare their predictions with the actual information that they read. On the board or overhead check off each prediction that is validated.

❏ Finish by reading or displaying samples of student summaries and giving positive feedback.

❏ Review the process for previewing a text assignment and discuss the benefits of this five-step approach:

1. Predict from title.

2. Scan the major subheadings (usually bolded).

3. Predict after reviewing opening and closing paragraphs.

4. Read each section and compare to predictions.

5. Summarize the chapter.

VARIATIONS

1. Have students work in pairs throughout the process. Let pairs discuss the predictions before they share with the class.

2. Have each student keep his own list in a journal.

3. Follow up with an assignment using and documenting the process with the next chapter in the text.

4. Have students learn the process by using magazine articles.

Other Intelligences

- Visual/spatial
- Intrapersonal

ACTIVITY 3

Issue Editorial

Targeted Grades: Middle and Secondary

ACTIVITY AT A GLANCE

Purpose

- To formulate and support a conclusion or point of view using factual information

When to Use

- When introducing a new lesson or new information

What You'll Need

- Several copies of newspaper editorials

WHAT-TO-DO CHECKLIST

❏ Arrange students in pairs. Give each pair a copy of an editorial from the local newspaper. After students have read the editorial, ask them to list what information was used to argue the point of view.

❏ Ask the pairs to identify how they think the editorial was organized (for instance, "Gives main topic and then three follow up reasons.") Discuss the various formats in the editorials.

❏ Identify a key topic, issue, or concept from the lesson or unit students will next study.

❏ **Brainstorm** with the class a list of what they know about the topic. Clarify all items on the list and assign one item to each pair of students. Instruct pairs to read the text and use additional resource materials to look for information that will expand or extend their basic knowledge.

❏ When they have finished gathering information, instruct each pair to write an editorial that uses the research to support these two students' point of view. They should draw upon the model formats from the start of this activity (in class or for homework).

❏ Invite pairs to read their editorials aloud and explain the format used. Review the format for an editorial.

VARIATIONS

1. Divide class into three to five groups of mixed ability (see Activity 145). Have each group organize itself as a newspaper or magazine team. Give each team a different set of resource materials on a topic they are studying. Review the format for an editorial. Have the team then prepare a newsletter with an editorial and several short articles on the topic.

2. At the end of a lesson, brainstorm current related topics. Create a class newspaper with editorials on subtopics, cartoons, ads, and news articles. Assign groups of three to each element.

3. In place of written material, allow students to select from other media (for instance, a pair may elect to write a song satirizing a topic, and another pair may create a cartoon or an ad).

Other Intelligences

- Visual/spatial
- Musical/rhythmic
- Intrapersonal

ACTIVITY 4

The Big Picture

A Textbook Walkthrough

Targeted Grades: Middle and Secondary

ACTIVITY AT A GLANCE

Purpose

- To gain an overview of course or unit content by becoming familiar with the textbook layout and subtopics
- To learn how to scan a text and its chapters to predict the course or topic, and to make learning goals

When to Use

- At the start of the semester for a class that will use a textbook on a regular basis
- At the start of a chapter so that students see the relationship of subconcepts to the main idea as shown through the text headers, and so they learn to make predictions about what they will learn

What You'll Need

- Chart paper

WHAT-TO-DO CHECKLIST

- ☐ Invite students to **walk through** their textbooks or a single chapter and preview the major text headings. If you are previewing the entire textbook, introduce students to the book's table of contents.

- ☐ Ask them to scan the chapter titles, index, and format of the chapters, including highlighted vocabulary; visuals, including graphs and charts; questions; and references. If you are previewing a chapter, ask them to identify the major headers (topics and subtopics) and key vocabulary words.

- ☐ Post four to six learning objectives for the course or chapter on the board or overhead and ask students to tell how these relate to the material they have previewed. Seek several responses for each objective.

- ☐ After this walkthrough, ask students to describe how the material is organized (for instance, sequentially, conceptually, by topic, and so on) and what highlights relate to the course's objectives.

- ☐ Provide students with chart paper. If the text uses a sequential format, assign pairs of students to construct a timeline for the course using the chapter titles. If the text uses a topical or conceptual format, work with students to construct a concept map (see Activity 18) for the course from the chapter titles. Post timelines or concept maps as a reference for use throughout the course.

Concept Map

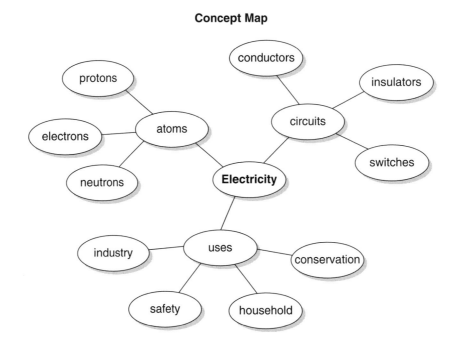

VARIATIONS

1. Assign students to complete the walkthrough in pairs.
2. Use the walkthrough process with a chapter instead of the entire textbook.
3. Assign students to use a **sequence chart** (see Activity 29) to track ideas through a chapter.
4. Assign students to construct chapter-by-chapter concept maps of content.

Other Intelligences

- Visual/spatial
- Intrapersonal

ACTIVITY 5

Bag of Knowledge

Targeted Grades: Elementary

ACTIVITY AT A GLANCE

Purpose

- To bridge prior knowledge to new information

When to Use

- When tying existing knowledge to an upcoming lesson
- During a lesson to check that students are connecting new information to prior knowledge

What You'll Need

- Paper lunch bags
- Three-by-five-inch index cards

WHAT-TO-DO CHECKLIST

☐ Give each student a paper lunch bag. List five key names, places, events, or concepts from the upcoming lesson on the board for all to see.

☐ On the outside of the lunch bag, invite students to write words or draw sketches or symbols to tell one thing they already know about each of the key words or concepts listed. Students may leave a blank if they don't have any ideas for a specific word.

☐ After students have answered the questions, arrange the students in small groups of two to four and have them share what they wrote or drew. Invite the groups to share what they know about each example.

☐ Give each student five to ten index cards. As the class progresses through the lesson or unit, invite students to write on the cards any new information they learn about the key words or concepts. Students may keep the cards inside their lunch bags. At the end of the lesson, have small groups reconvene and share their bags of new knowledge.

VARIATIONS

1. Create an all-class concept map (see Activity 18) on the bulletin board using the key words.

2. Hang a clothesline across the classroom, high enough so it will not be a hazard or distraction. Invite students to make mobiles with their cards and hang the mobiles from the clothesline (see Activity 59).

3. Prepare a people search (see Activity 27) from the completed cards and use as a closure activity.

Other Intelligences

- Visual/spatial
- Intrapersonal

ACTIVITY 6

Question Web

Targeted Grades: All

ACTIVITY AT A GLANCE

Purpose

- To clarify key concepts introduced in the first half of a unit or lesson

When to Use

- In the middle of a lesson or unit to check for student understanding of what they're learning

What You'll Need

- Newsprint and markers, or blackboard and chalk
- Journals

WHAT-TO-DO CHECKLIST

❏ Draw a web on the board or overhead for all to see. Write the unit title in the center of the web.

❏ Ask students to review the unit's concepts by volunteering information they have learned so far.

❏ Instruct them to identify parts of the unit for which they need further explanation and to construct questions for any items they do not fully understand.

❏ Use a round-robin questioning pattern (see Activity 24); write each question on the web. After all questions are posted work around the web asking students to suggest answers and recording them next to the corresponding questions.

❏ Invite students to replicate the web in their journals (see Activity 153).

❏ If a student gives a partial or incorrect answer, ask another volunteer to add to it or to correct it. Answer the questions only when no one else can.

❏ Check to make sure everyone has understood each answer.

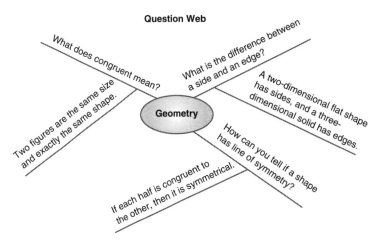

Question Web

VARIATIONS

1. Pair students and have them construct a critical question.

2. Identify students who believe they can answer one of the questions.

3. List each selected question on a separate sheet of chart paper and tape sheets of this paper around the room.

4. Arrange students in small groups. Send the volunteer student who can answer the question to stand under the question selected. Assign a different group to discuss each question. Have each group decide on an answer and record it under the question. Check to be sure they have answered all questions accurately.

5. Invite the students to take a carousel (see Activity 10), moving from question to question, confirming, expanding on, or correcting answers. Gather as a class to discuss additions and revisions to each chart paper.

Other Intelligences

- Visual/spatial
- Intrapersonal

ACTIVITY 7

Explain Why

Targeted Grades: All

ACTIVITY AT A GLANCE

Purpose

- To extend thinking and expand understanding by elaborating on answers

When to Use

- In class discussions when students give one-word responses

What You'll Need

- Journals

WHAT-TO-DO CHECKLIST

❐ Arrange students in pairs to complete a task, such as solving a math problem, conducting an experiment, or completing a project. As they work, ask students to record the steps they take in their journals (see Activity 153).

❐ Invite each pair to share its process with the class and explain why each step was necessary.

❐ Ask students to tell what steps they would change if they were to attempt the task again, and why they would change them. Whenever possible, ask students for additional explanations.

❐ Seek multiple responses to each question. Encourage students to build on each other's explanations.

❐ Write a list of "why" questions on the board or overhead. Have pairs answer them and share with the class.

Why? Questions

Why are you changing the title of your story?

Why did you decide to work backward to solve that problem?

Why are you rearranging your exercise schedule?

VARIATIONS

1. Have a "Why?" marathon. Gather students into pairs to see how many "why" questions each group can list about the topic. Then have groups exchange lists and answer as many questions as they can, making sure explanations are thorough.

2. Ask pairs to write out explanations and attach them to their task sheets for grading.

Other Intelligences

- Visual/spatial
- Intrapersonal

ACTIVITY 8

What It Looks Like

Targeted Grades: Middle and Secondary

ACTIVITY AT A GLANCE

Purpose

- To create a rubric for students' self-assessment by using performance rubrics

When to Use

- At the beginning of a lesson, task, or project to help students develop success criteria for their work
- At the end of the task to help students reflect on and evaluate their work

What You'll Need

- No materials necessary

WHAT-TO-DO CHECKLIST

☐ On the board or overhead, sketch a T-chart (see Activity 139).

☐ Select a performance not related to your class, such as taming wild animals or figure skating. Ask the class to brainstorm the actions needed to perform the activity well. Write these criteria or characteristics of excellence in the appropriate columns on the T-chart.

☐ Have the class vote on the three most important criteria for high performance. For example, if a figure skater does a triple axel, what characteristics determine whether he has done it well? Height? Revolutions? Balance?

☐ Arrange students in groups of three and assign one characteristic to each group.

☐ Invite each group to create a rubric for its characteristic that details four levels, or indicators, of success. Have each group explain its rubric to the class.

☐ At the end of the task, invite groups to self-assess with the rubric. Identify three characteristics of excellence.

☐ Find four indicators of success for each characteristic.

❏ Chart the indicators.

❏ Discuss how the rubrics helped them complete the task.

❏ Discuss how else they might use a rubric to improve their school performance.

❏ In future assignments that require students to demonstrate or use knowledge in a performance, include the preparation and use of a rubric.

Sample Rubric for a Research Project

1	2	3	4
Project shows that the accuracy of research needs to be increased, and sources need to be cited.	Project shows evidence of some accurate research, but sources need to be cited.	Project shows evidence of accurate research, and adequate sources are cited.	Project shows evidence of detailed, thorough, accurate research, and many sources are cited.

VARIATIONS

1. Reduce the number of criteria and indicators required for the rubric. As students increase their proficiency with rubrics, expand the number of criteria and indicators.

2. Provide the completed rubric for younger students.

Other Intelligences

- Logical/mathematical
- Visual/spatial
- Intrapersonal

ACTIVITY 9

Lead-In Statements

Targeted Grades: All

ACTIVITY AT A GLANCE

Purpose

- To develop self-assessment to reflect on learning content or on the process of learning

When to Use

- After a lesson, unit, or project
- At the end of a class period

What You'll Need

- Journals
- Three-by-five-inch index cards

WHAT-TO-DO CHECKLIST

- ❏ Write a lead-in statement on the board or overhead, such as
  - *Today, I learned . . .*
  - *In this lesson, I discovered . . .*
  - *In this lesson, I was pleased that I . . .*
  - *In this task, I found it easy (difficult) to . . .*
  - *The most important thing I learned in this lesson was . . .*

- ❏ Let students know that they will have the chance to use the lead-in as a way of reflecting about how and what they have learned in a lesson or unit. Have them write in their journals (see Activity 153).

- ❏ Share an example of a completed reflection the first time you use this tactic. Explain that this is an open-ended reflection without a correct answer. All that is needed is an honest response.

- ❏ Let students know before they begin to write whether or not the reflections will be collected or shared. As students become more comfortable with the process, they may take more time and may write lengthier reflections.

- ❏ When sharing, ask for a volunteer to start a round-robin questioning pattern (see Activity 24). Encourage all to listen to each idea.

- ❏ Proceed in order to the right or left of the first response. Allow but do not encourage students to say "I pass." Allow as many students to share as time allows.

VARIATIONS

1. Change the medium. The most common medium is a journal. Have students write in the journal at the end of the day to summarize the key points that they learned, to evaluate their own performance, or to select favorite learning experiences. Do spot samples from volunteer students who elect to share.

2. Have students attach completed reflections to assignments as a way of assessing what they learned or how well they succeeded.

3. Have students write on index cards and collect the completed statements. Read random cards to the class. Instead of having students write down their reflections, arrange students in small groups and use lead-in statements as discussion starters.

4. Use a lead-in that enables students to share their prior knowledge (see Activity 54).

5. Use fun lead-in statements that encourage students to share a fun weekend experience such as a visit to the zoo, a play seen, or a sports accomplishment.

Other Intelligences

- Visual/spatial
- Interpersonal
- Intrapersonal

ACTIVITY 10

Carousel

Targeted Grades: Middle and Secondary

ACTIVITY AT A GLANCE

Purpose

- To select the most important material or concepts learned in a lesson and construct an evaluative summary

When to Use

- At the end of a lesson to evaluate what students learned
- At the end of a lesson or unit to identify points that students may need reinforced or reviewed

What You'll Need

- Chart paper
- Journals

WHAT-TO-DO CHECKLIST

❐ On sheets of chart paper taped to the classroom walls, write the following statements and questions:
- *What is the most important thing you learned in this lesson?*
- *What did you like most about this lesson?*
- *What did you like least about this lesson?*
- *What did you learn in this lesson that will help you in other classes?*
- *A contribution I made to the class during this lesson was . . .*
- *What I learned in this lesson will help me because . . .*

❐ Invite each student to choose a statement or question and move to its location.

❐ Students at each location will form a group with a recorder. Try to get a comparable number of students at each position.

❏ Invite each group to think of as many true endings for its statement as possible in three minutes. Have the group recorder list all the ideas in response to the statement or question.

❏ After three to five minutes, invite the groups to rotate to the next statement's position and repeat the process. Encourage each group to rotate the role of recorder.

❏ Rotate several times around the carousel before asking students to return to their seats.

❏ Ask each student to write a summary (see Activity 118) in their journals (see Activity 153) about one of the statements the group discussed. Have students put quotation marks around direct quotes. Instruct them to edit and sign their summaries before sharing with a partner.

VARIATIONS

1. Instead of rotating the groups, call for a random remix.

2. Reseat the students in **base groups** or some other configuration and instruct each group to write the summary together. Collect and read each group's summary.

3. Reseat students in new random pairs. After each has written a summary in a journal, encourage students to share with each other and proofread each other's completed summaries.

4. Provide a model summary and point out its structure and format. Encourage students to replicate the structure or format with their own ideas.

5. Use a rubric (see Activity 8) before students write the summaries. Ask them to follow the rubric. Use the rubric to assess the final summaries.

Other Intelligences

- Logical/mathematical
- Visual/spatial
- Bodily/kinesthetic
- Interpersonal
- Intrapersonal

ACTIVITY 11

Letter to the Editor

Targeted Grades: Middle and Secondary

ACTIVITY AT A GLANCE

Purpose

- To develop and support a point of view through letter writing

When to Use

- In the middle or at the end of a unit to assess what students have learned

What You'll Need

- Examples of letters to a newspaper or magazine editor

WHAT-TO-DO CHECKLIST

❑ Show students an example of a letter to the editor of a newspaper or magazine that takes a point of view related to the unit's content. For example, if the topic is "pollution in the environment," show a letter taking a point of view about pollution in the local community. If the topic is *To Kill a Mockingbird,* show a letter taking a point of view about treating others with fairness.

❑ Present a rubric (see Activity 8) to guide their writing. Check for understanding (see Activity 43) of the criteria.

❑ After showing the letter, discuss how to write a point-of-view letter. Remind students that they need to explain their points of view using facts or research to support their thinking.

❑ Brainstorm with students possible issues that relate to the unit, and have each student write a letter expressing her opinion about an issue.

❑ Use peer editing to review the letters, and then invite students to read their letters aloud.

❑ Collect and grade by the rubric. Return papers with rubric attached.

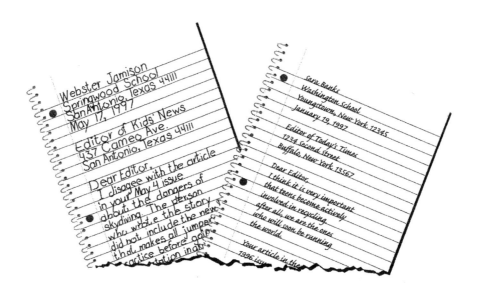

VARIATIONS

1. Instead of grading the letters, write a brief response to each letter.
2. Pair students with contrasting or different points of view and ask them to write a response to each other's letter.
3. Instead of grading the letters, help students complete a final edit and encourage each student to send his or her letter to the editor of the local newspaper.
4. If used in the middle of a unit, have students predict what the remainder of the unit will cover.
5. Use at the start of a lesson or unit as the advanced organizer. Have students focus on prior knowledge (see Activity 54) of the topic.
6. Have students write the letter to a political candidate regarding one of his positions.

Other Intelligences

- Logical/mathematical
- Visual/spatial
- Interpersonal
- Intrapersonal

ACTIVITY 12

Pointed Paragraphs

Targeted Grades: All

ACTIVITY AT A GLANCE

Purpose

- To synthesize the relevance of a topic in everyday life and apply new information to a real-world issue

When to Use

- As an advanced organizer to a lesson or unit so that students can call up prior knowledge for the selected topic, concept, or issue
- With a topic that has relevance for your students in order to help them process what they have learned in a pointed paragraph

What You'll Need

- Examples of pointed paragraphs from the textbook your students are using in your class
- A rubric or list of criteria for evaluating student-written paragraphs

WHAT-TO-DO CHECKLIST

❏ Follow Checklist 1 or Checklist 2.

Checklist 1

❏ After the class has completed work on a topic, arrange students in small cooperative groups (see Activity 128).

❏ Present a rubric (see Activity 8) to guide the paragraph writing.

❏ Ask each group to write an opening paragraph that synthesizes what the students have learned.

❏ Review the paragraphs and read aloud two or three that capture the core ideas of the topic.

❏ Encourage each group to rewrite and improve its paragraph by the rubric.

❏ Collect and assess each paragraph.

Checklist 2

❏ Set up cooperative groups (see Activity 128) of three.

❏ Identify the topic or concept they are going to study.

❏ Ask groups to brainstorm why the topic is important for them to study. Help them list authentic situations in which they might need to apply the new information.

❏ Generate a class list from each group's ideas.

❏ Show a model paragraph. Discuss the format and the elements of a well-written opening paragraph.

❏ Assign each student to complete a paragraph according to the model.

Natural Resources

If we don't learn to conserve, we won't be able to support life on this planet.

We could invent new kinds of fuels that don't pollute.

We need to find a way to eliminate garbage and waste.

We need to be aware of how much water we are using.

❏ When the lesson is complete, show students how to expand the paragraph to a three to five paragraph essay.

❏ Give students a rubric or list of criteria for a successful editorial that you will use to evaluate the completed works.

❏ Ask each student to write a complete essay on the importance of the topic that the class has been studying, using the list of criteria or the rubric as a guide.

  • States the problem or concern.

  • States the writer's opinion or point of view.

- Elaborates, providing supporting facts.
- Closes with a concluding statement.

VARIATIONS

1. For middle school students, assign a three-paragraph format.

2. Have students work individually rather than in groups to complete all steps of this process.

3. For younger children, do entire preparation with the whole class. Make the criteria and models for a single paragraph. Elicit ideas for each sentence from the class and construct a single essay that they can copy.

Other Intelligences

- Logical/mathematical
- Visual/spatial
- Interpersonal
- Intrapersonal
- Naturalist

ACTIVITY 13

Democratic Dots

Targeted Grades: Secondary

ACTIVITY AT A GLANCE

Purpose

- To reach consensus in the assessment of important vocabulary or concepts in a lesson or unit through the use of a nonverbal voting system

When to Use

- To determine the most important vocabulary words or concepts for a lesson or unit
- To emphasize connections between the concepts or words and the lesson's goals

What You'll Need

- Dot stickers
- Chart paper

WHAT-TO-DO CHECKLIST

☐ Arrange students into cooperative groups (see Activity 128) of five and provide each group with chart paper.

☐ Explain that each group should make a list of the ten most important vocabulary words or concepts studied, and that each group then should define and review the definitions of each of these ten words.

☐ Explain the purpose of the activity.

☐ Assign roles: recorder, reporter, facilitator, materials manager, and checker. Encourage groups to determine responsibilities of each role.

☐ Give each student three dot stickers. Ask students to vote for the three most important words on their group's list by placing the dots next to their choices.

☐ Before voting, group members may debate for five minutes. After all have placed their dots, have groups total their results by allocating five points for the first choice, three for the second, and one for the third.

☐ Make an all-class list of the winning words from each small group. Repeat the dot process until the class has created a top-ten list.

☐ Instruct the groups to construct a concept map (see Activity 53) of the words around the central concept of the lesson.

☐ Post the maps and ask group reporters to respond to questions from other groups.

Important Vocabulary

** prejudice—opinion formed without sufficient knowledge

*** *The North Star*—newspaper started by Frederick Douglass

* orator—public speaker

* amendment—addition to something, such as to the Constitution

**** abolition—eliminate something, such as slavery

*** Underground Railroad—a system that helped slaves escape to the North or Canada

* to liberate—to free

VARIATIONS

1. For middle or elementary students, use a smaller group and a shorter list of words.

2. Conclude the top-ten list by requiring all students to recall the correct spelling, the meaning in context, and a reason why the selected words are the most important to the lesson or unit.

3. Have students use a different medium (such as collage, pantomime, or mobile) to communicate the relation of the top-ten words to the lesson or unit goals.

Other Intelligences

- Visual/spatial
- Interpersonal
- Intrapersonal

ACTIVITY 14

Fishbowl

Targeted Grades: Elementary

ACTIVITY AT A GLANCE

Purpose

- To read for the understanding of key concepts
- To learn from listening

When to Use

- When teaching concepts from textbooks or other written sources

What You'll Need

- Cardboard fish figures
- Bowl
- Checklist of three presentation requirements

WHAT-TO-DO CHECKLIST

- ❐ Cut out several small cardboard fish figures and write a subheading from the textbook chapter on each. Put all fish in the bowl.

- ❐ After students have read the chapter, arrange them in small groups or pairs.

- ❐ Explain the activity's purpose.

- ❐ Allow each group to choose a fish from the bowl; each fish indicates the section of the chapter for which the group is responsible. Each group is to
  - summarize the key idea of its section,
  - explain the meaning of new vocabulary or important facts, and
  - explain how its section fits into the main idea of the chapter.

- ❐ Invite each group to present its chapter section to the class. Ask listeners to use the checklist to assess how well each presentation covers the material, according to the three presentation requirements.

❏ Ask listeners to take notes during each presentation in preparation for a class discussion and review of the chapter.

❏ Close by asking students how the presentations helped them identify the key components to study in the chapter. Encourage them to use a checklist.

Checklist

___ Summary completed

___ New words explained

___ Fit to chapter explained

VARIATIONS

1. Make and label a fish with the name of a section of the chapter. Make as many fish as you have students, then have students who chose similar sections form into groups to complete the task.

2. Make a bulletin board with a giant fishbowl. Add the fish with the names of the sections as you assign a section to a group

3. Make a giant fishbowl map. Place it on the floor. Have each student come to the map and explain a fish (the chapter section).

4. Have each student work independently to write a summary for her section.

5. After a demonstration chapter is completed, assign students to cover an entire chapter.

Other Intelligences

- Visual/spatial
- Bodily/kinesthetic
- Intrapersonal

ACTIVITY 15

Rank Order Ladder

Targeted Grades: All

ACTIVITY AT A GLANCE

Purpose

- To identify the relative importance of one concept to another

When to Use

- At the start, in the middle, or at the end of a lesson or unit when helping students distinguish and prioritize the importance or value of concepts learned

What You'll Need

- Model of a rank order ladder on the overhead (optional)

WHAT-TO-DO CHECKLIST

- ❏ Brainstorm with the class a list of concepts or items that students are to assess such as the characters in a novel, problem-solving methods, key concepts (such as fractions, whole numbers, or numerators), or causes leading to an event.

- ❏ Have students vote to determine the three most important items on the list in relation to the main idea of the lesson or unit.

- ❏ Explain that each student votes three times. They begin with closed fists, but as the list of items is read aloud, they hold up one finger to indicate a first-place vote, two fingers to indicate a second-place vote, and three fingers to indicate a third-place vote.

- ❏ A class recorder tallies the votes and writes the score beside each item. A final count will give the rank order. Conclude with a class discussion of the top three choices, eliciting from students their reasons for making their choices.

- ❏ If used as an advanced organizer or predictor at the start of a lesson, put the rank order on a ladder visual and post it for all to see. During and at the end of the lesson, check back to the first **ranking** made at the lesson's start.

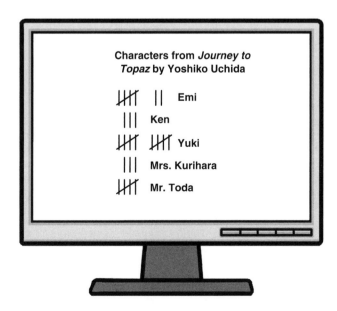

Characters from *Journey to Topaz* by Yoshiko Uchida

||||| || Emi
||| Ken
||||| ||||| Yuki
||| Mrs. Kurihara
||||| Mr. Toda

VARIATIONS

1. Use straight voting of one vote per person. The items are ranked based on the number of votes they receive.

2. Before voting, have students debate the issues, explaining the reasoning behind each of their first choices.

3. At the end of the lesson, invite students to stand in front of the class and move to show the ranking changes they made during the lesson.

Other Intelligences

- Logical/mathematical
- Visual/spatial
- Bodily/kinesthetic
- Intrapersonal

ACTIVITY 16

Exemplary Examples

Targeted Grades: Middle and Secondary

ACTIVITY AT A GLANCE

Purpose

- To determine interpersonal attributes by using narrative examples

When to Use

- When developing expository or narrative writing skills
- When introducing public speaking

What You'll Need

- No materials necessary

WHAT-TO-DO CHECKLIST

☐ Brainstorm with students a list of characters from a novel or a list of famous persons studied in previous units. For each name, have students highlight key character attributes, such as honesty, industriousness, sneakiness, or deceitfulness.

☐ Tell a sample personal story to illustrate one of the character's attributes. Discuss the advantages of using a concrete story or narrative to illustrate an abstract attribute (such as honesty, with the story of George Washington and the cherry tree).

❏ Explain the activity's purpose.

❏ Invite one or two volunteers to tell similar personal stories to the class. Ask other students to identify the strengths of each student's example. Make a list of attributes for all to see.

❏ Ask each student to select one attribute from the list and write a personal story or paragraph to illustrate that attribute. Discuss the criteria for the stories in advance or provide students with a rubric (see Activity 8).

❏ Collect and provide feedback for each story.

Hans Christian Andersen

sensitive

creative

intelligent

humorous

philosophical

hard working

VARIATIONS

1. Use a matrix (see Activity 179) for detailing character attributes.

2. For elementary students, use a web (see Activity 6) to show attributes. Post the web on the bulletin board.

3. Have students illustrate unit concepts by telling personal or fictional stories.

4. Instead of providing students with the criteria for a quality story or paragraph, have students brainstorm standards for success.

5. Use a peer-editing system for revising paragraphs.

6. Invite students to share their stories in small groups or by reading aloud to the class.

Other Intelligences

- Visual/spatial
- Logical/mathematical
- Interpersonal
- Intrapersonal

ACTIVITY 17

Three-Legged Stool

Targeted Grades: Middle and Secondary

ACTIVITY AT A GLANCE

Purpose

- To understand the basic design of a three-paragraph expository essay

When to Use

- When introducing the structure of an expository essay or when emphasizing the importance of providing supporting facts for ideas in an essay

What You'll Need

- Picture of three-legged stool

WHAT-TO-DO CHECKLIST

❐ Show students a picture of a three-legged stool. Explain the metaphor of the stool in relation to a well-organized essay with a central or main idea (the seat), supporting examples (the legs), and conclusion (surface stool sits on).

❐ Draw the three-legged stool on the board or overhead and write an example of a main idea, its three supporting ideas, and a conclusion in the appropriate parts.

❐ Use the example to model how to write a five-paragraph essay that includes an introductory paragraph, three supporting paragraphs, and a concluding paragraph.

❐ Discuss the criteria for the essays in advance or provide students with a rubric (see Activity 8). You may want to include grammar, punctuation, sentence structure, and spelling criteria as well as the number of detail sentences per paragraph, interest, and accuracy of information.

❐ Provide feedback based on established criteria. Discuss the best essays with the class.

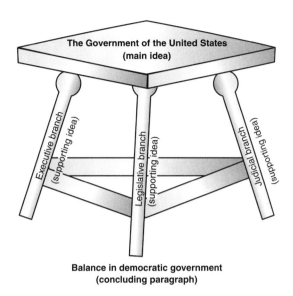

**The Government of the United States
(main idea)**

Executive branch
(supporting idea)

Legislative branch
(supporting idea)

Judicial branch
(supporting idea)

**Balance in democratic government
(concluding paragraph)**

VARIATIONS

1. Use peer-review teams comprising students who are familiar with the basic paragraph structure to critique outlines and drafts.

2. Emphasize the steps in the writing process by providing due dates for each stage (outline or prewriting, first draft, revision, and final edit).

Other Intelligences

- Logical/mathematical
- Visual/spatial
- Interpersonal
- Intrapersonal

ACTIVITY 18

Concept Connections

Targeted Grades: Middle and Secondary

ACTIVITY AT A GLANCE

Purpose

- To develop words and phrases that bridge ideas in writing

When to Use

- When guiding students to improve expository, persuasive, or narrative writing

What You'll Need

- Copies of Bridging Ideas
- Sample essay that uses bridging words
- Books and magazines
- Picture of a bridge (optional)

WHAT-TO-DO CHECKLIST

❏ Show students a picture of a bridge (or draw one on the board) and ask them to explain its purpose. Use the bridge as a metaphor for words or phrases that connect ideas in writing.

❏ Hand out to students a copy of a three-paragraph essay that uses bridging words. After they have read the essay, discuss how the author used language to connect ideas. Explain to students that they will be looking in books and magazines to find examples of bridging words.

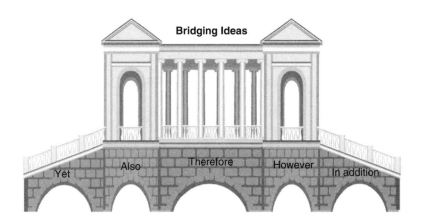

❏ Provide each student with a copy of "Bridging Ideas." Invite students to choose a book or magazine and to look for the words that the author used to bridge, or connect, ideas.

❏ Ask students to write the words and phrases they find on their copies of "Bridging Ideas." Invite volunteers to share their bridging words and phrases, and to read the passages in which they found them.

❏ Ask students to write a three- to five-paragraph essay. Establish criteria that call for appropriate use of bridging words.

❏ Use a peer-editing system for reviewing the words used and revising paragraphs.

VARIATIONS

1. Create an all-class list of bridging words and post for reference throughout the year.

2. Find examples of bridging words in class textbooks.

3. Use this activity after students have written an essay. Ask students to review their essays and find any bridging words they used. Have students identify one to three examples where they could use bridging words and rewrite those sentences using bridging words.

Other Intelligences

- Logical/mathematical
- Visual/spatial
- Interpersonal
- Intrapersonal

ACTIVITY 19

Newspaper Graphic

Targeted Grades: Middle and Secondary

ACTIVITY AT A GLANCE

Purpose

- To compile information and to organize an expository essay or narrative through the use of a visual format

When to Use

- When introducing expository essays or the key components of a news story

What You'll Need

- One newspaper article per group
- Chart paper
- Copies of the Newspaper Model

WHAT-TO-DO CHECKLIST

☐ Arrange students into cooperative groups (see Activity 128) of three. Assign cooperative group roles: one student is the reader, one is the recorder, and one is the encourager (who makes sure each student has an opportunity to speak).

☐ Provide each group with a newspaper article and a large sheet of chart paper labeled with the following headings: who, what, when, where, why, and how.

☐ Instruct students to read their assigned article and list the facts that they find under the appropriate headings.

❑ Post the completed lists with their corresponding articles at different locations around the room.

❑ Rotate groups from station to station, so that students can discuss several of the articles and lists of facts. Review two to three examples with the class.

❑ Ask volunteers to explain why the six questions are important.

The Newspaper Model

Who	*What*	*When*	*Where*	*Why*	*How*
Patriots	American Revolution	1776	Boston, MA	Rebel against taxation without represen-tation	Disposed of tea in harbor

Write a paragraph using the information from this inverted pyramid form.

The Patriots were colonists opposing the British government in the late 1700s. In 1773, they protested the issue of "taxation without representation" by dumping a shipment of tea overboard into the Boston harbor. This event and others led to the American Revolutionary War, in which we gained our independence as a nation.

❑ Explain to students that they will be writing their own newspaper articles. Brainstorm a list of current school and community events that could be used as topics.

❑ Select one topic to use as an example. Model listing facts for each of the six headings on the Newspaper Model and writing a paragraph using those facts.

❑ Invite each student to choose a topic, complete a copy of the Newspaper Model, and write his own article.

❑ Provide corrective feedback on the completed articles and review two to three samples with the class, pointing out the strengths of each.

❑ Invite students to reflect on their experience using the Newspaper Model by listing the pluses, minuses, and interesting aspects (**PMI** assessment; see Activity 158) of using this graphic organizer.

VARIATIONS

1. Students can remain in their original groups for the last three steps above.

2. Use peer-editing pairs for the revising and editing stages of the writing process.

3. Ask students to name other classes or subjects for which this graphic organizer could be helpful.

Other Intelligences

- Visual/spatial
- Bodily/kinesthetic
- Interpersonal
- Intrapersonal

ACTIVITY 20

Story Tree

Targeted Grades: All

ACTIVITY AT A GLANCE

Purpose

- To identify and list the major elements of a story by using a visual organizer

When to Use

- When introducing or expanding students' abilities to analyze fiction according to the elements of a story

What You'll Need

- Copies of the Story Tree Graphic
- Copies of the story

WHAT-TO-DO CHECKLIST

❏ Invite volunteers to identify the elements of a story (characters, setting, theme, events, and conflicts). Work together to clarify the terms.

❏ Give students copies of the Story Tree graphic. Invite them to use the graphic organizer as they read a short story or part of a novel. Have students record examples on the tree as they identify specific elements.

❏ After all students have read the selection, project a blank copy of the Story Tree on the overhead or draw it on the board. Invite students to volunteer examples of each element and complete the story tree as a class.

❏ Make sure the class agrees with the placement of the ideas. If there is a disagreement, encourage discussion.

❏ Ask each student to write a summary paragraph about one of the story's elements, such as its characters. Before students begin to write, brainstorm criteria for a good summation.

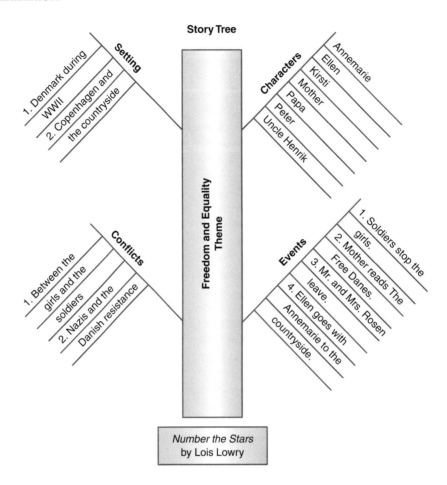

❏ Invite students to tell what they have learned about the elements of a story.

VARIATIONS

1. Delay recording on the story trees until the entire story is read.
2. For elementary and middle school students, substitute "problem and solution" for the conflict element.
3. For elementary students, make a bulletin board with a giant tree and post responses on it.
4. For elementary students, outline a tree on the floor. Ask students to represent different branches and leaves as they stand on the outline.

Other Intelligences

- Visual/spatial
- Bodily/kinesthetic
- Interpersonal
- Intrapersonal

ACTIVITY 21

Class Magazine

A Project

Targeted Grades: Middle

ACTIVITY AT A GLANCE

Purpose

- To gain experience in creating stories, articles, and ads while writing for an authentic reason

When to Use

- At any time during the year to motivate student writing

What You'll Need

- Age-appropriate magazines
- Duplicating equipment
- Colored markers
- Three sheets of newsprint per group
- Masking tape
- Blank paper (eight inch by ten inch)
- Pencils

WHAT-TO-DO CHECKLIST

- ❐ Explain the project and its purpose.
- ❐ Give pairs of students age-appropriate magazines. (Different issues are fine.)
- ❐ Ask pairs to formulate a list of the magazine's components, such as the cover, table of contents, stories, articles, interviews, features, and ads. Discuss whether each component is found in every magazine or if it is found only in some.
- ❐ Explain the project: to create a class magazine. Appoint or elect students to the following jobs: editor-in-chief, associate editors, story writers, feature writers, graphic artists, ad writers, photographers (need cameras), and proofreaders.
- ❐ Hold a meeting to determine the class magazine's focus, theme, title, and each person's responsibilities. Create a large web with the key theme or issue in the center.
- ❐ Assign tasks and deadlines for each component.
- ❐ As each student revises her work, conference with individuals to ensure quality.
- ❐ Help the students assemble all the parts.
- ❐ Duplicate copies of the completed magazine for every student.
- ❐ Close with a discussion of problems that students may have encountered and the solutions they developed while working on the tasks.

VARIATIONS

1. For secondary students, use the project as the main tool for studying a unit in your content area. Add research elements so that students can better gather the information they need.

2. Create a newsletter or a brochure instead of a magazine. Arrange students in teams of five to seven and have each team create its own magazine. Identify the similarities and differences among the groups' different products.

3. Provide or develop a list of criteria for a good magazine, for well-written articles, and for ads. Use the criteria to assess individual work and the completed magazine.

Other Intelligences

- Logical/mathematical
- Visual/spatial
- Interpersonal
- Intrapersonal

ACTIVITY 22

Interviewing

Targeted Grades: Secondary

ACTIVITY AT A GLANCE

Purpose

- To develop questioning skills while gaining insight into the difference between closed and open-ended questions

When to Use

- When introducing a unit involving famous persons
- When studying biographies
- When investigating characters in literature
- At the end of a unit with interviews of real or fictional characters related to the study

What You'll Need

- Copies of Three-Story Intellect

WHAT-TO-DO CHECKLIST

❑ Discuss the difference between a closed question that elicits factual, right, or wrong answers and an open-ended question that elicits a variety of different responses.

❒ Show the class the Three-Story Intellect diagram below. Using the metaphor of a house, explain that the first story on the diagram shows verbs for factual, or closed, questions. The second story also shows verbs for open-ended questions that elicit answers involving comparing, reasoning, and generalizing. The third story also lists verbs for open-ended questions that invite imagining, predicting, and idealizing. Each level of question builds on the level below it.

❒ Explain that students will be developing interviews using these three types of questions and may use the listed verbs or any others that they choose.

The Three-Story Intellect

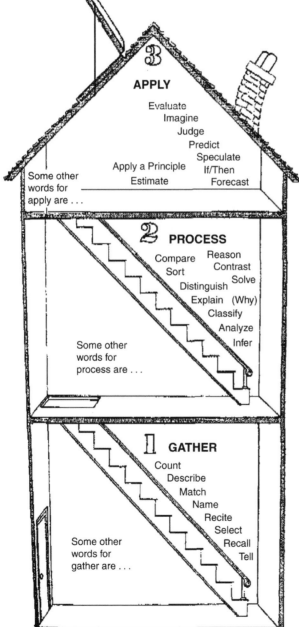

There are one-story intellects, two-story intellects, and three-story intellects with skylights. All fact collectors, who have no aim above their facts, are one-story men. Two-story men compare, reason, generalize, using the labors of the fact collectors as well as their own. Three-story men idealize, imagine, predict–their best Illumination comes from above, through the skylight.

–Oliver Wendell Holmes

SOURCE: Bellanca, J., & Fogarty, R. (2003). *Blueprints for Achievement in the Cooperative Classroom*, (3rd ed.). Thousand Oaks, CA: Corwin Press.

❏ Create a list of people the students would like to investigate, either famous people (or characters) or people (or characters) related to the unit's topic.

❏ Choose one person to use as a sample for modeling questioning strategies.

❏ Invite volunteers to pretend they are interviewing the person and to ask sample questions.

❏ Have each student explain the level (according to the diagram) at which his or her question would be categorized.

Questions for Helen Keller

How old were you when you learned to sign? (Level 1)

If you could live your life over, what would you change? (Level 3)

❏ Arrange students in pairs. Invite each pair to select one name from the class list and to prepare two closed and four open-ended questions about that person.

❏ Join pairs into cooperative groups (see Activity 128) of four students each. Have students share their interview questions and jointly decide the level of each question.

❏ Have volunteers share their questions and explanations with the class. Invite students to tell what they learned about asking questions.

VARIATIONS

1. Have students discuss authentic situations or class activities in which the different levels of questions would be most useful.

2. Use the diagram for a homework assignment. Instruct students to observe the kinds of questions their reports or essays answer.

3. Have middle school students work with only two levels of questions: factual questions, and questions that involve comparing, reasoning, and generalizing.

4. Have elementary students ask "why" questions.

Other Intelligences

- Interpersonal
- Intrapersonal

ACTIVITY 23

TV News Flash

Targeted Grades: Middle

ACTIVITY AT A GLANCE

Purpose

- To develop narrative, persuasive, and presentation skills while demonstrating knowledge on a topic

When to Use

- In the middle or at the end of a unit

What You'll Need

- Videotapes of news shows
- VCR player
- Copies of the Newspaper Model

WHAT-TO-DO CHECKLIST

☐ Play videotaped segments of TV news shows from different channels. Ask students to rate each segment on a scale from one to five, and to explain their reasoning.

☐ From their explanations, extract three to five criteria for judging the quality of content and presentation.

☐ Provide students with copies of the Newspaper Model and invite each to write a school-based news story. Explain that students will be creating their own news broadcasts. Review the students' drafts before they present them and encourage appropriate changes.

☐ Create a set for the class news station. Schedule presentations on successive days and assess each using class-developed criteria (see Activity 8).

☐ After the last presentation, discuss the overall pluses and minuses of the performances (see Activity 158).

VARIATIONS

1. Use teams of five students to copy the style of a specific station's news show.

2. Invite a news anchor or TV reporter from a local channel to speak to the class about his job.

3. Write letters to news anchors or TV reporters asking questions about their jobs. Invite them to respond to students' letters by enclosing self-addressed, stamped envelopes.

4. Videotape student presentations and play them for parents during open house.

Other Intelligences

- Logical/mathematical
- Visual/spatial
- Intrapersonal

ACTIVITY 24

Round-Robin Response in Turn

Targeted Grades: All

ACTIVITY AT A GLANCE

Purpose

- To contribute while working in large and small groups

When to Use

- After completing a task, lesson, or unit
- Before a lesson as an advanced organizer to check prior knowledge
- With lead-in responses
- At the end of a class period to review what was learned
- At the start of a class period to bridge from the previous day's work

What You'll Need

- No materials necessary

WHAT-TO-DO CHECKLIST

- ❑ Invite students to summarize key points in a lesson or unit by
  - completing a lead-in (see Activity 9) statement such as *In this lesson . . . , I was pleased that . . .* ;
  - answering an open-ended question, such as "If you were to imagine a different outcome, what would it be?";
  - listing the pluses, minuses, and interesting aspects (PMI assessment; see Activity 158) of the lesson; or
  - sharing at the end of a think-pair-share or write-pair-share.
- ❑ Allow students time to think for at least three seconds before inviting volunteers to share their responses.
- ❑ Start with a volunteer (vary the starters) and proceed to the right or left for the second response and those that follow.
- ❑ Allow for the pass right but encourage all to respond in their own words.
- ❑ Encourage different answers and active listening.
- ❑ If appropriate, ask clarifying questions to extend a student's thinking.
- ❑ In a large class, vary the statement or question after every seven to eight students.
- ❑ Make no comments.
- ❑ Conclude by asking a volunteer to summarize the responses.

VARIATIONS

1. Use the technique in small groups and have one student from each group summarize or highlight the group's responses for the class. After all groups have responded, conclude with a summary.

2. Allow each student to write a response on a card and read it in turn.

3. Use a web on the board (see Activity 6) for all to see. Record unduplicated responses.

Other Intelligences

- Logical/mathematical
- Visual/spatial
- Interpersonal
- Intrapersonal

ACTIVITY 25

Solve a Story Problem

Targeted Grades: Middle

ACTIVITY AT A GLANCE

Purpose

- To identify problems in a story to determine best solutions

When to Use

- During or at the end of a lesson or unit

What You'll Need

- Three-by-five-inch index cards
- Copies of scenarios
- Copies of Problem-Solving Chart

WHAT-TO-DO CHECKLIST

- ❐ With the whole class, brainstorm a list of favorite television shows and invite students to share why they chose them.

- ❐ On the overhead or board, draw a two-column T-chart (see Activity 139) with the headings "Problem" and "Strategies to Use." Choose one show from the list and invite a volunteer to discuss a problem situation that occurs in the show.

- ❐ Brainstorm possible solutions to the problem and complete the chart.

- ❐ Explain that students will be acting out a problem situation and deciding on a solution to the problem.

- ❐ Arrange students in groups of three and assign the following cooperative group (see Activity 128) roles: reader, recorder, and encourager. The reader will read a scenario aloud. The recorder will take notes on the group's discussion. The encourager will make sure each student has an opportunity to speak.

Problem

Lily needs money to
buy her mother a present.

Strategies to Use

Lily could baby sit
Work for her grandfather
Ask her uncle for a loan

❑ Provide each group with a scenario to dramatize. Have students discuss the situation, identify the problem, and agree on how they will solve it.

❑ Group members should decide who will play each character and then practice the skit. Allow students to use props.

❑ Invite groups to present their skits and explain the rationale behind the solutions.

❑ Give each group a copy of the Problem-Solving Chart and ask students to work together to complete it.

VARIATIONS

1. Select a short story for each group to dramatize.

2. Have one member other than the reader summarize the story for the class, and have a different member explain how the group used problem solving in the task.

3. For elementary students, read a story to the class and then form mixed-ability groups (see Activity 145) to dramatize it for the whole class. If you have sufficient strong readers, form the groups around those readers. The reader will be the director and the others will act out the story after hearing it read.

Other Intelligences

- Logical/mathematical
- Visual/spatial
- Bodily/kinesthetic
- Interpersonal
- Intrapersonal

Problem-Solving Chart

1. Character and Problem

Lily needs money to buy her mother a present.

2. Our Solution

Lily should baby sit to earn money.

3. Reasons for Our Choice of Solution

1. She knows lots of people who need babysitters.
2. She knows how to do it.

4. Signatures

Noelle
Andrew
Gerry

PART II

Logical/Mathematical Intelligence

ACTIVITY 26

WAY TO GO!

A Rubric

Target Grades: All

ACTIVITY AT A GLANCE

Purpose

- To improve understanding of mathematical concepts as identified in a guide or rubric with criteria and indicators through the use of specific criteria

When to Use

- Before, during, and following a lesson

What You'll Need

- Model rubric on PowerPoint or overhead projector

WHAT-TO-DO CHECKLIST

- ❑ Provide a model rubric for all to see. Be sure that the model details the key concepts students will develop in the lesson or unit (see Activity 8).

- ❑ Walk students through the model rubric.

- ❑ Explain the activity's purpose and check for understanding.

- ❑ Keep the model rubric posted during the lesson or unit.

- ❑ Use the model rubric during the lesson or unit to conference with students and mark progress.

- ❑ Use the model rubric at the end of the lesson or unit for final assessment.

- ❑ Provide a completed rubric for each student, to be used at parent conferences.

Math Skills: Long Division

Criteria	1	2	3	4
Accurate	Few correct	Some correct	Most correct	All correct
Process steps clearly used	Doesn't know steps	Skips steps	Most correct	All correct
Work is checked	Never	Seldom	Often	Always

VARIATIONS

1. Ask students to identify criteria to be used in the rubric.

2. Have students create individual rubrics for specific math tasks and use them as self-assessment tools upon completion of the task or tasks.

3. Use with other content areas.

Other Intelligences

- Visual/spatial

ACTIVITY 27

People Search

Targeted Grades: All

ACTIVITY AT A GLANCE

Purpose

- To access prior knowledge when introduced to a new topic in mathematics

When to Use

- When introducing students to a math topic or a unit in another subject area, or as an icebreaker with a new class
- As a lesson review

What You'll Need

- Copy of people search for each student

WHAT-TO-DO CHECKLIST

❐ Use the blank people search to create a scavenger hunt that relates to your topic or unit.

❐ Complete the statements in each square to provide clues as shown in the sample.

❐ Distribute a copy of your completed people search to each student and explain the rules:
  - In ten minutes, students must obtain a signature for as many of the squares as possible.
  - Students must first introduce themselves before asking for correct answers.
  - Students may use the signature of each student only once.
  - When students have obtained a signature for every square, they should return to their seats.

People Search

Find a person who . . .

1. has cut a pie into equal-sized pieces.	2. has broken a limb.	3. can find the sum of 1/4 + 1/2.
4. knows how many nickels are in one dollar.	5. has used a recipe with fractions.	6. knows who said, "A job half done is well begun."
7. can tell how many students are in one-fifth of this class.	8. can multiply 5/2 × 2/5 correctly.	9. who knows which is larger: 8/32 or 5/16.

❐ At the end of ten minutes, ask for volunteers to share some of the responses they recorded.

❐ Introduce the new unit's topic and bridge from what students already know to what they will be studying.

VARIATIONS

1. Develop a variety of searches for use with different lessons in all or mixed-content areas. Make language age-appropriate.

2. Use the search at the end of a lesson to tie knowledge together.

3. When students have completed their searches, invite them to make up new questions for their own people searches.

Other Intelligences

- All

ACTIVITY 28

Math Jigsaw

Targeted Grades: Middle and Secondary

ACTIVITY AT A GLANCE

Purpose

- To complete a variety of practice problems presented in a lesson

When to Use

- During guided practice and with a range of problems at the start of a lesson
- As a check for understanding prior to independent practice
- With students who benefit from sequential, step-by-step instruction or from working in a mixed-ability group

What You'll Need

- No materials necessary
- Optional materials
  ○ Math problems of a single type (such as single step or distance)
  ○ Journals (optional)

WHAT-TO-DO CHECKLIST

❐ After modeling a sample problem, explain the purpose of the activity.

❐ Give students multiple problems of the same type (such as single step or distance). Have them start with the easiest problem.

❐ After all have completed the first problem, match students in pairs to discuss how they each solved the problem.

❐ Call on volunteers to explain the methods. Identify the successful processes.

❏ Repeat this procedure through three more difficult problems until students have a clear list of how they are to think through the problem-solving process.

❏ Provide three additional but more difficult problems of the same type.

❏ Divide the number of practice problems for the assignment by the number of pairs or trios. Assign problems to each group.

❏ Encourage students to plan the steps they will take for each problem and to review what they did afterwards. Coach individuals or groups as needed.

❏ Discuss the process and procedures that worked best. Have students record these in a visual journal (see Activity 76).

❏ Teach the model formally by showing it in different formats (such as visual or spatial formats).

❏ Check for understanding or the process and the procedures. Be sure students can explain why they used each of the procedures.

❏ Assign independent practice with problems of the same type that are more difficult.

VARIATIONS

1. With same-ability groups, assign practice problems that are the appropriate level of difficulty.

2. Assign two pairs of students the same set of practice problems, writing them in their journals (see Activity 153). After each pair completes its work, invite pairs to check each other's work.

3. Add different types of problems of increasing difficulty.

Other Intelligences

- Verbal/linguistic
- Visual/spatial
- Interpersonal

ACTIVITY 29

Sequence Chart

Targeted Grades: All

ACTIVITY AT A GLANCE

Purpose

- To organize the steps for solving a problem
- To build analytical thinking skills through the use of the problem-solving process

When to Use

- At the beginning of a lesson or unit involving problem solving
- As a review during the lesson
- At the end of the lesson to summarize

What You'll Need

- Three-by-five-inch index cards
- Sequence chart of the problem-solving process
- Journals

WHAT-TO-DO CHECKLIST

☐ Review the steps for solving a math problem of a specific type (such as two-step or distance problems) using the problem-solving process taught in a previous lesson.

☐ Post the steps in a sequence chart for all to see. Write key words or phrases for each step on index cards and attach to the chart in the proper order.

☐ Encourage students to copy the chart in their journals (see Activity 153).

☐ Check for understanding by removing different cards and asking students to tell what steps are missing and why the step is important.

☐ Arrange students in pairs or trios. Give each group a word problem to solve and a set of five blank index cards. As they complete each step, have students label the front of an index card with the step completed, then on the back of the card explain why they used the step for their specific math problem.

☐ Select a group of students to model how they solved their problem. Instruct them to tape their work to the displayed sequence chart and explain why they chose to complete each step the way they did.

☐ Instruct students to explain what they learned using the sequence chart by writing in their journals.

The Problem-Solving Process

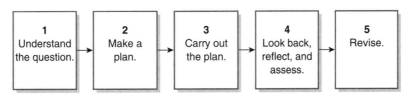

☐ Assign additional types of problems to be solved using the sequence chart.

VARIATIONS

1. Instead of having students label the problem-solving steps on index cards, have them write only the explanation for each step. Then ask each group to mix up its set of completed cards and exchange it with another group's set. Ask students to put their new set of cards in the correct sequential order and to name each problem-solving step.

2. Test for individual knowledge of the process sequence by mixing up the steps and inviting students to rearrange them to show the proper order.

3. Shorten or lengthen the number of steps based on the readiness of the students.

Other Intelligences

- Verbal/linguistic
- Visual/spatial
- Interpersonal
- Intrapersonal

ACTIVITY 30

Paired-Partner Problem Solving

Targeted Grades: Middle and Secondary

ACTIVITY AT A GLANCE

Purpose

- To apply the mathematical problem-solving process by using peer mediation

When to Use

- Throughout a math unit or lesson to help students review the explicit steps necessary for problem solving

What You'll Need

- Three-by-five-inch index cards

WHAT-TO-DO CHECKLIST

❐ Review the problem-solving processes that students have learned for each type of problem.

❏ Review students' ability to follow the procedures.

❏ Arrange students in pairs and assign two familiar problem types (such as finding circumference or radius) to each pair.

❏ Hand out two index cards per pair of students.

❏ Explain that one student is to solve Problem 1, identifying the problem-solving processes already learned for this type of problem as she completes them. The other student is to record the first student's thinking on an index card.

❏ Monitor student work and coach as needed (see Introduction, p. 11).

❏ Instruct students to repeat the process for the second problem but to reverse their roles.

❏ Randomly select two to three pairs to demonstrate their problem-solving steps for the class. Ask questions to mediate accuracy and complete use of the process.

❏ Reteach any steps students find difficult. Remix partners, assign two new problems to each pair, and repeat the problem-solving sequence.

Problem: I filled my new car's tank with 15.4 gallons of gasoline. It holds 16 gallons. I drove 534 miles, at which point I had one-fourth of a tank of gas. What was my miles per gallon?	
Step 1 What is the problem asking me to find out?	How many gallons of gas the car uses per mile?
Step 2 My plan	Decide how much gas equals one-fourth tank and subtract from what I bought. Determine how many gallons I used. Take the total number of miles the car traveled and divide it by the number of gallons of gas it used.

VARIATIONS

1. Use the problem-solving process *after* the students finish a problem to assess their thinking.

2. Invite pairs of students to create a math puzzle by writing the steps to solve a problem and leaving out some steps. Have different pairs try to determine the missing steps.

Other Intelligences

- Verbal/linguistic
- Interpersonal

ACTIVITY 31

Pizza Pizza

Targeted Grades: All

ACTIVITY AT A GLANCE

Purpose

- To represent an abstract concept in mathematics through the use of a visual tool

When to Use

- Throughout a unit to illustrate a concept in mathematics

What You'll Need

- Chart paper
- Several pizzas for students to eat

WHAT-TO-DO CHECKLIST

- ❏ On the overhead or board, draw a round pizza. Invite the class to brainstorm possible math problems (such as the cost for one pizza multiplied by the number of pizzas for a class, cost of a whole pizza (eight slices) versus the cost of eight slices, cost of ingredients plus labor versus profit margin, gross margin versus net after taxes and other overhead).
- ❏ Create mixed-ability groups (see Activity 145) of two to three students and provide each group with a sheet of chart paper. Demonstrate how to write one- and two-step word problems from the generated list of "pizza problems."
- ❏ Check for understanding (see Activity 43) and invite each group to create its own word visual problem with the pizza and write it or show it on chart paper.
- ❏ Ask each group to exchange its problem with another group for solving.
- ❏ Invite students to share their methods for solving the problems using only the pizza picture. Have the original groups check computation.
- ❏ Discuss what students learned from creating the word problems with the pizza image.
- ❏ Show students the real pizzas and challenge them to divide the pizza pies equally among the class.
- ❏ Have a party!

VARIATIONS

1. Have students think of other practical situations that involve steps, such as making a pair of jeans, baking a cake, or building a model airplane.

2. Have students set up problems involving money. Have students use play dollars and coins to solve them, recording the steps they take.

Other Intelligences

- Visual/spatial
- Verbal/linguistic
- Interpersonal

ACTIVITY 32
Understanding Circles

Targeted Grades: Secondary

ACTIVITY AT A GLANCE

Purpose

- To understand measurement terms of circles by using teamwork

When to Use

- To teach key concepts in the measurement of circles
  1. Circumference (πr^2)
  2. Diameter
  3. Radius

What You'll Need

- Newsprint
- For each group of three students
  1. Ruler
  2. Compass
  3. String
  4. Pencil
- Journals (optional)

WHAT-TO-DO CHECKLIST

❑ Divide the class into groups of three. Give each group the materials listed.

❑ Assign roles: compass holder, string holder, recorder.

❑ On the overhead, show the activity's purpose and key words to be understood.

❑ Call a volunteer to the overhead. Ask the student to estimate the distance around the outer circle on the overhead glass. Use the glass to draw a circle on the overhead. Ask if the distance around the circle is the same as the estimated distance. Explain the term "circumference."

❏ Explain πr^2 and why it is important.

❏ Introduce and define the words radius and diameter. Explain why each is important.

❏ Give instructions to the group so they can use the words in constructing circles on the newsprint. (Compass stuck into newsprint with twelve inches of string tied to compass point. Pencil tied to other end and used to trace a circle.)

❏ Instruct students how to calculate radius with the circles they have made.

❏ Change length of string and create and calculate new circles with identified circumference, radius, and diameter.

❏ Again change length of string and create and calculate new circles.

❏ Discuss what the groups learned about the similarities and differences among the circles. What rule can they formulate?

❏ Construct the formula for measuring circumference and give each student a different-size circle to calculate (such as a plate, drinking glass, wheel, and so on).

VARIATIONS

1. Adjust the size of the groups.

2. Use different types of triangles as the models to measure. For each type, what are the critical attributes?

3. Have students track the process in math journals (see Activity 153).

Other Intelligences

- Visual/spatial
- Verbal/linguistic
- Interpersonal

ACTIVITY 33

Number Survey

Targeted Grades: Middle and Secondary

ACTIVITY AT A GLANCE

Purpose

- To use surveys of familiar items as a basis for calculation

When to Use

- At the beginning of a lesson or unit to prepare students for gathering data or to introduce statistics as a tool

What You'll Need

- Calculators

WHAT-TO-DO CHECKLIST

☐ On the board or overhead, show samples of number-based survey questions (such as, "How many students are in the class? How tall is a favorite tree?").

☐ Ask the class to brainstorm some number-based questions they might ask their family members. List these questions.

☐ Select six questions for each student to ask his family.

☐ Construct a tally sheet for each question. Divide the class into six groups. Assign each group to tally one set of responses.

☐ Show students how to calculate range, mode, median, and mean (average).

    o Range: difference between highest and lowest number
    o Mode: number recurring most often
    o Median: middle number of a set in numerical order
    o Mean (average): the sum of all numbers divided by the number of units

☐ Invite students to calculate and verbalize their conclusions based on the results.

☐ Have students draw their representation of the generalizations they make for each type of calculation.

VARIATIONS

1. Make the number surveys more or less complex based on student ability.

2. Combine with a science or social studies issue to gather statistical data for a hypothesis.

Other Intelligences

- Verbal/linguistic
- Visual/spatial
- Interpersonal

ACTIVITY 34

Scale It

Targeted Grades: Middle and Secondary

ACTIVITY AT A GLANCE

Purpose

- To learn to estimate

When to Use

- At the beginning of a lesson or unit to introduce proportion and scale
- Throughout a unit to provide the foundation for more complex problems of scale

What You'll Need

- Grids
- Rulers

WHAT-TO-DO CHECKLIST

- ❏ Ask students what they know about the word "scale" (such as fish scales, weight scales, a measurement of proportion).
- ❏ Identify the scale they will work with.
- ❏ Investigate the word "proportion." What does it mean when proportion is associated with scale?
- ❏ Present a grid in a scale of ten feet by twenty feet, with each square one inch by one inch. Point out the size of each square ("one foot square") and ask students to determine the grid size.
- ❏ Tell students that the grid represents a classroom. Provide each student with a ruler to measure the size of her desk and place it on the grid in proportion.
- ❏ Ask students to calculate how many desks can fit in a ten- by twenty-foot classroom with at least 30 percent of the space not used for student desks. Have students discuss how they solved the problem.
- ❏ Discuss the meaning and value of proportion.

VARIATIONS

1. Do the measurement tasks in pairs.

2. Provide scaled cutouts of desks and so on for students to arrange on the grid.

3. Invite cooperative groups (see Activity 128) to measure furniture in the classroom or at home and to scale these on a grid.

Other Intelligences
- Verbal/linguistic
- Visual/spatial
- Interpersonal

ACTIVITY 35

Pie Chart

Targeted Grades: Middle and Secondary

ACTIVITY AT A GLANCE

Purpose

- To calculate percentages through the use of the pie chart tool

When to Use

- Prior to conducting a survey or when beginning a research project in any content area

What You'll Need

- Newsprint and markers

WHAT-TO-DO CHECKLIST

❏ Show a pie chart on the board or overhead. Invite three students to agree on how much "pie" each can eat. Mark the answers.

❏ Do a second pie chart. Invite four students to "eat some pie" and mark their answers.

❏ Explain the pie chart. Show students how they can use it to illustrate statistical results.

❏ Assign a statistical task in another content area such as social studies. Require the use of a pie chart to display results.

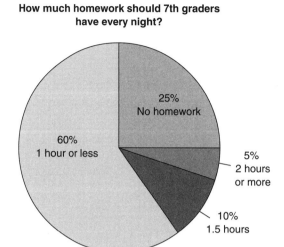

How much homework should 7th graders have every night?

VARIATIONS

1. Increase the number of samples included in the pie chart for variety.
2. Have students work in pairs or trios to create pie charts related to events, opinions, or objects in the classroom.
3. Use pie charts with research projects in science and social studies.

Other Intelligences

- Verbal/linguistic
- Visual/spatial
- Interpersonal

ACTIVITY 36

Recipe Magic

Targeted Grades: Elementary and Middle

ACTIVITY AT A GLANCE

Purpose

- To use metric and customary English (traditional U.S.) measures of capacity

When to Use

- Throughout a unit or lesson to practice calculations or to reinforce knowledge of a measurement system

What You'll Need

- Recipe
- Ingredients

- Cooking utensils
- Kitchen facilities

WHAT-TO-DO CHECKLIST

☐ Select a recipe appropriate for students by age and mathematical readiness (such as cookies for elementary students, soups for middle school students).

☐ Teach the measurement table.

☐ Provide pairs with copies of the recipe, the ingredients, and the necessary cooking utensils.

☐ Demonstrate how to use the recipe. Discuss proper measurements and check for understanding.

☐ Have student pairs combine ingredients and cook.

☐ Take time for additional problems (such as fifty cookies at one ounce per cookie is how heavy?) using the prepared items.

☐ Let students eat the snack while discussing what they learned.

VARIATIONS

1. Repeat the activity, selecting increasingly difficult recipes.

2. Have students double, halve, or triple the recipe size (use calculators).

3. Give different recipes to each group.

4. Ask students to rewrite the recipe by converting customary English measures to metric units or vice versa.

Other Intelligences
- Interpersonal
- Visual/spatial
- Verbal/linguistic

ACTIVITY 37

Collect, Count, and Classify

Targeted Grades: Elementary

ACTIVITY AT A GLANCE

Purpose

- To apply the mathematical thinking skills of counting, attributing, classifying, comparing, and contrasting

When to Use

- Throughout a unit or lesson to practice counting with real objects, to integrate mathematics with science study, and to practice analytical thinking

What You'll Need

- Several items to classify
- Containers
- Sheets of cardboard
- Straight pins
- Glue

WHAT-TO-DO CHECKLIST

- ❏ Select an item to classify (such as stones, seeds, insects, bark, leaves, or feathers). Pick one that is easy for students to scavenge.
- ❏ Provide each student with a small container, a sheet of cardboard, straight pins, and glue.
- ❏ Go on a scavenger hunt to collect the targeted objects. After all students have a set number, return to the classroom.
- ❏ Identify attributes of the object that allow classification. Set a minimum number per class. Arrange the objects by class on the cardboard. Label the classes.
- ❏ Use the classification board for counting tasks (for example, have them add the number of items in Class A and Class B, or divide the number of items in Class C into the total).
- ❏ Discuss the attributes used for forming each class. Ask about similarities and differences.

VARIATIONS

1. Use pairs and trios during the scavenger hunt.

2. Use teams to gather different, specific items.

3. Combine individual collections for larger calculations.

4. Provide students with several related items (such as books or buttons). Ask students to sort items into groups based on shared characteristics and to brainstorm as many ways to group items as possible (books with indexes, hardcover books, books with pictures, books with blue covers, and so on).

Other Intelligences

- Verbal/linguistic
- Naturalist
- Interpersonal
- Visual/spatial

ACTIVITY 38

Patterns

Targeted Grades: Elementary

ACTIVITY AT A GLANCE

Purpose

- To understand the concept of patterns

When to Use

- With elementary students prior to introducing or reviewing number patterns

What You'll Need

- Toy building blocks, such as Legos, in a variety of colors

WHAT-TO-DO CHECKLIST

- ❐ Provide each student with a set of colored building blocks. Each set will need at least two colors.

- ❐ Demonstrate how students can make a sequenced pattern using two different colors of blocks. Explain the principle of patterns so they don't just copy the example.

- ❐ Ask students to create patterns using the colored building blocks.

- ❐ Invite students to share their constructions with the class and explain the patterns they created.

- ❐ Locate patterns in buildings and other places. Discuss with students.

- ❐ Use this activity to bridge to number patterns.

VARIATIONS

1. Have students use pairs of building blocks to make the patterns.

2. Have students use three or four different colors to create more complex patterns.

3. Ask students to identify one to three examples of patterns in objects found outside the classroom. Ask them to either sketch the patterns or write a paragraph describing each pattern. Use the round-robin tactic (see Activity 24).

Other Intelligences

- Verbal/linguistic
- Visual/spatial
- Interpersonal

ACTIVITY 39

Stock Exchange

Targeted Grades: Middle and Secondary

ACTIVITY AT A GLANCE

Purpose

- To motivate students to think about mathematical applications in the real world

When to Use

- During lessons or units to practice calculations in a real-world context

What You'll Need

- Play money
- Newspapers, brochures, or financial magazines containing information on stocks

WHAT-TO-DO CHECKLIST

- ❐ Explain to students how the stock market works. Engage them with prior knowledge checks (see Activity 54).

- ❐ Provide each student with $1,000 of play money.

- ❐ Provide students with materials to research stocks such as newspapers, brochures, or financial magazines.

- ❐ Have students purchase and record their stock selections.

- ❐ One day a week, have students trade, purchase, or sell stocks and calculate their gains and losses.

- ❐ End the project after nine weeks with a discussion about what they learned using mathematics for buying and selling stocks.

- ❐ Have students post their records on newsprint around the room and do a carousel (see Activity 10).

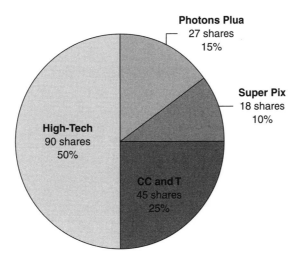

Total Number of Shares: 180

VARIATIONS

1. Use mixed-ability groups (see Activity 145) of three to five students.

2. Use mutual funds or bonds instead of stocks.

3. Visit a stock exchange and talk with a stockbroker about numbers.

4. Create an all-class line graph so students can track gains and losses of individual stocks.

5. Create pie charts (see Activity 35) that show a student's investment portfolio, or the specific stocks purchased and percentage of overall investment.

Other Intelligences

- Verbal/linguistic
- Interpersonal

ACTIVITY 40

Measure My Garden

Targeted Grades: Middle

ACTIVITY AT A GLANCE

Purpose

- To engage students in the use of measurement by laying out a garden

When to Use

- As a project to teach measurement

What You'll Need

For each pair of students:

- Tape measure
- Ruler
- Three-by-five-inch index cards
- Ball of string
- Stake
- Journal
- Garden catalog

WHAT-TO-DO CHECKLIST

- ❒ Randomly assign students as partners to work together throughout the project.
- ❒ Take students to a local garden or show a slide show of a garden.
- ❒ Explain the activity and its purpose.
- ❒ Give each pair several garden supply catalogs. (Write to a garden supply catalog company ahead of time and request the number you need.)
- ❒ Have students identify how the catalog is categorized.
- ❒ Have each pair select a category that will be the heart of their garden. Have each pair select twelve to twenty-four varieties of plant for their garden from that category.
- ❒ Show students where they will find the recommendations for how to space the plants (in inches).
- ❒ Designate the size of the garden plot (in feet) for each pair. Make the garden size appropriate to the students' age.
- ❒ Have students calculate the space layout for the plants selected. They may plant from three to twelve plants per variety selected in each category. The lot size will determine how many plants they can plant of each variety.
- ❒ Using rulers and pencils, each pair will sketch in their journals (see Activity 153) its garden in proportion to the full site.
- ❒ Coach and check all calculations.
- ❒ Take the class to a local park where they will all have room to stake out their plots and place markers for each type of plant.
- ❒ On each stake, attach an index card with a picture of the variety.
- ❒ Take pictures of the final gardens that students can share with their parents and explain what they learned.
- ❒ Take up the stakes and leave the park as it was.
- ❒ Use a round-robin (see Activity 24) with a lead-in (see Activity 9) to conclude the project.

VARIATIONS

1. Use a site where the students can actually plant and care for a spring garden. Have them estimate the products they will gather at the spring harvest.
2. Make a single garden plan to which all students contribute.

Other Intelligences
- Visual/spatial
- Naturalist
- Verbal/linguistic
- Interpersonal

ACTIVITY 41

Problem-Solving Strategy Wheel

Targeted Grades: All

ACTIVITY AT A GLANCE

Purpose
- To learn to use multiple problem-solving strategies

When to Use
- Each time students practice problem solving in a unit or lesson, use to select a different model

What You'll Need
- Problem-solving strategies wheel
- Journals

WHAT-TO-DO CHECKLIST

☐ Create a cardboard problem-solving strategies wheel prior to actual classroom usage (see sample).

☐ Provide a mathematics problem from the textbook. Spin the spinner and ask a student to follow the instructions given on the wheel.

☐ Review how the student demonstrated the technique.

☐ Spin the spinner again to select another strategy to use for the same mathematics problem. Repeat until several strategies have been demonstrated.

☐ Encourage students to keep a page in their journals (see Activity 153) for each strategy: What it is. How it works. When to use it. Helpful hints. (See Activity 152.)

Problem-Solving Startegies Wheel

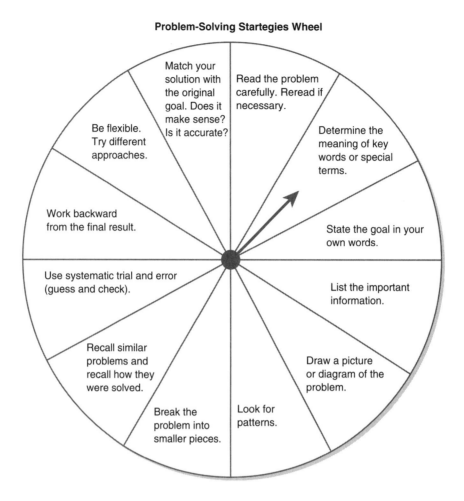

VARIATIONS

1. Use the wheel before students work on a mathematics problem. Assign the selected strategy to the entire class.

2. Use the wheel after students have completed an assignment.

3. Use pairs to practice the techniques.

4. Provide each student with a wheel to use during homework tasks.

5. Create a people search (see Activity 27) as a final review of the strategies used.

Other Intelligences

- Visual/spatial
- Verbal/linguistic
- Interpersonal
- Intrapersonal

ACTIVITY 42

Treasure Map

Targeted Grades: Middle

ACTIVITY AT A GLANCE

Purpose

- To complete a problem-solving task and mathematical computations through the use of a game format or physical activity

When to Use

- To motivate student interest by providing a series of challenging tasks to complete
- To review material before a test

What You'll Need

- Cardboard sets of mathematical questions or problem-solving activities
- Copies of a treasure map

WHAT-TO-DO CHECKLIST

- ❏ Create four sets of mathematical computations or problem-solving tasks. Write them on cardboard and hide cards around the room.
- ❏ Form four mixed-ability groups (see Activity 145) of students.
- ❏ Give each group a treasure map with clues for finding all the hidden cards. When they find a card students must perform the task or complete the mathematical computation on that card. Successful completion can earn students points for a grade or a team prize.
- ❏ Set a time limit.
- ❏ After the hunt is done, review the results with a **jigsaw** grouping (see Activity 28) of students assembled from teams.

VARIATIONS

1. Make this an individual search. Each day, hide clues for the new tasks. When an individual finds a clue or task, she completes it.

2. Hide parts of a problem on different days. Over several days, have students find the pieces so they can eventually solve the entire problem.

Other Intelligences

- Visual/spatial
- Interpersonal

ACTIVITY 43

Check for Understanding

A Tool for Differentiating Instruction

Targeted Grades: All

ACTIVITY AT A GLANCE

Purpose

- To ensure understanding of meaning for key concepts taught

When to Use

- Throughout a lesson or unit, or at the end of an explanation or set of instructions to check for student understanding and to differentiate students by understanding

What You'll Need

- Journals

WHAT-TO-DO CHECKLIST

- ☐ Provide students with specific problems to solve based on a key concept (such as fractions, right triangles, equations).
- ☐ Demonstrate how to solve one example.
- ☐ Check for understanding by asking for show of hands that indicate "yes, I understand how to do this" (hands up), "I am not sure how to do this" (hands halfway up), or "I definitely do not know how to do this" (hands on the desk).
- ☐ Demonstrate the procedure.
- ☐ At appropriate steps in the procedure, ask students to show understanding by indicating thumbs up for yes, to the side for unsure, or down for no.
- ☐ Ask students who are signaling uncertainty to tell what they *do* understand so far. Clarify as needed.
- ☐ Ask students who don't understand to pinpoint the spots of confusion. Reteach as needed or call on students to coach each other or explain to the class.
- ☐ Ask those who are unsure what they do not understand or what is confusing them. List these points on the board for all to see.

❏ Ask those who are sure to explain the listed items one by one.

❏ Using a show of fingers (one low to five high) ask students to revote. Ask those with low scores to explain what is confusing them and students with high scores to respond.

❏ Recheck with show of fingers. Group students with high and low scores in their own differentiated groups.

❏ Provide those with high scores (four to five) with five to seven additional problems that they will solve.

❏ Take other students and reinstruct problem model with concrete representations (such as pie charts for fractions; see Activity 35).

❏ After students are ready, assign additional problems.

❏ When all students are finished with sample problems, select volunteers to put their solutions on the board and explain what/how/why they solved the problem.

❏ Identify general principles for solving this problem.

❏ Have students record the general principles in journals (see Activity 153) and save for use with independent practice.

❏ Assign independent practice.

VARIATIONS

1. Give students a cue card with different colors on each side (such as red, yellow, and green) to use instead of raising their hands.

2. After you end the first check for understanding, divide the students into groups (a) green cards (b) yellow cards, (c) red cards.

Other Intelligences

- Visual/spatial
- Bodily/kinesthetic
- Verbal/linguistic
- Interpersonal

ACTIVITY 44

The Fishbone Chart

Targeted Grades: Secondary

ACTIVITY AT A GLANCE

Purpose

- To distinguish between causes and effects

When to Use

- Throughout or at the end of a lesson to prepare students to examine important events from a cause-effect perspective

What You'll Need

- Match, candle, lighter
- Chart paper

WHAT-TO-DO CHECKLIST

- ❏ Invite a student to the front of the classroom. Light a match, and have the student blow it out. Repeat this with a candle and then with a lighter. On the board or overhead, list the student blowing as a cause and the extinguished flames as effects.

- ❏ Ask volunteers to explain why they think the student was listed as a cause and why the extinguished flames were effects. Use questions to elicit definitions for and examples of cause and effect.

- ❏ Explain that they are going to use a tool, the **fishbone** diagram, to help them understand more complex causes and effects. Display a model of the fishbone diagram. Show examples and gather ideas to fill in the blanks.

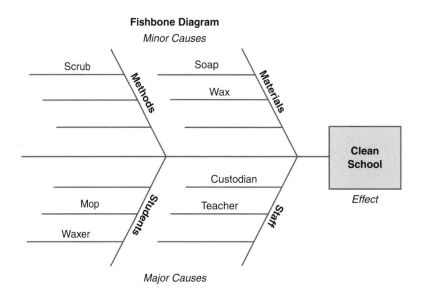

- ❏ Create mixed-ability groups (see Activity 145) of three to five students.

- ❏ Assign roles (facilitator, materials manager, and recorder).

- ❏ Supply chart paper and marker to materials manager.

- ❏ Have the recorder outline the fishbone diagram.

- ❏ Brainstorm a list of familiar effects in the school or community.

- ❏ Let each group select its effect, place it on the diagram, and then build causes and examples. The facilitator guides the group and double checks the responses.

❐ Post the completed diagrams.

❐ Use a rotating system so that each group has the opportunity to inspect all the diagrams.

❐ Brainstorm situations for which students might find this tool to be useful. Here are same examples:
  ○ Language arts: causes of a conflict between characters
  ○ History: causes of a major historic event such as a war
  ○ Science: causes of a chemical reaction
  ○ Health: damage from drug use

❐ Select an appropriate cause-effect issue in the next unit of study. Review the fishbone diagram process before having students create the pattern for the chosen issue. Post and carousel (see Activity 10) the pattern before discussing the unit through the perspective of cause and effect.

❐ Conclude the unit lesson by assessing
  ○ individual ability to use the fishbone diagram with a new cause-effect topic,
  ○ each student's understanding of the terms, and
  ○ students' understanding of the unit material examined through the cause-effect pattern.

VARIATIONS

1. Move from the simple model to complex examples using the course content.

2. Challenge students to explain various connections and their importance. Debate priority selections, causes, and effects.

3. Introduce "correlation" as a concept that is different from "causation." Have students create a **Venn diagram** (see Activity 66) of the two concepts.

Other Intelligences

- Visual/spatial
- Interpersonal
- Verbal/linguistic

ACTIVITY 45

Go Figure

Targeted Grades: Secondary

ACTIVITY AT A GLANCE

Purpose

- To reinforce the ability to distinguish geometric shapes

When to Use

- At the end of a course

What You'll Need

- Journals
- Pencils

WHAT-TO-DO CHECKLIST

- ☐ Select a site where building facades show a plethora of examples.

- ☐ During the course review at the end of the year, announce the project: a field trip to identify geometric shapes.

- ☐ Prepare for the field trip according to school regulations (permission slips, arrangement for a bus, lunches, and so on).

- ☐ Explain the task's purpose to the students.

- ☐ Divide the students into pairs. Instruct them to find and record in their journals (see Activity 153) the geometric shapes they see, label them, and note locations.

- ☐ Travel to the site.

- ☐ Back in the classroom, do a people search (see Activity 27) of the various possible figures.

- ☐ Review the distinguishing attributes of each geometric form and check for understanding (see Activity 43).

VARIATIONS

1. Provide students with a list of shapes to find (names only). Review the list before leaving on the field trip.

2. If there are insufficient geometric figures available to see at your selected site, create a PowerPoint presentation, including photographs of buildings. Show in class and have students pick out the figures they see.

Other Intelligences

- Visual/spatial
- Verbal/linguistic
- Interpersonal

ACTIVITY 46

Math Career Collage

Targeted Grades: Middle

ACTIVITY AT A GLANCE

Purpose

- To motivate interest in study of mathematics

When to Use

- At a teachable moment when students object to studying math as a useless subject

What You'll Need

- Computer and projector
- PowerPoint presentation
- Sheets of cardboard
- Magazines
- Scissors
- Paste or glue

WHAT-TO-DO CHECKLIST

- ❐ Set up the computer and projector with your prepared presentation that shows pictures of people at work in fields where math is central (such as insurance, banking, sports reporting, cooking, and so on).

- ❐ Identify math needed in the field. Show examples (doubling recipes, showing standings of individuals in sports, keeping track of account activity, and so on).

- ❐ After your presentation, form mixed-ability groups (see Activity 145) of three and identify their roles.

- ❐ Ask teams of students to make a poster ad about what they learned about math careers (see Activity 61).

- ❐ Distribute materials to each group and give instructions for making a collage that shows the use of numbers in one or more careers.

- ❐ Display completed collages.

VARIATIONS

1. Invite a series of speakers from different fields (start with parent volunteers) to talk about math in their field.

2. In place of math in a field, ask the PowerPoint or speaker to address the use of logic in a career field.

Other Intelligences

- Visual/spatial
- Verbal/linguistic
- Interpersonal

ACTIVITY 47

Logic Organizers

Targeted Grades: All

ACTIVITY AT A GLANCE

Purpose

- To develop specific thinking skills

When to Use

- In lessons to introduce a specific thinking operation that is important in that lesson
- In lessons to help students solve a thinking problem
- In lessons to help students see the thinking they are asked to do

What You'll Need

- Newsprint
- Markers
- Demonstration graphic organizer

WHAT-TO-DO CHECKLIST

❏ Select the graphic organizer that matches the thinking operation that students will do in the lesson, unit, or project. Examples of graphic organizers can be found throughout the text: Venn diagram (see Activity 66), musical styles (see Activity 111), classification matrixes (see Activity 179), concept maps (see Activities 4, 113, and 163), T-Chart (see Activity 163).

❏ Explain the thinking operation and ask students why it is important in school or life situations.

❏ Show the selected graphic and connect it to the thinking operation.

❏ Divide the class into mixed-ability groups (see Activity 145) of three and assign roles.

❏ Distribute materials to each group.

❏ Select a concrete example and show the students how to use the organizer.

❏ Use the text or other resource materials. Invite the students to construct their organizer.

❏ When all students have completed their organizers, have two groups pair to make a group of six. Have them compare the organizers and help each other correct or add items.

❏ Use the overhead and invite group reporters to help you complete a master organizer for all to see. Discuss disagreements.

❏ Discuss how the organizer helped the students develop the targeted thinking operation. From their points, form a definition or description of the operation.

❏ Repeat the operation or organizer with additional material later in the unit.

VARIATIONS

1. Give the students an age-appropriate text to read before starting the activity. Select the text so that it matches the thinking operation you want to teach. After reading, present the organizer on the overhead and call for volunteers to provide information.

2. Discuss the thinking operation and other places that they might use it in the curriculum.

3. Use this process with various organizers appropriate to the thinking operations in your standards.

Other Intelligences

- Visual/spatial
- Verbal/linguistic
- Interpersonal

ACTIVITY 48

The Magic Mediator

Targeted Grades: All

ACTIVITY AT A GLANCE

Purpose

- To develop the quality of logic
- To strengthen deficient or weak cognitive functions

When to Use

- At teachable moments when you notice weak logic or poor use of thinking operations (such as when comparing or hypothesizing)

What You'll Need

- Chart board
- Journals

WHAT-TO-DO CHECKLIST

☐ Introduce the noticed function (see chart of cognitive functions) to the class with examples.

Chart of Selected Cognitive Functions

- Restrained impulsivity
- Connected ideas
- Precision
- Accuracy
- Sharp perception
- Spontaneous comparative behavior
- Problem recognition
- Simultaneous use of multiple information sources
- Deciphering of key points
- Conservation of constancies
- Provision of detail
- Summative behavior

(Feuerstein, 2007)

☐ Define the desired function (such as precise thought).

☐ Give examples for the lesson you are teaching (for example, whole numbers).

☐ Students to identify other similar examples.

☐ In journals (see Activity 153), have each student make a goal for improving the targeted function. Be sure that the goals are specific, measurable, and related to your content.

☐ Each day, match pairs to share how each is doing with the common goal (see Activity 127).

☐ Give positive feedback to instances of student performance related to the function.

VARIATIONS

1. Change the targeted function at least once per quarter.

2. Make a classroom chart showing progress on improving the function.

3. Once a week, ask students to share their progress in a think-pair-share (see Activity 148).

4. Expand the list of functions to target (Feuerstein et al., 2007).

Other Intelligences

- Visual/spatial
- Verbal/linguistic
- Interpersonal
- Intrapersonal

ACTIVITY 49

Getting to the Big Idea

Targeted Grades: Middle and Secondary

ACTIVITY AT A GLANCE

Purpose

- To be able to transcend facts and form in content areas

When to Use

- In each lesson so that students understand key concepts

What You'll Need

- Five-by-eight-inch index cards
- Markers
- Tape

WHAT-TO-DO CHECKLIST

❏ Introduce the class to the key objectives of the lesson. Highlight the core concept in each objective (such as, "To understand the causes of the Civil War").

❏ Explain the core concepts and develop a definition of each.

❏ Rephrase the core concepts as questions (such as, "Why are these causes important?").

❏ Form mixed-ability groups (see Activity 145) of three. Instruct them to use the text material to find the answers to each question and record the answers on which they agree.

❏ Have the groups reduce their answers for each question or objective to a single word or phrase and write the phrase on an index card. Post the cards for all to see.

❏ Start with the first concept or question. Invite one group to post the question card with the answer cards underneath. Ask other groups in turn to add any missing cards or answers.

❏ Repeat with a new group starting the responses to each question.

❏ Check for agreement that the answer cards are appropriate and that they answer the questions completely.

❏ Solicit ideas from the class for a header card that will encompass all the answer cards. This card should state the big ideas that tie the unit together.

❏ Ask each group to put the big ideas into their own words and to share these with one other group.

VARIATIONS

1. Use resource materials (film, magazine articles, and so on) to provide the information.

2. Shorten the number of objectives used to three for middle school students.

3. Designate specific roles and responsibilities in each group.

4. End with each student making a poster (see Activity 61) about one of the big ideas.

Other Intelligences

- Verbal/linguistic
- Interpersonal
- Visual/spatial

ACTIVITY 50

Hypothesis Test

Targeted Grades: Secondary

ACTIVITY AT A GLANCE

Purpose

- To learn how to make and check hypotheses

When to Use

- At the start of a lesson or project

What You'll Need

- Journals
- Newsprint
- Markers

WHAT-TO-DO CHECKLIST

❒ At the start of the lesson or unit, explain that the purpose is to learn the content (give the content objective) by creating and testing a hypotheses. Define and explain the value of this approach.

❒ Ask the students to do a read-through of the chapter material they will study. They should record the key concepts and ideas in their journals (see Activity 153).

❒ With the class, generate a list of six to eight important "what if" questions based on what the students have read in their content.

　○ Social studies: "What if Washington had decided not to cross the Delaware? What do you think might have happened?"

　○ English: "What if Scout (in *To Kill a Mockingbird*) had not _____?"

　○ Science: "What if you mix _____with ____?"

❒ Group students in trios of mixed ability (see Activity 145). Assign roles of reader, recorder, and reporter.

❒ Give each group the markers and newsprint it will need to write its results.

❒ Instruct groups to find the answer to the two questions you assign them. Do a random mix of the questions and round-robin (see Activity 24) the responses.

❒ Facilitate "explain why" responses (see Activity 7).

❒ Have students write out their conclusions and provide their evidence they have developed for each.

❒ Have reporters from each group present the responses. Ask the other groups to discuss whether the evidence provided does or does not test the hypothesis.

❒ Ask each group to make a rubric (see Activity 8) and then self-assess itself on the thinking processes involved in hypothesizing.

VARIATIONS

1. Use groups from the start of the task.

2. Explore with the students what other resources they could use to test the hypothesis.

3. Complete the rubric at the start of the project so students can follow it throughout the project.

4. Use a carousel (see Activity 10) to display groups' work.

Other Intelligences

- Visual/spatial
- Verbal/linguistic
- Interpersonal
- Naturalist

ACTIVITY 51

Gallery Walk

Targeted Grades: Middle and Secondary

ACTIVITY AT A GLANCE

Purpose

- To display visual work by teams for examination

When to Use

- At the completion of the central task in a research project

What You'll Need

- Overhead projector
- Overhead transparencies
- Poster board
- Art supplies
- Journals
- Newsprint
- Markers

WHAT-TO-DO CHECKLIST

❐ Introduce the lesson or project by stating its purpose and outcomes.

❐ Create mixed-ability groups (see Activity 145) of three to five students.

❐ Present the research launch question (see Activity 182) for the project in the targeted content areas (science, language arts, social studies, mathematics, and so on).

❐ Check for prior knowledge (see Activity 54).

❐ Introduce journal use (see Activity 153) with a daily lead-in (see Activity 9) to end each class period.

❐ Set timelines for interim reports and present a rubric for the reports (see Activity 8).

☐ Use a snapshot sequence chart (see Activity 72) to outline the procedures and their order in the research project. Make the procedures appropriate to your content.

☐ Coach the groups as they do the research and assemble the project (see Introduction, p. 11).

☐ At prescheduled points, check for understanding (see Activity 43) using appropriate lead-in statements and "explain why" questions (see Activity 7).

☐ When teams have finished research, instruct them to select a visual display (such as 28 [math jigsaw], 35 [pie chart], 47 [logic organizers], 61 [make a poster], 68 [create a collage]) or other appropriate visual representation.

☐ Instruct students to create the visual representation of their research. Show some examples.

☐ Post the completed visuals around the room. Have each team select one member to "host" and answer questions as other students walk through the gallery.

☐ After the walk is complete, have each team assess its research process, its product, and its understanding with the prepared rubric.

VARIATIONS

1. Select a different prior knowledge assessment strategy (see Activity 54).

2. Allow teams to frame their own launch question at the end of a unit just completed.

3. Allow select individuals to work alone.

4. Use like-ability groups.

Other Intelligences
- All

PART III

Visual/Spatial Intelligence

ACTIVITY 52

Hourglass Graphic

Targeted Grades: Middle and Secondary

ACTIVITY AT A GLANCE

Purpose

- To construct "what if" questions based on prior knowledge of a topic or an idea

When to Use

- At the start of a new lesson, unit, or project or to bridge between subtopics

What You'll Need

- Hourglass graphic

WHAT-TO-DO CHECKLIST

- ☐ Introduce the central idea or topic of the new lesson, unit, or project. Explain the purpose of this activity.

- ☐ Display an hourglass graphic on the board or overhead. Write the topic in the center of the image. Describe how the hourglass shape can be used as a visual organizer for recalling prior knowledge (see Activity 54) (convergent thinking) and for building hypothetical "what if" questions (divergent thinking).

- ☐ Invite the class to brainstorm what they know about the topic you have selected. Write these items in the upper portion of the hourglass. Then brainstorm "what if" questions about these ideas and write them in the lower portion.

- ☐ Encourage students to combine ideas from the list to frame "what if" questions that will help them investigate the topic further.

- ☐ Using their list, provide examples of "what if" questions from their list.

- ☐ After the "what if" list is complete, assign one question to each student to track responses given throughout the unit.

- ☐ At the end of the lesson, unit, or project, show a sample summary statement for the information tracked for a specific hypothetical question. Point out the organizing principles for the statement.

- ☐ Provide a rubric (see Activity 8) for a summarizing statement.

- ☐ Assign students the task of summarizing the selected "what if" hypotheses.

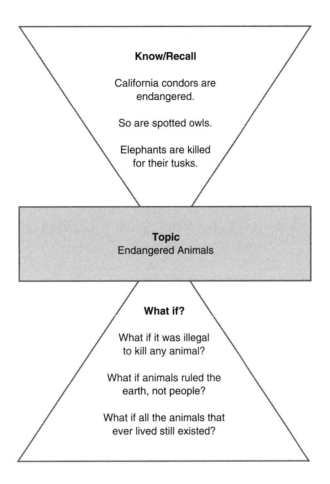

VARIATIONS

1. Brainstorm in cooperative groups (see Activity 128) of three students each.

2. Have students create "what if" questions in pairs before making the all-class list. Instruct each pair to construct several questions and select its best question for the list.

3. After listing prior knowledge (see Activity 54), use texts or other resource materials to help construct the "what if" questions.

4. Assign cooperative pairs or trios to search out answers to one of the "what if" questions. Have students work together to prepare an all-class report.

5. Do a round-robin reading (see Activity 24) of summary statements in groups of five. Invite students to use the summarizing rubric to give feedback to each other.

Other Intelligences

- Verbal/linguistic
- Logical/mathematical
- Intrapersonal

ACTIVITY 53

Concept Connections

Targeted Grades: Middle and Secondary

ACTIVITY AT A GLANCE

Purpose

- To connect prior knowledge on a topic by using a concept map

When to Use

- With students familiar with concept maps

What You'll Need

- Chart paper
- Markers

WHAT-TO-DO CHECKLIST

- ❐ On the overhead or board, identify the topic or concept students will explore in a new lesson, unit, or project. Draw a circle, and put the key word inside that circle.

- ❐ Invite students to tell something they know about the topic. Branch each item they suggest from the circle. Invite students to give more ideas to branch from the central idea or from the other ideas.

- ❐ After ten to twelve items have formed the basis of a concept map, divide the class into cooperative groups (see Activity 128) of five students each.

- ❐ After all groups have copied the beginning portion of the map, invite them to continue the map's development on sheets of chart paper. Allow ten to twenty minutes.

- ❐ When the groups are finished, post the maps for a gallery walk (see Activity 51) and discuss their similarities and differences.

- ❐ Display a list of the key subconcepts to the topic of the lesson or unit. Show how these connect to students' prior knowledge (see Activity 54) or ask students how they think the ideas connect.

VARIATIONS

1. Arrange students in groups of three to five at the beginning of the project.

2. Post the completed group maps and do a carousel review (see Activity 10).

3. After students learn to use the strategy in groups, use it with individual research projects.

4. As the study of the topic continues, have groups use colored markers to add new knowledge to the maps. This technique is especially appropriate for individual or collaborative group research or inquiry projects.

Other Intelligences

- Verbal/linguistic
- Bodily/kinesthetic
- Intrapersonal

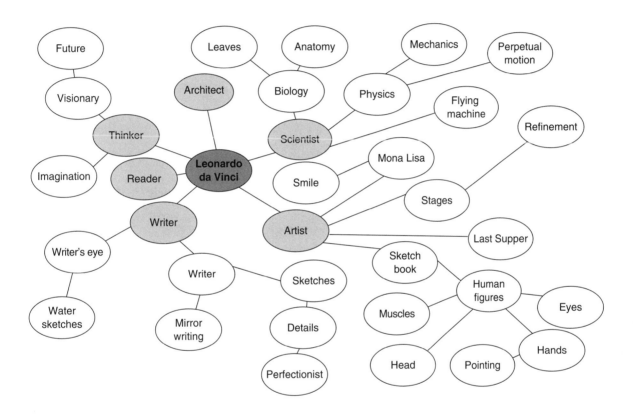

ACTIVITY 54

KWL: A Prior Knowledge Check

Targeted Grades: All

ACTIVITY AT A GLANCE

Purpose

- To remember prior knowledge before investigating a new topic, lesson, unit, or problem
- To reflect on new learning after the investigation

When to Use

- At the beginning of a new lesson or unit to connect prior knowledge to or increase excitement about a new topic
- After the completion of the lesson or unit, to assess learning

What You'll Need

- Chart paper
- Markers

WHAT-TO-DO CHECKLIST

- ☐ On a sheet of large chart paper, sketch a KWL chart (see figure). Explain or review the meaning for each letter of KWL (what we **K**now, what we **W**ant to know, and what we **L**earned).

- ☐ Introduce a topic and ask the class to brainstorm what they already know about it. Record the ideas in the first column of the chart. Encourage every student to respond.

- ☐ When the "K" column is full, repeat the brainstorming process for the "W" column. Remember to provide wait time (at least three seconds of thinking time after each question and after each response) as necessary. Ask for clarification for meanings of terms that don't seem to fit.

- ☐ On the last day of the lesson, reflect on student learning by brainstorming items to list in the "L" column.

The Planets in Our Solar System

What we Know	What we Want to Know	What we Learned
Earth is one. Some have rings.	Are there any we can't see with a telescope?	The rings around Saturn are gases with pieces of lead.
Some are hot and some are cold.	Could there be life on other planets?	Some planets have more than one moon.

VARIATIONS

1. Invite each student (or pair of students) to pick an item from the "W" column. The student then becomes the expert "researcher" for that item during the lesson. She should report on the item when the class completes the "L" column.

2. Instead of listing "What we want to know" in the second column, change the "W" to "P" (What we predict we'll learn) and list the students' predictions.

3. Invite students to write a strong summary statement (see Activity 157) based on the L column.

Other Intelligences

- Verbal/linguistic
- Interpersonal
- Intrapersonal

ACTIVITY 55

Web Check

Targeted Grades: All

ACTIVITY AT A GLANCE

Purpose

- To remember prior knowledge about a new topic being introduced in a lesson or unit
- To check on knowledge or questions about content in the middle of a lesson or unit

When to Use

- At the beginning of a lesson or unit to connect or bridge students' prior knowledge to the new topic
- In the middle of a lesson to check for understanding with statements or questions

What You'll Need

- Board and chalk or newsprint
- Marker with web illustration

WHAT-TO-DO CHECKLIST

❏ Draw a web on the overhead, chart paper, or board for all to see.

❏ Put the topic to be introduced in the center of the web.

❏ Invite students to recall what they know or have previously learned about the topic. Ask each student to provide one new idea. Record each new idea on a branch of the web. Adjust the lesson according to what the prior knowledge (see Activity 54) check reveals.

❏ If activity is taking place in the middle of a lesson, ask the students to generate questions on the material so far about which they need more information or clarification.

❏ Invite volunteers to summarize common points on the web. Explain the connections to the lesson being introduced. Keep the web visible throughout the lesson or unit and add to it daily to keep students focused on key concepts. If you use it as a question web in the middle of a lesson, ask volunteers to try and answer each question.

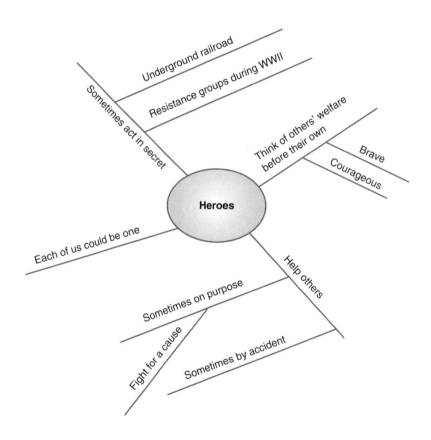

VARIATIONS

1. Use a concept map (see Activity 53) rather than a web. Fill in what the students already know, and then add new ideas.

2. Use with a short story or a fairy tale for elementary grades.

3. Use pairs of students in the middle of the lesson to generate questions.

4. Invite students to work in small groups to create their own Webs. Post these with a carousel (see Activity 10) or gallery walk (see Activity 51).

Other Intelligences

- Verbal/linguistic
- Bodily/kinesthetic
- Intrapersonal

ACTIVITY 56

Learning Links

Targeted Grades: All

ACTIVITY AT A GLANCE

Purpose

- To connect or bridge past experiences to new ideas

When to Use

- When reviewing a previous unit
- When introducing a new concept to the class

What You'll Need

- Visual aids
- Strips of paper (six inch by one inch)
- Glue

WHAT-TO-DO CHECKLIST

❒ Write a word on the overhead or board that introduces the key concept or idea of a new lesson, unit, or project.

❒ Use visual aids to help students understand the idea (such as photographs, PowerPoint presentation, collage, montage, sketches, video, and so on).

❒ Place students in cooperative groups of three (see Activity 128). Ask them to think of experiences they have had with the key concept of the lesson. For example, if the concept is "respect," the students can recall times when others were respectful toward them.

❏ Give each group a six-inch strip of paper on which to write examples of the key word or key words.

❏ Have groups glue their strips to other groups' strips to form one chain. This chain shows all the links to the original concept.

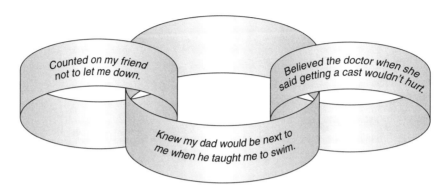

Concept: Trust

VARIATIONS

1. Have group members tell about the experience using a think-pair-share (see Activity 148) and how it connects to the new idea.

2. Have each student create her own link in the chain and hang the all-class chain across the classroom, high enough so it will not be a hazard or distraction.

3. Form new groups of three. Have each group prepare a strong summary statement (see Activity 157) of how the members' experiences connect to the core idea.

Other Intelligences

- Verbal/linguistic
- Interpersonal
- Intrapersonal

ACTIVITY 57

Create an Ad

Targeted Grades: All

ACTIVITY AT A GLANCE

Purpose

- To build on prior knowledge by learning more about a topic or concept

When to Use

- At the beginning of a new lesson, topic, unit, or semester

What You'll Need

- Resource materials for the topic of study
- Construction paper

WHAT-TO-DO CHECKLIST

❏ Divide the class into cooperative groups (see Activity 128) of three to five students each.

❏ Assemble a collection of visual materials that provide information on the topic of study (pictures cut from magazines, newspapers, sketches, and so on).

❏ Instruct each group to select four to six visuals that reflect different aspects of the topic.

❏ Let the students review the materials and make two lists: what they know and what they want to know about the topic (see Activity 54). At they end, they will make a third list about what they have learned.

❏ Show students sample ads from a magazine or newspaper. Discuss what each is selling and how the ad sells the product or service.

❏ Ask each group to use the ideas to create a newspaper or magazine ad, "selling" the study of the topic.

❏ Post the ads and discuss their content and method of selling.

❏ Make the third list: "What have I learned?"

VARIATIONS

1. Use when previewing a story with elementary students.

2. Use when previewing a research topic with middle or secondary students.

3. Use at the end of a lesson to "sell" the lesson to next year's students.

Other Intelligences

- Verbal/linguistic
- Interpersonal
- Intrapersonal

ACTIVITY 58

We-Know Parachute

Targeted Grades: Elementary and Middle

ACTIVITY AT A GLANCE

Purpose

- To build on prior knowledge while working through a unit or lesson

When to Use

- At the introduction of a lesson or unit to help elementary and middle school students build on prior knowledge in a purposeful way

What You'll Need

- Construction paper
- String
- Scissors
- Glue
- Three-by-five-inch index cards

WHAT-TO-DO CHECKLIST

- ☐ Divide the class into pairs.

- ☐ Explain the purpose of the activity.

- ☐ Have students construct a parachute using string, construction paper, and index cards. Do not prediscuss or model other then to ask the students to use their creativity.

- ☐ Instruct students to write on each index card something they know about the lesson, unit, or topic being introduced.

- ☐ Hang the parachutes around the room. As students learn something new about the topic, they may add new cards to their parachutes.

- ☐ At the end of the lesson, ask each student to reflect on what was learned and to write and send a card that summarizes the ideas (see Activity 75).

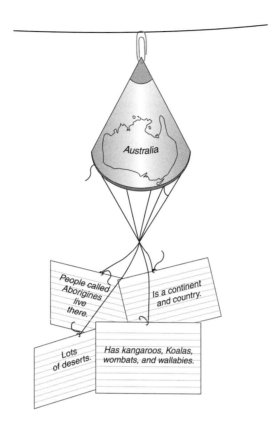

VARIATIONS

1. End each lesson of the unit with students adding new cards.

2. Have middle school students compete for the number of cards added each day.

Other Intelligences

- Verbal/linguistic
- Interpersonal
- Intrapersonal

ACTIVITY 59

Mindful Mobile

Targeted Grades: Elementary and Middle

ACTIVITY AT A GLANCE

Purpose

- To connect prior knowledge to a new topic

When to Use

- When introducing a new topic or unit to check prior knowledge and to prepare students for new information

What You'll Need

- Wire coat hangers
- String
- Three-by-five-inch index cards
- Magazines
- Sample mobile

WHAT-TO-DO CHECKLIST

❏ Make a mobile from coat hangers, index cards, string, and magazine pictures. Show it to students as a model for this task.

❏ Divide the class into groups of three students each. Explain the purpose of this activity and introduce the concept for use on the mobiles.

❏ Instruct each group to make a mobile that illustrates what it knows about the concept to be studied.

❏ Hang the mobiles and encourage each group to explain its own mobile. As you take the class through the lesson, connect ideas on the mobiles to subconcepts that emerge in the lesson

❏ Revisit the mobiles to review the lesson. Ask students to explain what they have learned about a subconcept and connect it to the key concept by using the round-robin questioning pattern (see Activity 24).

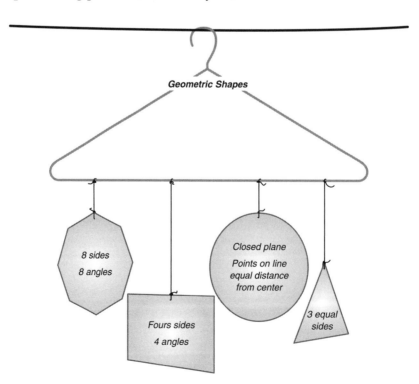

VARIATIONS

1. Let students explore the resources and text before making the mobiles.

2. Have students paste a picture illustrating the concept on one side of an index card and record information on the other side.

3. Create mobiles by cutting out shapes of related objects (such as types of butterflies) and listing or sketching unique features of each.

4. Conclude the lesson by having each student create an "I learned" mobile. Match students in pairs to explain their mobiles to each other.

Other Intelligences

- Verbal/linguistic
- Interpersonal
- Intrapersonal
- Naturalist

ACTIVITY 60

Topical Museum

Targeted Grades: Elementary and Middle

ACTIVITY AT A GLANCE

Purpose

- To make thoughtful connections between prior knowledge and a new lesson, concept, topic, or unit

When to Use

- When introducing a topic as well as during a unit to collect **artifacts** of the lesson or unit

What You'll Need

- Various art supplies

WHAT-TO-DO CHECKLIST

❑ Invite students to tell what they already know about museums (see Activity 54). Discuss different types and purposes of museums. Connect the purpose of this activity to the metaphor of the museum as a storehouse of artifacts.

❑ Introduce the topic or concept for the lesson or unit by previewing the materials or text they will use (see Activity 2).

❑ Form cooperative groups (see Activity 128) of three students each. Assign roles of museum director, artifact registrar, and compiler. Discuss the roles of each as if in a museum.

❑ Invite each group to brainstorm a list of what its members know about the topic or concept they are going to study. Explain that each group is to select one of the "what we know" statements from its list and make an artifact (such as a sketch, sculpture, writing sample, mobile, and so on) to represent it.

❑ Provide students with the art supplies.

❑ Complete the study of the unit. At the end of the unit, invite students to modify the artifacts based on what they learned.

❑ Invite the groups to make a second artifact based on what new subconcepts they learned about the key idea.

❑ Label and display the artifacts in a class museum, and have groups explain the connections between their artifacts and the topic.

VARIATIONS

1. Take students to a museum related to the topic of study before they make their first artifacts (see Activity 45).

2. Display artifacts in a public area of the school such as a hallway or the cafeteria.

3. Invite parents to the class museum. Have students guide the parents on a museum tour.

4. Instead of a museum, use the activity to create a science exhibition with lab projects displayed.

5. Use the gallery walk (see Activity 51) or the carousel (see Activity 10) for an in-class display.

Other Intelligences

- Verbal/linguistic
- Interpersonal
- Intrapersonal
- Naturalist

ACTIVITY 61

Make a Poster

Targeted Grades: Elementary and Secondary

ACTIVITY AT A GLANCE

Purpose

- To express understanding of a topic through the creation of a product that expresses a clear central idea or several subconcepts

When to Use

- At the end of a unit as an assessment piece or as an opportunity for students to synthesize new information

What You'll Need

- Poster boards
- Sample poster
- Crayons or markers

WHAT-TO-DO CHECKLIST

- ❏ Teach a lesson, unit, or project with an emphasis on the core ideas and subconcepts.
- ❏ At the end of the lesson, unit, or project, brainstorm a list of what the students learned and post it for all to see.
- ❏ Show students a completed sample of a poster. Provide a checklist of key ingredients or a rubric that you will use to assess the poster. Key items in the poster should include a clear and original expression of the ideas, color, visual appeal, and so on.
- ❏ Have students make a poster that expresses what they learned in the lesson.
- ❏ Use the rubric or checklist to assess the posters.
- ❏ Hang the posters in the room or hallway.
- ❏ Randomly select three to four posters and ask the creators to explain the ideas behind the compositions.

VARIATIONS

1. Have students make posters about specific historical figures, periods, literary characters and settings, cultures, mathematics concepts, science concepts, or musical figures.

2. Use a carousel (Activity 10), gallery walk (Activity 51) or museum (Activity 60) to organize peer assessments of the posters.

3. Hang the posters in the hallway for passers-by to see.

Other Intelligences

- Verbal/linguistic
- Interpersonal
- Intrapersonal

ACTIVITY 62

Make a Graph

Targeted Grades: Middle and Early Secondary

ACTIVITY AT A GLANCE

Purpose

- To demonstrate changes in quantity by using graphs

When to Use

- When integrating mathematics into other curricular areas (such as social studies, language arts, and science) as a visual representation of quantity

What You'll Need

- Rulers
- Protractors
- Newsprint
- Markers
- Computer
- Projector

WHAT-TO-DO CHECKLIST

☐ Pose a question, issue, or problem related to a current event (such as population growth, building heights, age spans, career choices, or global warming).

☐ Brainstorm subtopics related to the question posed. Arrange students in pairs and instruct each pair to conduct research and gather data on one subtopic.

☐ Select the type of graph students will use, such as a bar graph, line graph, pie chart, and so on. Demonstrate an example.

❐ Monitor pairs as they create their graphs for their subtopics.

❐ Invite volunteers to show their graphs and explain their findings. Use a computer projector, newsprint, or other media that will show the graph to the whole class.

VARIATIONS

1. Assign each group to create two different types of graphs based on the same data.

2. Assign different questions to be researched and graphed by different groups of students.

3. Display graphs for public show. Invite parents to review the results.

Other Intelligences

- Logical/mathematical
- Interpersonal
- Intrapersonal

ACTIVITY 63
Nonsensical Creations Outside the Box

Targeted Grades: Middle and Secondary

ACTIVITY AT A GLANCE

Purpose

- To teach the higher-order thinking skill by synthesizing disparate ideas in a visual medium

When to Use

- When middle-grade students need to develop the ability to synthesize ideas
- When secondary students need to develop artistic expression and generate new ideas by improving how they synthesize

What You'll Need

- Newsprint
- Markers or crayons

WHAT-TO-DO CHECKLIST

❏ Discuss with students the meaning of the word "synthesize." Explore jobs, careers, and situations where it might be beneficial to synthesize ideas, such as in marketing, inventing, or integrating two or more fields of knowledge.

❏ Explain the purpose of this activity with regard to the thinking skill of synthesis.

❏ Challenge students to create a synthetic name for an unusual combination, such as an alligator and a drummer, or an eagle and a racecar driver.

❏ Ask a student to sketch a rendition of the "alli-drummer" or the "flying-racer" on the board or an overhead.

❏ Have students brainstorm two lists: one of animals and another of people or common objects.

❏ Instruct students to select one item from each list and combine them to make nonsensical creations. It is important that students know that being "silly" or outlandish is important to stretch their divergent thinking or thinking "outside the box."

❏ The creation should have some of the characteristics from each of the original items and could have new characteristics as well.

❏ Give students the newsprint and markers to draw their creations and to title their drawings.

❏ Post the completed drawings and allow students to take turns introducing their new creations to the class. Use a gallery walk (see Activity 51) or carousel (see Activity 10).

❏ Ask students to reflect on how their outside-the-box thinking was helped by this activity. Use a round-robin questioning pattern (see Activity 24) to share.

VARIATIONS

1. Allow students to work in pairs or trios.

2. Invite students to make paintings, sculptures, or construction-paper collages of their creations.

3. Use computer slideware software such as PowerPoint and a projector to show the completed images.

4. Create an art museum in the school's entryway to show the completed works signed by the artist.

5. Have students write stories about their creations.

Other Intelligences

- Verbal/linguistic
- Interpersonal
- Intrapersonal
- Naturalist

ACTIVITY 64

Design a Machine

Targeted Grades: Middle and Secondary

ACTIVITY AT A GLANCE

Purpose

- To understand a concept or topic by using Visual/spatial intelligence

When to Use

- Throughout a lesson or unit to encourage students to visualize a concept, to deepen students' understanding of a concept, or to invite expression through a Visual/spatial medium

What You'll Need

- Copies of some of Leonardo da Vinci's sketches

WHAT-TO-DO CHECKLIST

- ❐ Show samples of Leonardo da Vinci's sketches of some of his inventions (such as the water lift, machine gun, paddleboat, and retractable bridge). Discuss design as a medium of expression, citing examples from architecture, consumer products, and fiction writing.

- ❐ Identify for the class the big idea they will study in a complete lesson, unit, or project.

- ❐ Brainstorm with the class a list of the key subconcepts they will learn in this lesson, unit, or project.

- ❐ Show these on the overhead within a concept map (see Activity 53).

- ❐ Give students the art materials they will use to design their invention.

- ❐ Have each student select one idea from the list and design a machine representing that idea.

- ❐ Post the completed designs and prepare a paragraph explaining why the machine connects to the idea they selected. Use the carousel (Activity 10) or the gallery walk (Activity 51).

- ❐ Put students into groups of three to read their paragraphs round-robin style (see Activity 24).

VARIATIONS

1. Form mixed-ability design groups (see Activity 145) to work together on the project.

2. Replace the "machine" design with an animal, vegetable, or consumer product design.

3. Require a written explanation of the finished design.

4. Form design pairs to create both a sketch and written explanation of a designed object. Collect all sketches and display them so they are visible to the entire class. Ask students to read their explanations in turn and have the class identify the corresponding sketch based on the written description.

5. At the end of a unit or lesson, have students construct a model of a design that symbolizes the key concept studied. Make a class museum to display the models.

Other Intelligences

- Verbal/linguistic
- Interpersonal
- Intrapersonal
- Naturalist

ACTIVITY 65

Picture Vocabulary

Targeted Grades: Middle

ACTIVITY AT A GLANCE

Purpose

- To reinforce the meanings of vocabulary words by using Visual/spatial intelligence

When to Use

- At the end of a unit or lesson to ensure that all students know the definitions of key words

What You'll Need

- No materials necessary

WHAT-TO-DO CHECKLIST

❏ On the overhead or board, post these three words: socdroop, toehole, and linebind.

❏ Explain that Lewis Carroll took an old word—portmanteau, a suitcase divided into compartments that carries ("port" from *porter*, the French word for "to carry") more goods ("*manteau*," the French word for "coat")—and used it in his book *Alice in Wonderland* to mean the joining of two or more words.

❏ Provide the definitions and ask students to draw pictures of each word:
  o Socdroop—a sock that has lost its elasticity and falls down
  o Toehole—a hole in one's sock that expands as one's toe plays with it
  o Linebind—when there is only one person in front of you at a fast-food restaurant, but he orders twenty-five sandwiches

❏ Ask students to invent portmanteau words and ask volunteers to sketch pictures of them on the board.

❏ Discuss how pictorial images can help us remember the meanings of words.

❏ Introduce six to nine vocabulary words from a unit students are studying. For homework, have students find the definitions in the dictionary and create pictures to express each meaning.

❏ Pair students. Ask them to exchange their picture definitions with their partners and to identify the corresponding vocabulary word and give a verbal definition.

❏ Quiz students on the definitions of assigned words.

VARIATIONS

1. Change the difficulty of the sample words to suit the age of the students.

2. Assign students to cooperative groups (see Activity 128) and jigsaw (see Activity 28) the assigned words.

3. Restrict combination to words in a specific discipline such as mathematics or science.

Other Intelligences
- Verbal/linguistic
- Logical/mathematical
- Interpersonal
- Intrapersonal
- Naturalist

ACTIVITY 66

Working With Venn Diagrams

Targeted Grades: All

ACTIVITY AT A GLANCE

Purpose

- To compare and contrast two or more items or concepts by using Venn diagrams

When to Use

- When promoting reading comprehension with material that calls for comparison and contrast (Marzano et al., 2001)

What You'll Need

- Chart paper
- Markers

WHAT-TO-DO CHECKLIST

- ❏ Show a sample Venn diagram and review the process for using it.

- ❏ Assign reading from a class textbook, fiction story, or other age-appropriate resource material. Select material that invites comparison and contrast (such as the differences between African and Asian elephants, acute and obtuse triangles, two characters in a novel, two cultures, and so on).

- ❏ Brainstorm with the class a list of elements of the reading assignment that could be compared and contrasted, such as two plots, two characters, two settings, two themes, two situations, and so on.

- ❏ Arrange students in pairs and assign each pair a topic from the list. Instruct students to compare and contrast items within their topic and to work together to make a Venn diagram that shows the similarities in the overlapping center and the differences in the outer spaces.

- ❏ Coach and assist without giving answers (see Introduction, p. 11).

- ❏ Invite volunteer pairs to present their Venn diagrams to the class. Post the others on a bulletin board.

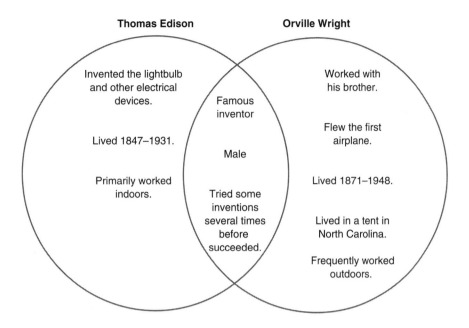

Thomas Edison — Invented the lightbulb and other electrical devices. Lived 1847–1931. Primarily worked indoors.

Famous inventor / Male / Tried some inventions several times before succeeded.

Orville Wright — Worked with his brother. Flew the first airplane. Lived 1871–1948. Lived in a tent in North Carolina. Frequently worked outdoors.

VARIATIONS

1. Before beginning the activity, form cooperative trios and use chart paper to record a checklist of the steps needed to make a Venn diagram.

2. For elementary students, start with a Venn diagram about two students in the class.

3. Identify other graphic organizers (see Activity 47) that facilitate comparing and contrasting, or see Bellanca (2007).

4. For secondary students, extend this activity to each succeeding lesson in your content. After a lesson is finished, elicit from the students what the core concepts are that they could compare or contrast from the lesson. Brainstorm the list and assign pairs to make a Venn diagram.

5. Share the Venn diagrams with the class as the lesson review.

Other Intelligences

- Verbal/linguistic
- Interpersonal
- Intrapersonal

ACTIVITY 67

Map Making

Targeted Grades: Elementary and Middle

ACTIVITY AT A GLANCE

Purpose

- To organize information by constructing maps

When to Use

- In units in which location is an important element for understanding the relationship of place to place or place to event
- When integrating map skills into nongeographic curricula

What You'll Need

- Chart paper or poster boards
- Rulers
- Protractors
- Art supplies (such as paint and magic markers)

WHAT-TO-DO CHECKLIST

- ☐ Assess students' prior knowledge (see Activity 54) of maps (such as road maps, museum maps, zoo maps, and so on).

- ☐ Review or outline the importance of maps (exploration, driving to a new place, and so on).

- ☐ Demonstrate to students how to make a map of one geographic location (such as the lion house in the zoo, or the area around the school).

- ☐ Provide chart paper or poster boards and other necessary art supplies based on desired sophistication of final maps.

- ☐ Target the area to be mapped by the students.

- ☐ Brainstorm a list of items that might be included in each map, as well as the criteria for success (see Activity 8).

- ☐ Arrange students in groups of three to create the maps. Coach their work (see Introduction, p. 25).

- ☐ Have each group share its completed map with the class. Instruct students to explain their maps' pluses and minuses according to the established criteria. Post completed maps signed by the mapmakers in the room or hallway.

- ☐ Invite students to explain how and when they will be able to use maps more skillfully.

VARIATIONS

1. In elementary grades, integrate this project into a study of the local community or use as a preactivity for making a community diorama.

2. In social studies units involving multiple locations (such as Revolutionary War Battles or the countries of a continent), assign each group a different area to map. Make a giant bulletin board that combines all the smaller maps.

Other Intelligences

- Interpersonal
- Intrapersonal

ACTIVITY 68

Create a Collage

Targeted Grades: All

ACTIVITY AT A GLANCE

Purpose

- To show the topic and subtopics in a lesson or unit by using a visual format

When to Use

- At the end of a lesson or unit to review concepts, or to assess each student's understanding of key ideas

What You'll Need

- Scissors
- Glue
- Poster boards
- Magazines
- Sample collages

WHAT-TO-DO CHECKLIST

❏ Brainstorm with the class a list of concepts students learned during the unit or lesson.

❏ Introduce or review the collage format. Show samples of previous student collages or works by professional artists.

❏ Present or develop with the class the criteria for a collage.

❏ Explain that the pictures represent ideas and are accompanied with a minimum of words. They form a pattern that connects ideas and may use a color scheme.

❏ Ask each student to make a collage showing the most important aspects of what she has learned.

❏ Display completed collages. Allow each student a chance to explain his work in relation to the set criteria in a carousel (see Activity 10) or gallery walk (see Activity 51).

❏ Provide feedback that highlights the connections students made with their collages and the concepts of the lesson.

VARIATIONS

1. Allow students to work in cooperative pairs or trios.

2. Have students work on their collages throughout the lesson.

3. Assign the collage as task to be done at home. Show students how to involve parents in the discussion about creation of the collage.

4. Create a hallway display or school museum (see Activity 60) of the collages.

Other Intelligences

- Verbal/linguistic
- Logical/mathematical
- Interpersonal
- Intrapersonal

ACTIVITY 69

Model Building

Targeted Grades: Middle and Secondary

ACTIVITY AT A GLANCE

Purpose

- To visually portray ideas in a lesson or unit by creating a model

When to Use

- In lessons that lend themselves to creating visual models to portray the topic, ideas, or concepts studied

What You'll Need

- Legos or building blocks
- Various materials for building models

WHAT-TO-DO CHECKLIST

❏ Check students' prior knowledge (see Activity 54) of models.

❏ Use Legos or other building blocks to demonstrate how to build a simple model. Show a model used in science (such as neurons or the space system).

❏ Explore ideas for models in other areas (such as roads, bridges, or skyscrapers). Invite students to discuss materials they would need to use to build such a model.

❏ Brainstorm with students the criteria for a successful model. Make a rubric (see Activity 8) for all to keep and use during the project.

❏ Assign students construction of models to illustrate concepts or ideas related to a particular unit or topic that they are going to study.

❏ Allow time for the building of the models at home.

❏ Display the models around the classroom.

❏ Review the rubric for each model and give it to the makers.

VARIATIONS

1. Use Legos or other toy building blocks to explore patterns with elementary students as they make model roadways, towers, and geometric designs.

2. Use pairs or trios to build models together.

3. Invite volunteers to explain the connections between their models and the lesson or unit's main ideas.

Other Intelligences

- Verbal/linguistic
- Interpersonal
- Intrapersonal
- Naturalist

ACTIVITY 70

PowerPoint Reports

Targeted Grades: Middle and Secondary

ACTIVITY AT A GLANCE

Purpose

- To make a class report using PowerPoint

When to Use

- At the end of a lesson, unit, or project to communicate the key ideas learned

What You'll Need

- Computer
- Microsoft PowerPoint
- Video projector
- Screen

WHAT-TO-DO CHECKLIST

- ❏ At the beginning of a lesson, unit, or project, introduce students to the expectation that they will be showing what they learned via a PowerPoint.

- ❏ Explain the criteria for creating a strong visual to use in a presentation:

  - ○ Coordinated colors

  - ○ Large print size

  - ○ Three short lines of print per page

  - ○ Graphics and other visuals that illustrate ideas

- ❏ Display the final rubric (see Activity 8) that you will use to assess the report.

- ❏ Illustrate good and bad examples of what you expect in each presentation.

- ❏ If students are unfamiliar with a PowerPoint presentation and software, prepare them:

  - ○ Provide each student with a paragraph of text or a short article to read.

  - ○ Ask students to prepare individual reports about their reading assignments. Each student should pick out the main idea and three supporting details. Assist as needed.

  - ○ Show students how to set up a single PowerPoint frame using this information and other features of the software.

  - ○ Explain that each student will make a complete presentation using the PowerPoint to communicate the information from the project. Review the rubric.

- ❏ Complete the lesson or project.

- ❏ Review the PowerPoint use and expectation. Set the time limits and schedule for reports.

- ❏ As students individually present their reports, highlight the positive aspects of each slide using the rubric presented at the start of the lesson.

VARIATIONS

1. Assign pairs to make the first visual.

2. Use nontext material for the topics.

3. Assign longer presentations throughout the year.

4. Use pairs or trios to make the final PowerPoint presentations. Set up guidelines so that each student has an equitable chance to present.

5. Use in conjunction with a project on charts or graphs (see Activity 35).

Other Intelligences

- Verbal/linguistic
- Logical/mathematical
- Interpersonal
- Intrapersonal

ACTIVITY 71

Storyboard Concepts

Targeted Grades: Middle and Secondary

ACTIVITY AT A GLANCE

Purpose

- To construct a visual story line related to the content of a unit or lesson

When to Use

- Throughout a lesson or unit to connect and sequence events or to develop students' understanding of the parts of a story (beginning, middle, end)

What You'll Need

- Poster boards
- Three-by-five-inch index cards
- Guest speaker (an artist)

WHAT-TO-DO CHECKLIST

❐ Invite an artist from an advertising agency or graphic arts company to introduce **storyboards** to the class.

❐ Brainstorm concepts to storyboard related to a unit or lesson you are teaching (such as historic events, literature, math concepts, or science procedures).

❏ Identify the concept for the story. Identify characters, conflict, scene, and timeframe.

❏ Brainstorm events in the conflict between the two main characters.

❏ Instruct students to write the events on index cards. Limit the number of frames to be used. For example, elementary students might storyboard "The Three Billy Goats Gruff" in three to five frames. Secondary students might have as many as twelve to twenty-five frames for a story about the "Division of Fractions."

❏ Ask students to assemble their index cards in sequence and attach them to poster boards (see Activity 61).

❏ Hang the poster boards around the room and invite students to walk around and view them (see Activities 10 [carousel] and 51 [gallery walk]).

❏ Lead an all-class discussion about the activity and the displayed storyboards. What did students learn (see Activities 9 [lead-in statements] and 24 [round-robins])?

VARIATIONS

1. Have pairs or trios create a storyboard.

2. Assign the same idea or topic to everyone.

3. Have the class create storyboards for different periods in history. Post them in sequence around the room.

4. Have students create a written or video story from the storyboards.

5. Have students create storyboards to show specific steps and their order for a sequential activity, such as lab experiments, cooking, or building projects.

Other Intelligences

- Verbal/linguistic
- Logical/mathematical
- Interpersonal
- Intrapersonal
- Naturalist

ACTIVITY 72

Snapshot Sequence Chart

Targeted Grades: Middle

ACTIVITY AT A GLANCE

Purpose

- To arrange pictures of key learning events in order to connect subtopics in the proper sequence

When to Use

- To review a lesson or to check prior knowledge before beginning a new lesson

What You'll Need

- Chart paper (optional)
- Journals (optional)

WHAT-TO-DO CHECKLIST

❏ On an overhead or chart paper, draw a blank sequence chart. Provide as many blanks as appropriate for the lesson's objectives.

❏ As each step in the learning sequence is completed, invite a student to draw a picture, symbol, or sign representing the object of the lesson. Have the student explain its meaning in relation to the objective.

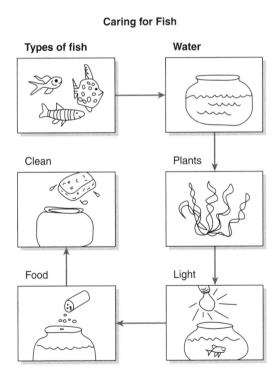

Caring for Fish

VARIATIONS

1. Form base groups of three students to keep their own snapshot charts.

2. Adjust the chart to fit the age of the students. Elementary students may use a straight-line chart with five to seven blocks. Secondary students may have a dozen snapshots.

3. Have students keep a snapshot sequence in their journals (see Activity 153).

4. Discuss the connections between and among snapshots.

Other Intelligences

- Verbal/linguistic
- Interpersonal
- Intrapersonal

ACTIVITY 73

Cartoon Stories

Targeted Grades: Secondary

ACTIVITY AT A GLANCE

Purpose

- To increase understanding and encourage expression of important concepts through the creation of dialogue in a visual story

When to Use

- At end of a unit or lesson as a review of a topic

What You'll Need

- Samples of cartoon strips
- Photocopies of a cartoon strip with the dialogue removed

WHAT-TO-DO CHECKLIST

- ❏ Using correction fluid, cover the dialogue from an age-appropriate cartoon strip, leaving the bubbles empty. Photocopy the cartoon, making one copy for each student.

- ❏ On the overhead or board, show several age-appropriate cartoon strip samples from a newspaper. For each sample, explain the use of dialogue or thought balloons.

- ❏ Discuss how dialogue differs from other kinds of writing.

- ❏ Select a topic from a unit or lesson the class has been studying. Brainstorm a list of problems, issues, or dilemmas related to the topic. Post the list for all to see.

- ❏ Invite each student to choose an issue from the list and develop a point of view about it. Have students write new dialogue in the blank bubbles on their cartoon strips to express the issues and their points of view.

- ❏ Select a way to share all cartoons with all the class members (see Activities 10 [carousel] and 51 [gallery walk]).

VARIATIONS

1. Structure pairs or trios to work on the cartoon strips.

2. Have groups of six share and critique their completed cartoon strips.

3. Establish quality criteria and have students vote on the three best cartoon strips. Include these in a class newspaper.

Other Intelligences

- Verbal/linguistic
- Interpersonal
- Intrapersonal

ACTIVITY 74

Symbolic Sense

Targeted Grades: Secondary

ACTIVITY AT A GLANCE

Purpose

- To understand symbols as a form of visual communication

When to Use

- At the end of a lesson or unit to stimulate creative thinking about the topic and to structure alternate ways of thinking about the course content

What You'll Need

- Scissors
- Glue
- Magazines
- Poster boards

WHAT-TO-DO CHECKLIST

❑ Brainstorm with the class a list of important concepts learned in a lesson or unit.

❑ Show samples of visual symbols that are found in school (+, x, H_2O) or in society (six-pointed star, cross, IBM logo). Discuss with the class what each represents literally and figuratively.

❏ Arrange students in pairs and provide newsprint and markers to each pair.

❏ Instruct each pair to make a symbol that represents one of the core ideas in the lesson.

❏ Display completed symbols and invite students to view other pairs' posters. Ask students to explain why they selected the symbols they used.

VARIATIONS

1. Use this activity to lead into a discussion of symbols in literature (such as *The Scarlet Letter* or *The Red Badge of Courage*).

2. Make constructing symbols an individual assignment rather than a group task.

Other Intelligences

- Logical/mathematical
- Visual/spatial
- Interpersonal
- Intrapersonal

ACTIVITY 75

Write a Card

Targeted Grades: Elementary

ACTIVITY AT A GLANCE

Purpose

- To evaluate the content of a lesson or unit and transfer the information to a visual medium

When to Use

- After students have investigated a topic or when students need to examine a topic from several points of view

What You'll Need

- Sample greeting cards
- Three-by-five-inch index cards
- Colored pencils or crayons

WHAT-TO-DO CHECKLIST

❑ Explain that at the end of the unit students will evaluate what they learned in the lessons. Encourage them to keep this in mind as they work through the unit's lessons.

❑ At the end of each lesson in the unit, add the key ideas of the lesson to a list that all can see.

❑ After the list is finished, show sample greeting cards. Ask students to explain why they think people send these cards.

❑ Tell the class that they are going to create some greeting cards to send to their parents. The cards will be made around some of the key things they have learned in this last unit.

❑ Brainstorm a list of occasions for sending a card. Have the class vote on which occasion they want to use.

❑ Invite students to pick what ideas from the lesson they want to use.

❑ Give students the materials for drawing the pictures to put on their cards and to make the statement inside.

❑ Post the finished cards on the bulletin board for all to review.

❑ Have students take the cards home and explain them to their parents.

VARIATIONS

1. Let students work in pairs or threes.

2. Ask students to create cards that fit with a particular holiday.

Other Intelligences

- Verbal/linguistic
- Interpersonal
- Intrapersonal

ACTIVITY 76

Visual Journals

Targeted Grades: Middle and Secondary

ACTIVITY AT A GLANCE

Purpose

- To determine the importance of ideas or reflect on an assignment

When to Use

- At the start of a lesson to visualize prior knowledge
- At the end of a lesson or unit to provide a visual image that indicates the degree to which a student has met the lesson goals
- Throughout the unit or lesson to picture ideas

What You'll Need

- Rubric
- Journals

WHAT-TO-DO CHECKLIST

- ☐ Before starting the lesson or unit, create a rubric (see Activity 8) for students with three indicators or benchmarks:
  - (1) The visual captures the student's key meaning of ideas gained from the unit or lesson.
  - (2) The visual is unique and fresh.
  - (3) The visual is strong and captivating.

- ☐ Explain each indicator with a four-point scale from "not yet" to "outstanding." Describe the point system that will be used for each indicator of success on the rubric and create a formula for translating the points.

- ☐ At the end of the lesson or unit, invite students to write or draw in their journals (see Activity 153) a visual representation of what they learned.

- ☐ Invite students to share the visuals and explain their relationship to what they learned.

VARIATIONS

1. Have students start a lesson with a reflection on prior knowledge (see Activity 54) of key concepts you provide. Have them record their ideas with a visual in the journal.

2. Have groups add the values of individual members' work to determine a group score.

Other Intelligences

- Interpersonal
- Intrapersonal

PART IV

Bodily/Kinesthetic Intelligence

ACTIVITY 77

Healthy Helpers

Targeted Grades: Elementary and Middle

ACTIVITY AT A GLANCE

Purpose

- To raise awareness on how to make healthy eating choices

When to Use

- Early in school year during science time, and each week thereafter

What You Will Need

- Newsprint and markers
- Journals

WHAT-TO-DO CHECKLIST

- ❏ Early in the school year, select a time slot during science instruction.
- ❏ Post this question for all to see: "What do you think is needed for you to eat more healthy lunches?"
- ❏ In pairs, have students brainstorm three to five answers.
- ❏ Use a question web (see Activity 6) on newsprint to record the answers. Elicit answers using a round-robin questioning pattern (see Activity 24).
- ❏ Ask each student to select three items and record them in journals (see Activity 153). Ask them to date each entry.
- ❏ Tell students this is a goal that you are encouraging them to achieve (see Activity 127). Tell them that each week you will ask them to assess their goal and give themselves a rating of zero (low) to five (high).
- ❏ Once a week, take time for the students to assess the goals and add new ones if they are doing well. On successive weeks, use a simple rubric (see Activity 8) to assess the students' goals.

VARIATIONS

1. After students review and assess their goals, have them talk with a partner to share the assessments.

2. Have pairs of students use a write-pair-share (see Activity 148) to record assessments in a journal, discuss them with a partner, and share them with the entire class.

My Health Goals		
Goal: _____		
How I did /_____/_____/		
Not yet	OK	Wow!
Goal: _____		
How I did /_____/_____/		
Not yet	OK	Wow!
Goal: _____		
How I did /_____/_____/		
Not yet	OK	Wow!

Other Intelligences

- Verbal/linguistic
- Logical/mathematical
- Interpersonal
- Intrapersonal
- Naturalist

ACTIVITY 78

Pantomime Pals

Targeted Grades: Elementary

ACTIVITY AT A GLANCE

Purpose

- To explore nonverbal expressions

When to Use

- At the end of a lesson or unit

What You'll Need

- No materials necessary

WHAT-TO-DO CHECKLIST

❏ Brainstorm a list of the information, ideas, and values learned in a lesson or from a story.

❏ Using an overhead or chalkboard, list these headings (Facts, Ideas, and Values) on a **triple T-chart** (see Activity 163). Discuss what each means with the class and give some examples to prompt the brainstorming.

❏ Arrange students into cooperative groups (see Activity 128) of three. Have each group randomly select four to six items from the chart.

❏ Introduce the idea of a pantomime. Demonstrate a pantomime from the lesson's material or the story.

❏ Instruct each group to prepare a three-minute pantomime using the selected items. The pantomime should show how each of the selected items is important to the other items and to the goals of the lesson. The pantomime should show how the items on the list are connected.

❏ Ask the students to explain how the pantomime helped them better understand what they learned from the lesson or story. Use a lead-in (see Activity 9) and round-robin questioning pattern (see Activity 24).

Information	Ideas	Values
Louis Pasteur developed pasteurization, a preserving technique.	Pasteur believed bacteria caused disease.	Scientists have to be persistent.
Some molds are helpful, like those that make blue cheese and penicillin.	He also proved that microbes could contaminate food.	People who study molds and bacteria help make a better society.

VARIATIONS

1. Arrange students in groups before brainstorming information, ideas, and values. Review the groups' charts before they begin their pantomimes.

2. For younger children, limit the pantomimes to one fact, idea, or value.

Other Intelligences

- Verbal/linguistic
- Visual/spatial
- Interpersonal
- Intrapersonal
- Naturalist

ACTIVITY 79

Stretch Goal

Targeted Grades: Elementary and Middle

ACTIVITY AT A GLANCE

Purpose

- To construct goals that challenge physical capabilities

When to Use

- At the beginning of a lesson, unit, course, or competitive sports game

What You'll Need

- Rubber bands
- Three-by-five-inch index cards
- Journals (optional)

WHAT-TO-DO CHECKLIST

❒ Draw a horizontal line across the chalkboard.

❒ Ask a volunteer to give a personal goal (see Activity 159) for improving physical fitness. Place this goal at the right end of the line.

❒ Ask the student how close she is to the goal now. Mark this response at the left end of the line.

❒ On index cards, instruct all students to make a goal and chart it with a line graph or other visual that shows student's progress to the goal.

❒ Have the students give a more ambitious but attainable goal. Add this stretched goal on the board example and lengthen the line to meet it. Invite students to replicate the extended line on the index cards.

❒ Use a rubber band to illustrate the idea of stretching. Discuss what happens when there is no stretch, or too much stretch.

❒ Pair up students. Have each share a fitness goal for the week. It should be attainable, specific, measurable, and a stretch (such as, if the student currently walks very little, "I will walk one mile each day").

Physical Fitness Goal

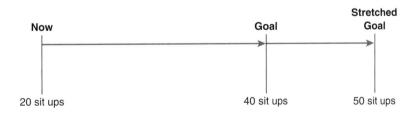

❒ Allow five minutes for sharing. Check to see if the goals meet the criteria. Give necessary feedback.

❒ At the end of a week, match pairs and have them revisit their accomplishments. Have them frame a new stretch goal for the next week.

VARIATIONS

1. Use journals (see Activity 153) or goal charts (see Activity 170) for students to track their improvements on a weekly basis.

2. Have students demonstrate, in pairs, the accomplishment of a stretched goal.

3. Use the process with team goals.

Other Intelligences

- Verbal/linguistic
- Logical/mathematical
- Visual/spatial
- Interpersonal
- Intrapersonal

ACTIVITY 80

Take A Hike

Targeted Grades: Elementary and Middle

ACTIVITY AT A GLANCE

Purpose

- To use daily walking as a form of exercise

When to Use

- Once a week in place of an unstructured recess or PE period

What You'll Need

- Suitable footwear and weather-appropriate clothing for each student
- Journals (optional)

WHAT-TO-DO CHECKLIST

❑ Plan a walk with the class near the school. Walk the route alone first to allow proper timing.

❑ Match elementary students in pairs. Put pairs in two straight lines (as in Ludwig Bemelmans' books about Madeline). For middle-grade students, plan a period walk around in the gym or playfield during PE.

❏ Discuss and demonstrate proper walking form. Practice in a hallway or on the playground.

❏ Before beginning the walk, use proper stretching and warm-up exercises.

❏ Walk at a pace that challenges the slowest walker. Keep the group together—it is not a race.

❏ After the walk, cool down with the students (see Activity 81).

VARIATIONS

1. Teach the students to sing a song or march as they walk.

2. Take the students to a place where they can walk extensively (such as a forest preserve, park, or zoo) as a group (see Activity 45). When on field trips, use the same prewalk and postwalk preparations.

3. Once a month, encourage students to make a journal entry (see Activity 153) tracking their improvements in physical well-being.

Other Intelligences

- Interpersonal
- Intrapersonal

ACTIVITY 81

Warm Up, Cool Down

Targeted Grades: Elementary and Middle

ACTIVITY AT A GLANCE

Purpose

- To understand the value of proper warm-up and cool-down procedures before and after conditioning or sports activities

When to Use

- Before all physical activity, allowing time for proper warm-up and cool-down

What You'll Need

- No materials necessary

WHAT-TO-DO CHECKLIST

☐ Ask students to identify what they know about warming up before a physical activity. After writing an all-class list on the board or overhead, ask students to identify the five most important warm-up tasks and explain why they are important.

☐ Repeat by compiling a list for the cool-down at the end of a physical activity.

☐ Provide a demonstration of each warm-up activity. Follow this with a guided practice and corrective feedback.

☐ Repeat the demonstration, practice, and feedback for each cool-down activity.

☐ Make a class bulletin board or handout. Use this to review the top five warm-up and cool-down activities before and after each exercise period or sport event.

☐ Before each exercise, lead the students in doing the warm-ups. Allow time at the end to lead the students in the cool-down.

VARIATIONS

1. Use a coach, professional trainer, or adult athlete to demonstrate proper warm-up and cool-down procedures, and talk with students about the value of such procedures.

2. Invite students to work in pairs, and to observe and assist each other during the warm-ups and cool-downs.

Other Intelligences

• Interpersonal

ACTIVITY 82

Silly Walk

Targeted Grades: Elementary

ACTIVITY AT A GLANCE

Purpose

• To enjoy daily aerobic exercise

When to Use

• After lunch to restore students' energy
• As a break from everyday activities

What You'll Need

- A long rope

WHAT-TO-DO CHECKLIST

☐ Tell students that they are going to take a walk roped together. Pick the path. If the school has a gym or cafeteria, lead them on a winding walk there, especially if the outside weather is bad. If there isn't an access to a large, closed room, lead the walk inside the classroom or the hallways. If there's a playground or a safe area in the school neighborhood, plan outdoor walks when the weather is suitable.

☐ Line students up and have them hold on to a rope with their right hands. Encourage an arm's length of spacing.

☐ Announce the behavior guidelines for the walk:
  ○ Keep one hand on the rope at all times.
  ○ Keep your distance from your neighbor.
  ○ Make only the sounds that the leader makes.
  ○ Copy the movements of the person in front of you.
  ○ Have fun. It's okay to be silly on the walk.

☐ Take the lead. On the way, make silly sounds and motions. Each student will imitate and pass the sound or motion down the line. Keep walking, making the sounds and motions (such as animal sounds, car sounds, waving hands, one hand on head, hops).

☐ Start slowly and gradually increase the speed of the walk and motions. On the first walk, four to five minutes will be okay. Add fifteen seconds each day, up to ten minutes.

☐ At the walk's end, have students sit for one minute without talking so they can cool down and reflect on the exercise.

VARIATIONS

1. Sing a choral song such as sing "Do Re Mi" and accompany with movements during the walk.

2. Pick different locales each week.

3. Select a student leader to head up the line and make the lead movements and sounds.

4. Play a counting game as the sound.

Other Intelligences

- Logical/mathematical
- Musical/rhythmic
- Interpersonal

ACTIVITY 83

Shadow Play

Targeted Grades: Elementary

ACTIVITY AT A GLANCE

Purpose

- To improve reading comprehension by using mime

When to Use

- After students have read a story

What You'll Need

- Spotlight or portable plant light
- White sheet

WHAT-TO-DO CHECKLIST

- ❏ Set up the classroom with a spotlight or portable plant light. Shine the light on a light-colored wall or hang a white sheet with enough room for a student to stand between the light and the wall and cast a shadow on the wall.

- ❏ Show students how to make finger shapes on the wall screen. Let them come up with more ideas by asking, "Who has an idea to show?" List for all to see the ideas that will best work.

- ❏ Show how to create shadows on the wall. Start with one student and a stationary shadow. Next, add moving shadows and groups of students who can strike shadow poses. Rather than tell the class who or what each is doing, allow the class to guess.

- ❏ Arrange students into groups of three to seven (depends on the story). Have a strong reader in each group. Assign the roles of reader, director, storyteller, and actors.

- ❏ Give each group a story to read. Instruct the reader to read aloud to the team.

- ❏ After the reading is done, have each team think about how they will mime the story for the class. The director will select the roles. One will retell the story as the others act behind the screen.

VARIATIONS

1. Tell the story of *Peter Pan*, J. M. Barrie's book. Tell how the children used mime in that story. Pick some volunteers to mime events from the story as they remember it.

2. Invite all groups to use the same one. Each will give its interpretation. For younger students, make a list of characters and brainstorm the story's events. Use a snapshot sequence chart (see Activity 72) on the board for all to see and put the events in order before the groups interpret the story in mime.

Other Intelligences

- Verbal/linguistic
- Visual/spatial
- Interpersonal

ACTIVITY 84

Posture Popcorn Party

Targeted Grades: Elementary and Middle

ACTIVITY AT A GLANCE

Purpose

- To develop healthy posture

When to Use

- When students slouch
- As an introductory conditioning lesson

What You'll Need

- Pictures showing good posture

WHAT-TO-DO CHECKLIST

- ❏ Ask students to tell what they know about the word "posture." Enter on a question web for all to see (see Activity 6).

- ❏ Add to their ideas with additional information about the importance of standing and sitting straight.

- ❏ Tell them about a possible popcorn party at the end of the quarter. Explain what they have to learn and do to earn the party.

- ❏ Show a sketch of good standing and sitting postures. Point out what good posture looks like and demonstrate it.

- ❏ Coach a guided practice (see Introduction, p. 25). Use pairs to check and coach each other. Visit among the pairs to give constructive feedback.

- ❏ During the first week, call on pairs several times to check postures. Do spot checks.

❑ In the following weeks, make a common goal (see Activity 127) for the entire class.

❑ Celebrate Good Posture Week with a popcorn party in which students eat popcorn in good posture positions.

❑ Ask the students to make a list of reasons or a series of posters (see Activity 61), collages (see Activity 68), or mobiles (see Activity 59) showing why good posture is important.

VARIATIONS

1. Arrange the class into mixed-ability groups (see Activity 145) of six to eight students. Make a competition chart and award points for observed good posture at surprise times. Each week, give a special award to the group with the highest points or to all groups that meet the criteria for success.

2. Have pairs of middle-grade students go to elementary classes to introduce the Good Posture Week popcorn party.

3. Set up a graph (see Activity 62) on the bulletin board. Have students chart their progress each week from points earned for good posture.

Other Intelligences

- Verbal/linguistic
- Logical/mathematical
- Visual/spatial
- Interpersonal
- Intrapersonal

ACTIVITY 85

Monthly Dancercise

Targeted Grades: Middle

ACTIVITY AT A GLANCE

Purpose

- To exercise through dance

When to Use

- At any time for conditioning and recreation

What You'll Need

- Music cassettes or CDs
- Cassette tape or CD player

WHAT-TO-DO CHECKLIST

☐ Select a dance of the month, such as a square dance, break dance, modern dance, line dance, or exercise dance.

☐ Set up the tape or CD player in a large-enough space for all students to participate.

☐ Play the music for the easiest dance selected and demonstrate the dance steps.

☐ Step-by-step, coach (see Introduction, p. 11) practice through each element of the dance. When all students can do the basic moves in each step, practice the entire dance.

☐ Using a variety of music. Have students practice the dance for a week before introducing the next version of the same dance. Continue through the month until the students can do four or five versions of the dance of the month.

VARIATIONS

1. Ask a parent or community member to teach the dances to the students.

2. Thirty minutes a day will provide the best use of this activity as a conditioning exercise, and one to three days a week will make it a recreational activity.

3. For elementary students, teach them how to do a freeform dance in which they imagine being forces of nature (such as wind or a storm) or animals (such as birds or giraffes).

4. Discuss with students the aerobic value of dancercise.

Other Intelligences

- Interpersonal

ACTIVITY 86

Build a Tower

Targeted Grades: Elementary and Middle

ACTIVITY AT A GLANCE

Purpose

- To enhance small-motor development

When to Use

- As a rainy day activity (elementary grades)
- During an advisory period to facilitate teamwork (middle grades)
- As a prebuilding activity for a subsequent model-building activity, such as building pyramids or inventions

What You'll Need

- Wooden blocks
- Tinkertoys
- Legos or other toy building blocks
- Kitchen items, such as coffee stirrers or paper cups

WHAT-TO-DO CHECKLIST

- ❏ Collect enough tower materials for all students in the class.
- ❏ Arrange students into mixed-ability groups (see Activity 145) of three.
- ❏ Explain that the purpose of the task is to work together to build the highest free-standing tower possible within a ten-minute period using the available materials (see Activity 64).
- ❏ *Do not model a completed tower.* You can connect them to their prior knowledge (see Activity 54) of "tower," however, by asking, "What is a tower?," "What are towers you have seen?," and "What are towers used for?"
- ❏ Each group will have to agree on its own tower design and build its own tower using the available materials and all the hands in the group.
- ❏ Set up a timer showing their ten minutes and tell them that this is a competition. Ask the students why they think it will be so important for the members to work together. Solicit multiple responses.
- ❏ When the time is up, have groups sit by their models. Identify the highest free-standing and completed tower. Applaud the winner.
- ❏ Ask each group to discuss the contributions of its members. Allow three to four minutes for this before selecting one member of each group to share examples of cooperative behavior in completing the model.
- ❏ Make a list of everyone's contributions on the board or overhead.

VARIATIONS

1. Increase the number of blocks on successive towers. First, ask the teams to review what they did well on the previous tower and what they need to improve.

2. Do the activity with individuals instead of groups.

3. Mix the type of materials.

4. Vary the type of model by changing the criteria (such as widest or longest tower).

5. Change the time parameter by allowing more or less than ten minutes.

6. For older students, discuss the physics involved in building a standing tower.

Other Intelligences

- Visual/spatial
- Interpersonal
- Naturalist

ACTIVITY 87

Pattern Dances

Targeted Grades: Elementary and Middle

ACTIVITY AT A GLANCE

Purpose

- To explore movement patterns

When to Use

- As a wellness unit to promote aerobic conditioning

What You'll Need

Music cassettes or CDs
Cassette tape or CD player

WHAT-TO-DO CHECKLIST

- ❏ Organize students in a circle around an open space. Tell them the activity's purpose.
- ❏ Count off groups of four. Instruct each group to make a square in which all four students face inward but are still able to watch the demonstration.
- ❏ Use one group to demonstrate each new movement pattern (the repetition of a variety of movements in an organized sequence). Start with a simple pattern to familiar music:
  - ○ Elementary grades—"Itsy Bitsy Spider"
  - ○ Middle school—"Macarena"
- ❏ After the demonstration, coach the practice in the groups.
- ❏ Ask each group to invent its own pattern dance—with or without words. The dance must include repetition of movements.
- ❏ Allow each group to teach its dance to the class. Practice each dance.
- ❏ Hold a pattern dance festival for other classes or parents.
- ❏ Use cooperative groups (see Activity 128) so that all students are included. Establish guidelines that ensure physically challenged students can perform any of the invented pattern dances.

VARIATIONS

1. Invite a professional dancer to work with the students to choreograph a pattern dance using classical or show music.

2. Integrate the pattern dance lesson with a lesson on rhyme.

3. Prepare the dances for a show on Parents' Night.

Other Intelligences

- Visual/spatial
- Interpersonal

ACTIVITY 88

Playground Races

Targeted Grades: Elementary and Middle

ACTIVITY AT A GLANCE

Purpose

- To challenge a variety of physical capabilities through participation in cross-age races

When to Use

- In place of recess or as part of a full day of activities to promote teamwork and exercise

What You'll Need

- First-, second-, and third-place ribbons, and participation certificates
- Appropriate materials and equipment for the game you select (such as Frisbees for the toss or cloth strips for the dragon's tails)

What-to-Do Checklist

❒ Invite a class that is three to four years older (or younger) to join your class for this activity.

❒ Arrange students into six to eight teams. Ensure a cooperative balance of physical abilities on each team (see Activity 128). Ensure that physically challenged youngsters are distributed among the teams.

❒ Set the guidelines:
  ○ Students should arrange themselves in pairs made up of one older and one younger student.
  ○ Only positive encouragement (cheering) is allowed.
  ○ All team members must participate equally.

❏ Awards go to each finisher according to the number of teams in a race. If there are eight teams, the top team gets eight points and the bottom team gets one point. Each event's score will contribute to the team's total. First-, second-, and third-place ribbons will go to the three top-scoring teams. All who participate receive certificates.

❏ Have the class make the awards in advance of the competition.

❏ List the races:
   ○ Bean toss (greatest number tossed accurately in two minutes)
   ○ Three-legged race
   ○ Frisbee throw (greatest distance for throw and catch)
   ○ Basket shoot (greatest number in four minutes)
   ○ Club relay (fastest combined time for four members)
   ○ Wheelbarrow race (two-member teams)
   ○ Water balloon toss (gradually increasing distance between members until balloon breaks)
   ○ Push up, sit up, knee-bend relay (all members participate equally)
   ○ Catch the Dragon's Tail (all members)

❏ Before starting, allow teams time to practice, to pick a team name, team colors, team cheers (see Activity 91), and so on.

❏ Be sure participants understand and use safety precautions. Integrate proper warm-up and cool-down procedures (see Activity 81).

❏ Hold the competition, using parent volunteers if possible as judges and team managers.

❏ End with an awards ceremony.

VARIATIONS

1. Add or delete events based on suitability to students (such as age).

2. Add an Olympic flavor with team logos (see Activity 131), and so on.

3. Use games taken from New Games (www.inewgames.com).

4. For older students, have an "expeditionary learning" Olympics. (Search the Internet for games to include.)

5. Make posters (see Activity 61) to advertise the competition to the other classes in the school.

6. Hold an interclass competition so all grades or classrooms in a school are included.

Other Intelligences
- Visual/spatial
- Interpersonal

ACTIVITY 89

Who Is in My Zoo?

Targeted Grades: All

ACTIVITY AT A GLANCE

Purpose

- To participate in an energizing activity

When to Use

- When students need an energizer
- When it is necessary to form pairs for a task in a different way that will give a random and unpredictable mix of students in each pair

What You'll Need

Three-by-five-inch index cards

WHAT-TO-DO CHECKLIST

❑ Write the names of animals on index cards (such as monkeys, elephants, horses, lions, and wolves). Make two cards for each animal and make enough cards for all students in the class.

❑ Assemble the class in a circle around an open area. Walk around the circle with the handful of cards and have each student select a card, which is their "secret" animal.

❑ When all students have cards, invite them to pretend that they are a large group of animals. Each animal is looking for another of its own kind. Students are to call out animal sounds based on the animal specified on their cards and listen for a matching call of the same animal.

❑ When students find a matching animal, each pair should compare its cards to be sure the match is correct.

❑ After all students have found their matches, ask pairs to demonstrate their calls together so the class can guess what type of animal they are.

❑ Assign students to begin the next activity in these pairs.

VARIATIONS

1. Make four cards for each animal and have students find all the members of their new group.

2. Choose animals from only one category, such as birds or mammals.

3. Have students create cards that can be reused for other grouping activities. Brainstorm an all-class list of animals that make sounds. Write list on overhead or board. Form student pairs and assign an animal to each pair. Ask each pair to create two illustrated cards for its animal. Have students label their cards and write the sound the animal makes.

4. Use musical instruments, city sounds, or weather sounds as the identifiers.

Other Intelligences

- Visual/spatial
- Interpersonal
- Naturalist

ACTIVITY 90

Juggle Challenge

Targeted Grades: Middle

ACTIVITY AT A GLANCE

Purpose

- To increase hand-eye coordination

When to Use

- Any time as a fun coordination task

What You'll Need

- Beanbags, used tennis balls, or other objects to juggle

WHAT-TO-DO CHECKLIST

- ❏ Gather thirty-six to fifty-four juggling objects.
- ❏ Ask students to say what they know about juggling before explaining the purpose of this lesson.
- ❏ Demonstrate two-ball juggling before pairing students.
- ❏ Have students help each other practice.
- ❏ Encourage students to advance to three-ball juggling and juggling with mixed objects.

VARIATIONS

1. Bring a professional juggler to class for a demonstration.

2. Hold an elimination contest to determine the most proficient classroom juggler.

Other Intelligences

- Visual/spatial

ACTIVITY 91

Team Cheers

Targeted Grades: All

ACTIVITY AT A GLANCE

Purpose

- To develop teamwork by creating cheers that require movement

When to Use

- After any special team accomplishment or as a class energizer

What You'll Need

- No materials necessary

WHAT-TO-DO CHECKLIST

- ❏ Form base groups (see Activity 141) of five students each.
- ❏ Give each group the task of developing a team cheer with physical movements. The cheer must reflect some common characteristics of the members. The movements must fit the rhythm of the cheer.
- ❏ Allow planning and practice time. Coach as needed (see Introduction, p. 25).
- ❏ Ask each team to demonstrate its cheer and then to use it to lead an all-class cheer.
- ❏ Use each group's cheer when one of its members deserves a cheer.

VARIATIONS

1. Have teams construct cheers based on a specific theme or team accomplishment.

2. Hold a cheering contest for younger classes.

Other Intelligences
- Verbal/linguistic
- Interpersonal

ACTIVITY 92

Interpretive Role-Play

Targeted Grades: Middle and Secondary

ACTIVITY AT A GLANCE

Purpose

- To interpret ideas, events, and skills through the use of a role-playing strategy
- To develop a learning strategy called role-playing

When to Use

- During a unit or lesson as a form of interpretation

What You'll Need

- No materials necessary
- Journals (optional)

WHAT-TO-DO CHECKLIST

❑ Ask students to discuss what they think the term "playing a role" means. List generated ideas for all to see and decide on the most appropriate definition.

❑ Use a think-pair-share (see Activity 148) to help students come up with examples of when they have played roles or of when they have seen others playing roles.

❑ Explain the purpose that you have selected from above for this activity.

❑ Provide a conflict situation, such as a person who is angry with someone or a leader who is trying to inspire a neighbor to help sandbag an overflowing river. Ask two volunteers to role-play the situation.

❑ Brainstorm with the class social, historic, or literary scenarios or incidents that would make good role-plays. List these on the board or overhead.

❑ Divide the class into mixed-ability trios (see Activity 145). Allow each group to select a conflict with which it is familiar and prepare a role-play. One person will be the director and the others the actors.

❑ Invite each group to perform its role-play. Have the director introduce the group's scenario.

❐ After the last performance, ask the trios to list the criteria for a successful role-play. Build a class list and identify the three to four most important criteria.

❐ Ask each group to use the criteria to evaluate the group's performance.

❐ Discuss other times in school where a role-play would help them understand the material.

VARIATIONS

1. Pick a specific conflict for all groups to role-play.

2. Provide scenarios written out for the groups to use as the conflict situation. Take these from stories familiar to the students.

3. Take conflicts from the current chapter of the text you are using.

4. Send the students in pairs to the local library to find stories they can use.

5. End the role-playing by asking students to make a journal entry (see Activity 153) about what they learned through the role-play using an appropriate lead-in (see Activity 9) that you provide.

Other Intelligences

- Verbal/linguistic
- Visual/spatial
- Interpersonal
- Intrapersonal

ACTIVITY 93

Human Graph

Targeted Grades: All

ACTIVITY AT A GLANCE

Purpose

- To illustrate differences of opinion and points of view with movement

When to Use

- As a physical and visual organizer to identify prior knowledge
- As a mid-lesson check
- At the end of a unit as a knowledge assessment

What You'll Need

- No materials necessary

WHAT-TO-DO CHECKLIST

- ❏ Line up students side-by-side in a straight line. If the room is too small, alternate which students participate in each part.

- ❏ Show a bar graph on the board or newsprint for all to see. Review the concept of bar graph (see Activity 62).

- ❏ Tell students they are going to make a human bar graph. The line they have formed is the baseline.

- ❏ Tell them how to move to show their point of view.

- ❏ Test understanding with some of these samples:

Hate TV sports	vs.	Love TV sports
Junk-food junkie	vs.	Health-food nut
Early bird	vs.	Late riser
Couch potato	vs.	Exercise advocate

- ❏ Ask for one or two students to explain why they took a position.

- ❏ Provide two extreme positions on a topic from the material you are studying. If you have been reading *The Three Billy Goats Gruff*, one extreme position would be "The goats should escape the troll" and another would be "The goats should capture the troll." If you have been reading *The Scarlet Letter*, the two extreme positions might be, "It was a wise decision to make Hester wear the scarlet letter" and "It was self-destructive for the community to punish Hester in this way." Designate each end of the baseline as representing one of the extremes. Students who agree with either of the extremes should move to the corresponding end of the line. Students who hold an in-between position should remain at their original locations or move closer to either end of the line to indicate their measure of agreement with a particular viewpoint.

- ❏ Have students grouped at each location form a bar by forming a line vertical to the baseline.

- ❏ Ask several students who are at different points on the graph to explain their positions.

- ❏ Return students to their seats in the classroom and bridge what they have said to the current lesson (see Activity 5).

VARIATIONS

1. Fit the graphing strategy's questions to different ideas discussed in the unit or lesson content as a review at the lesson's end.

2. Ask the group of students at each location of the bar to discuss and then create a summary to explain what is common in their position.

3. Ask a student to draw a bar graph on the board or overhead of the human bar graph in the classroom.

4. Assign students to make a collage representing the opposing group's point of view (see Activity 68).

Other Intelligences

- Verbal/linguistic
- Logical/mathematical
- Visual/spatial
- Interpersonal
- Intrapersonal

ACTIVITY 94

Class Reunion Name Tags

Targeted Grades: Middle and Secondary

ACTIVITY AT A GLANCE

Purpose

- To ice-break introductions at the start of the school year

When to Use

- On the first or second day of class in a new school year

What You'll Need

- Three-by-five-inch index cards

WHAT-TO-DO CHECKLIST

- ❒ Provide each student with an index card.

- ❒ Use a question web (see Activity 6) to list what students know about class reunions. Fill in missing information that is important to define the term but that they might have forgotten.

- ❒ Tell students to imagine they are going to their twenty-fifth class reunion and have to prepare name tags that give specific information to remind their classmates who they were.

- ❒ Use the overhead or board to identify what information is needed and how to prepare the name tag (see example).

Name Tag (25 years in future)

1. Name an important idea you learned from this class or lesson.	2. Name way this class helped you to succeed.
Name **Occupation, Business, Title**	
3. Tell about a dream fulfilled or one recalled.	4. Name an event or high point in your life.

❏ After the cards are completed, instruct students to form pairs. Partners will introduce themselves using descriptions given in the center of the nametag and discuss Response 1. Remind students that they are twenty-five years older and looking back on the past.

❏ After one minute, ask students to remix and repeat the procedure for Response 2. Repeat for Responses 3 and 4.

❏ Regroup as a class and ask for volunteers to share ideas about what they heard for each response.

VARIATIONS

1. Keep the questions and nametags in the present.

2. Ask specific questions to stir up prior knowledge (see Activity 54) of a new lesson or to review key ideas in a lesson just completed.

3. Use the same questions at the start and end of a lesson.

Other Intelligences

- Verbal/linguistic
- Visual/spatial
- Interpersonal
- Intrapersonal

ACTIVITY 95

Silent Hurrahs

Targeted Grades: All

ACTIVITY AT A GLANCE

Purpose

- To celebrate classmates' successes
- To enable base groups to celebrate their own achievements

When to Use

- After an individual, group, all-class achievement, or special contribution

What You'll Need

- No materials necessary

WHAT-TO-DO CHECKLIST

☐ Form base groups (see Activity 141) of five students each.

☐ Introduce the class to a silent **hurrah** such as the Standing "O"vation: At a signal, all students stand, clasp their hands so their arms form a circle over their heads, and say, "Oohhh."

☐ Practice it.

☐ Call on students to use it at the opportune time for a special recognition of students' work.

VARIATIONS

1. The number of different types of hurrahs is limitless. Groups can invent their own as well. Here are some silent samples:
   - Double Clam Clap (two hands open and close like a clam)
   - Alaska Hurrah (silent shake of two hands overhead)
   - Yes, Yes, Yes (emphatic lip-sync statement while pulling right arm down quickly)
   - Thumbs Up
   - Whirly Bird (one hand whirls over head like a helicopter)
   - Silent Clap (hands swish by each other)
   - Silent Cheer (students stand, wave hands, sit)
   - Wave (silent cheer, row by row)
   - Brain Wave (flutter hand by side of head)

2. Designate a student to pick the moment for a silent hurrah and lead the class in it. Use student leaders on a daily basis or for specific types of activities and rotate so that all students have the opportunity to be a hurrah leader.

Other Intelligences

- Interpersonal

ACTIVITY 96

Four Corners

Targeted Grades: Middle and Secondary

ACTIVITY AT A GLANCE

Purpose

- To be comfortable moving to different groups representing different opinions or points of view

When to Use

- To start a lesson in order to determine students' point of view before the lesson starts
- In the middle of a lesson to distinguish students' point of view on an issue in a lesson or unit
- At the end of the lesson to see final points of view

What You'll Need

- Poster boards (four)
- Newsprint
- Markers

WHAT-TO-DO CHECKLIST

- ❏ Use the index cards to label four corners of the room. Make each card represent a point of view on a key idea or issue that you are teaching (such as the causes of global warming: (1) carbon dioxide from power plants, (2) the burning fossil fuels in cars and airplanes, (3) methane gas from herd animals, and (4) deforestation).

- ❏ Ask students to consider which element is the major cause and why. Tell them to proceed to the corner of their choice.

- ❏ Invite each group to compile its reasons for selecting their corner.

- ❏ Have each group select key roles: recorder, idea gatherer, and reporter.

- ❏ Have recorder list the key ideas on newsprint.

- ❏ When ideas are gathered, invite each reporter in turn to state the group's position.

- ❏ Encourage any who wish to switch groups to do so after the reports.

- ❏ Show students how to write a summary that includes all the arguments.

- ❏ Assign each student to write a summary. Remind them to include a topic sentence. Collect the summaries and give feedback on each before returning each student's composition.

VARIATIONS

1. Make six to eight corners for additional points of view.

2. Use the carousel (see Activity 10) so that students can rotate around the classroom and review each point of view.

3. Have students create a sketch of the key arguments and post the completed pictures as the end task.

Other Intelligences

- Verbal/linguistic
- Logical/mathematical
- Visual/spatial
- Interpersonal

ACTIVITY 97
Concept Treasure Hunt

Targeted Grades: Elementary and Middle

ACTIVITY AT A GLANCE

Purpose

- To find objects that represent or symbolize concepts in a lesson or unit being studied

When to Use

- At the end of the lesson or project when students have identified and studied the key concepts

What You'll Need

- Objects for the treasure hunt
- A shoebox for each group
- Crayons or colored markers
- Journals

WHAT-TO-DO CHECKLIST

❐ After you have completed a unit, use a question web (see Activity 6) or concept map (see Activity 53) to conduct an all-class review of the key ideas from the lesson or project.

❏ Around the classroom, hide ten symbols of the subconcepts from the lesson.

❏ Introduce the treasure hunt plan to the students.

❏ Form groups of three to five students. Give each group a shoebox and markers. Explain the meaning of a "symbol." Ask students for examples of symbols and what each represents.

❏ Have each group decorate the outside of the shoebox with their symbol for one of the key ideas of the lesson they completed.

❏ Explain that you have hidden symbols of the subconcepts around the classroom. Each group is to search for the ten symbols.

❏ Send the groups on the hunt. Allow ten minutes.

❏ After the time has elapsed, recall groups and ask them to prepare a presentation of their treasure chests. They will show what they have found, explain the symbolism of each object, and explain how the symbol connects to the key idea.

❏ After all ideas are presented, instruct each student to complete an "I learned . . ." lead-in (see Activity 9) in their journals (see Activity 153).

VARIATIONS

1. Increase the number of symbols.

2. Have each group compose a summary statement that connects the symbols they found with the key idea.

3. Have each group compose a poster (see Activity 61) or collage (see Activity 68) that connects the subconcepts found to the key idea.

Other Intelligences

- Verbal/linguistic
- Visual/spatial
- Interpersonal

ACTIVITY 98

Team Play

Targeted Grades: Middle

ACTIVITY AT A GLANCE

Purpose

- To learn the value of cooperation or teamwork

When to Use

- As students work in groups

What You'll Need

- Newsprint
- Markers
- Journals

WHAT-TO-DO CHECKLIST

❒ Select six team sports familiar to the students. Write the names for all to see.

❒ Create a matrix chart (see Activity 47).

❒ Brainstorm five to six possible elements common to all sports. Write these across the top of the matrix.

❒ Write the names of the sports down the left column.

❒ Check where the sport names and elements intersect.

❒ Divide the class into mixed-ability groups (see Activity 145) of five. Distribute the newsprint and markers to each group.

❒ Have each group assign themselves one of these roles: recorder, reporter, materials manager, facilitator, and timekeeper.

❒ Explain the goal that will guide each group's goal: to invent a new sport.

❒ Set a twenty-minute time limit.

❒ At the end of the time, invite each reporter to identify the sport by name and the common characteristics.

❒ After all have reported, discuss with the class the common elements that are needed for team play.

❒ Invite each student to complete this stem in an entry in journals (see Activity 153): "In team play, the most important element is _____because_____" (see Activity 9). If time allows, use a round-robin questioning pattern to share the completed stems (see Activity 24).

VARIATIONS:

1. Add each group's elements to the matrix.

2. Have each group compose a coach's speech encouraging team play for the sport it invented.

3. Make a Venn diagram (see Activity 66) so that students can contrast individual sport play with team sport play.

Other Intelligences

- Verbal/linguistic
- Visual/spatial
- Interpersonal
- Intrapersonal

ACTIVITY 99

Teamwork Collage

Targeted Grades: All

ACTIVITY AT A GLANCE

Purpose

- To learn the individual behaviors that contribute to teamwork

When to Use

- When introducing students to the values of teamwork before starting work with cooperative or mixed-ability groups

What You'll Need

- Magazines
- Poster board
- Scissors
- Glue
- Journals
- DVD player, including screen

WHAT-TO-DO CHECKLIST

❑ Form cooperative groups (see Activity 128) (mixed ability, mixed gender, and so on) of three students.

❑ Give each group a set of magazines, scissors, glue, and two sheets of poster board. Ask each group to use the materials to make two collages: one showing teamwork and one showing individual performance.

❑ Introduce T-charts (see Activity 163) that show what the behaviors look and sound like in each type of performance.

❑ After the groups are done, post the collages side by side around the classroom.

❑ Ask volunteers from each group to explain what behaviors are associated with each type of performance. Which are the same and which are different?

❑ Ask a student from each group in turn to pantomime a helpful or unhelpful team behavior.

❑ In journals (see Activity 153), have the students summarize (see Activity 129) the most noticeable characteristics of each type.

VARIATIONS

1. Use wire hangers and string to construct mobiles of each type.

2. Make an all-class bulletin board on teamwork with a collage of cutout pictures.

3. Have students make a checklist of team behaviors in their journals.

Other Intelligences

- Verbal/linguistic
- Logical/mathematical
- Visual/spatial
- Intrapersonal

ACTIVITY 100

Pass the Baton

Targeted Grades: Elementary

ACTIVITY AT A GLANCE

Purpose

- To exercise daily inside the classroom

When to Use

- When weather prevents outside activity

What You'll Need

- A cardboard baton for each team of four (such as the inner roll from paper towels, decorated)
- Journals (optional)

WHAT-TO-DO CHECKLIST

☐ At a set time each day when your students' energy gets low, form cooperative groups (by gender and athleticism) (see Activity 128) of four. Each day, a different member will be the team captain who leads the team's silent cheer. Keep teams together for no more than two weeks, then rearrange the team membership.

☐ Have each team give itself an animal name (such as the Bears or Jaguars) and make up a silent hurrah (see Activity 95).

☐ Captains direct one member of the team to each corner of the classroom.

☐ Name the race they will do and the number of laps. Each student will do the required exercise to the next station. The captain starts with the baton and passes it to the next station.

☐ Post the scoring system: five points for the winning team, four for second, and so forth.

☐ No cheering or put-downs are allowed during the race. Only silence. You may penalize any team one point if it breaks the silence or uses a put-down of another team.

☐ At the end of the race, award points and have each team give its cheer in turn.

☐ At the end of the week, give a class silent hurrah to the winning team.

A List of Challenges

1. One-legged hop
2. Hopscotch hop
3. Backwards walk
4. Sideways slide
5. Toe touches
6. Heel-toe fast walk
7. Arm rotation walk
8. Windmill walk

VARIATIONS

1. Make teams of eight and do the exercises in tandem.

2. Do individual exercises in place but rotate around the corners. As a student completes the given number of energy exercises (such as sit-ups, toe-stretches, jumping jacks, and so on), the student walks the baton to the next group.

3. Use stretching and balancing exercises (such as standing on one foot, reaching high, and so on) and pass the baton around the corners.

4. After the exercise, instruct students to make entries in their journals (see Activity 153) that track the exercises done.

Other Intelligences

- Interpersonal
- Intrapersonal

ACTIVITY 101

Vocabulary Basketball

Targeted Grades: Middle

ACTIVITY AT A GLANCE

Purpose

- To review vocabulary words in a physical game simulation

When to Use

- At any point in a lesson or unit for vocabulary practice

What You'll Need

- A scoreboard
- A timer
- Lists of team members

WHAT-TO-DO CHECKLIST

- ❑ Divide the class into two teams. Give each team a name and a silent hurrah cheer (see Activity 95) and allow its members time to check the meaning of the words.
- ❑ Identify the rules of the game. If a team member gives the meaning of the word correctly, it scores one, two, or three points. Identify a word's point value before giving the word. You are the only judge of the definition's correctness. You also should enforce a time limit (use a timer).
- ❑ The team captain designates the person to answer a question. The captain rotates answerers until all have answered in turn.
- ❑ Rounds are three minutes each. There are four rounds per game.
- ❑ You may give foul shots (one point) if a member of the other team fluffs a definition, speaks out, or cheers. Foul shots come from the lowest-value words on list.
- ❑ At the end of the game's time, tabulate the winner and have each team give its silent hurrah.

VARIATIONS

1. Change the game and the score system to fit (such as baseball or field hockey).
2. Change the content from vocabulary to other academic challenges (such as solving an equation, identifying and defining geometric figures, or identifying slides under the microscope).
3. Use "true or false" or "multiple choice" responses.

Other Intelligences

- Interpersonal

PART V

Musical/Rhythmic Intelligence

ACTIVITY 102

Recall Rap

Targeted Grades: Middle and Secondary

ACTIVITY AT A GLANCE

Purpose

- To use prior knowledge as a lead-in to a new topic
- To teach rhyme in poetry

When to Use

- At the beginning of a lesson or unit to help students connect prior knowledge with new learning

What You'll Need

- Music cassettes or CDs
- Cassette tape or CD player

WHAT-TO-DO CHECKLIST

- ❏ Play a popular, age-appropriate rap song with a narrative portion for the class.
- ❏ After the song, discuss the elements of rap.
- ❏ Tell students they are going to write a rap song about the next unit of study. Share a sample and discuss the components.
- ❏ Brainstorm what students already know about the new topic.
- ❏ Have students work in pairs to use the list to create the first two verses and the refrain. Stop at appropriate spots to add new ideas and facts to the class list.
- ❏ Invite pairs to perform the songs.

VARIATIONS

1. For younger students, use the list to write a nursery rhyme and teach the class to sing it.

2. Use other musical forms such as a ballad.

3. Use this strategy in the middle of a lesson to bridge subtopics.

Other Intelligences

- Verbal/linguistic
- Interpersonal

ACTIVITY 103

Assessment Rap

Targeted Grades: Middle and Secondary

ACTIVITY AT A GLANCE

Purpose

- To synthesize reflection in a musical manner

When to Use

- At the end of a lesson or unit to stimulate creative thinking and motivate student reflection, allowing an alternative mode of expression

What You'll Need

- Music cassettes or CDs
- Cassette tape or CD player

WHAT-TO-DO CHECKLIST

- ❏ Play a popular, age-appropriate rap song. Discuss how the song communicates its message.
- ❏ Divide the class into cooperative groups (see Activity 128) of three students each, and instruct groups to brainstorm and list what they learned in the lesson.
- ❏ Review several of the groups' lists with the entire class.
- ❏ Ask each group to create a rap song based on its list.
- ❏ Have each group perform its rap song.

VARIATIONS

1. Make this an individual assignment.
2. Leave out the performances.
3. Use a different musical form that is familiar to the students.

Other Intelligences

- Verbal/linguistic
- Interpersonal

ACTIVITY 104

Sing a Song to Remember

Targeted Grades: Elementary

ACTIVITY AT A GLANCE

Purpose

- To use music as a memory tool

When to Use

- Throughout a lesson or unit to help students memorize basic facts or components of a topic

What You'll Need

- *The Sound of Music* on audiotape, CD, or videotape
- Cassette, CD, or video player

WHAT-TO-DO CHECKLIST

- ❏ Play an audio or a video cut of "Do-Re-Mi" from *The Sound of Music*.
- ❏ Ask students what makes the song easy to remember and what the song teaches about music (such as the eight-note scale).
- ❏ Identify some other easy-to-remember songs the students know, such as the "Itsy Bitsy Spider."
- ❏ Bridge to a song that will teach students how to memorize an element of the curriculum. Teach and practice the song.

VARIATIONS

1. Use music-only tapes, and provide paper so the class can write lyrics to the music.
2. Use tapes with both words and music.
3. Invite students to make their own "remember" songs.

Other Intelligences

- Interpersonal

ACTIVITY 105

Music Connector

Targeted Grades: Middle and Secondary

ACTIVITY AT A GLANCE

Purpose

- To communicate ideas and facts through a song medium

When to Use

- As a lesson to teach students how to write lyrics to a song that fits a particular type of music
- At the end of a lesson or unit to provide an alternative medium to communicate ideas learned in a lesson with students who have learned how to create a song

What You'll Need

- Music cassettes or CDs
- Cassette tape or CD player

WHAT-TO-DO CHECKLIST

- ❏ Arrange students in pairs or trios.
- ❏ Have the class name popular songs and record the list. Have pairs classify the music by grouping the songs into categories by type (such as rap, pop, and so on) and labeling the groups.
- ❏ Have each pair select one category and list the criteria for a quality song of that type.
- ❏ Invite each pair to select a topic to be the theme for the lyrics to a song that it will write.
- ❏ Coach and monitor the song-writing process.
- ❏ Have each pair present its song to the class, either by singing or by playing a pre-recorded tape.
- ❏ After each performance, ask students to share the criteria they used while creating the song.

VARIATIONS

1. For elementary students, use nursery rhymes as the model.
2. Use a single type of music such as rap or pop for all groups.

3. Replace popular music models with classical music or show tunes. Have the class study the selected model before having students write their own samples.

4. Use the completed songs for a performance on Parents' Night.

Other Intelligences

- Verbal/linguistic
- Interpersonal

ACTIVITY 106

Play It

Targeted Grades: All

ACTIVITY AT A GLANCE

Purpose

- To explore different musical instruments

When to Use

- As a way to bring music into the curriculum
- To create a unit that culminates in a field trip to see a concert or musical theater

What You'll Need

- Pictures of musical instruments
- Journals
- Guest speakers (musicians)
- Presentation outline

WHAT-TO-DO CHECKLIST

❏ Invite several local musicians to demonstrate and discuss their instruments with the class.

❏ Prepare the class for the lesson and demonstration by showing pictures of the instruments and placing the pictures in a cluster with similar instruments (woodwinds, strings, percussion, and so on).

❏ Structure the presentations by providing an outline for the presenters and the students to follow.

❏ Encourage students to make entries in their journals (see Activity 153) after each presentation.

❏ Have the class complete lead-in statements (see Activity 9) about each instrument, such as
   ○ What I learned was . . .
   ○ What I like about _____ is . . .
   ○ What surprised me about _____ was . . .

Example

Name of instrument: Accordion
Family: Reed
Origin: Vienna, Austria, in 1829
Special features: Bellows and buttons similar to piano keys
Famous players: Drew Carey, Eddie Vedder (of Pearl Jam), Rick Wright
(of Pink Floyd), "Weird Al" Yankovic
Musical demonstration
Questions and answers
• What I learned was . . .
• What I like about the accordion is . . .
• What surprised me about the accordion was . . .

VARIATIONS

1. After hearing the various instruments, invite a quartet that blends instruments in different kinds of music to play for the class.

2. Identify students from the class who play instruments. These students can make the presentations as an individual project or for extra credit.

Other Intelligences

• Interpersonal

ACTIVITY 107

Instrument Inventor

Targeted Grades: Middle

ACTIVITY AT A GLANCE

Purpose

• To understand how musical instruments produce sound

When to Use

• As a unit or lesson in which students study sound as music

What You'll Need

- Variety of instruments
- Guest speaker (musician)
- Variety of construction materials

WHAT-TO-DO CHECKLIST

❏ Invite a musician to demonstrate and discuss his instrument.

❏ After the demonstration, create a list with the class of facts about the instrument and how it makes music. Use this list to develop criteria for student-created instruments.

❏ Invite students to bring in materials they can use to make instruments similar to the demonstrated one. Be sure everyone contributes at least one item (such as a shoebox, metal clothes hangers, string, and tin cans).

❏ Arrange students into groups and divide the materials. Each group will make its version of the model instrument.

❏ Ask each group to show its instrument and explain its features in relation to the criteria and the original instrument.

VARIATIONS

1. Start with demonstrations of different instruments from the same category (such as string instruments) or from several different categories (such as percussion, strings, and brass). Each group will select a different instrument to recreate.

2. Create several small bands with a mixture of instruments. Encourage each band to demonstrate a simple tune.

3. Create period instruments from American history or instruments from other cultures.

4. Use a question web (see Activity 6) for the original list.

Other Intelligences

- Visual/spatial
- Interpersonal

ACTIVITY 108

Rhythms to Recall

Targeted Grades: Middle

ACTIVITY AT A GLANCE

Purpose

- To explore a variety of musical rhythms

When to Use

- As part of a lesson on rhythm in poetry or songs
- As preparation for writing poetry and songs

What You'll Need

- Music cassettes or CDs
- Cassette tape or CD player
- Coffee cans

WHAT-TO-DO CHECKLIST

- ☐ Using the cassette tape or CD player, play three songs for the class, each with a different rhythm (such as ballad, tango, and bossa nova).

- ☐ Ask students to describe the different rhythms.

- ☐ Discuss the importance of the rhythms in relation to the music.

- ☐ Use a sonnet and ballad to show how rhythm is used to accent words in a poem or in lyrics. Contrast these with how rhythm is used to accent words in with a rap song.

- ☐ Have each student select a rhythm and mark it out with numbers (such as one, two; one, two; one, two).

- ☐ Tell students to indicate the stronger beat by circling the stronger number.

- ☐ Arrange students into random groups of five.

- ☐ Provide each group with an empty coffee can and invite each person, in turn, to demonstrate her rhythm.

VARIATIONS

1. Use pairs to create the rhythms.

2. Have each student or pair create several different rhythms.

3. After the first demonstration, pick several rhythms for a band of percussionists to play together, using empty coffee cans. The creators will teach five to six other students how to play the rhythm in concert.

Other Intelligences

- Verbal/linguistic
- Interpersonal

ACTIVITY 109

Listening Time

Targeted Grades: Elementary and Middle

ACTIVITY AT A GLANCE

Purpose

- To listen to music with a purpose or goal

When to Use

- To build listening skills with elementary students
- At the start of the day in order to initiate student focus
- After an activity period to restore student focus
- On a daily basis

What You'll Need

- Music cassettes or CDs
- Cassette tape or CD player

WHAT-TO-DO CHECKLIST

- ❏ Select a piece of music with a special feature. Point out that feature for the students.
- ❏ Introduce the musician or composer.
- ❏ Explain what the students should listen for: rhythm, feeling, tone, or a specific instrument.
- ❏ Ask for concentrated silence and play the piece.
- ❏ After the piece is completed, discuss what the students heard, felt, and thought.
- ❏ Study a different genre each week, such as jazz, musical comedy, or classical.

VARIATIONS

1. After studying several different genres of music, use a T-chart (see Activity 47) or Venn diagram (see Activity 66) to compare them.

2. Study a genre of music that is connected to other topics your class is studying, such as historical periods or literature selections.

Other Intelligences

- Visual/spatial
- Interpersonal

ACTIVITY 110

Concert Trip

Targeted Grades: Middle and Secondary

ACTIVITY AT A GLANCE

Purpose

- To experience a full musical concert

When to Use

- When studying a historic period (select a related concert)
- When studying various cultures (select related folk or classical music)
- When studying American literature (introduce musical comedy)

What You'll Need

- Music cassettes or CDs
- Cassette tape or CD player
- Tickets to an afternoon concert
- Journals

WHAT-TO-DO CHECKLIST

- ❏ Prepare students for the field trip (see Activity 45) by listening to the musical score, doing research about the composer, or reviewing the historic context.

- ❏ Prepare students for postconcert reflection by informing them in advance of the assessment method they will use, such as a PMI assessment (see Activity 158) or Venn diagram (see Activity 66).

- ❏ After the concert, discuss the experience by asking probing questions that uncover personal reactions.

- ❏ Arrange students in pairs or trios to assess the performance. For example, ask groups to discuss the pluses, minuses, and interesting questions about the experience, or to create a Venn diagram comparing the concert to a similar experience.

- ❏ Conclude with an entry in their journals (see Activity 153) or invite students to complete reflective statements, such as *I liked* . . . or *I discovered* . . . (see Activity 9).

VARIATIONS

1. Select the music that fits the historical period or culture being studied.

2. Compare folk and classical music from a given period.

Other Intelligences

- Visual/spatial
- Interpersonal

ACTIVITY 111

Musical Styles

Targeted Grades: Elementary and Middle

ACTIVITY AT A GLANCE

Purpose

- To teach students to hear the differences between styles of soloists
- To develop students' ability to compare

When to Use

- When comparing and contrasting musical pieces to help students determine differences in rhythm, pitch, tenor, timbre, and other musical elements

What You'll Need

- Music cassettes or CDs
- Cassette tape or CD player

WHAT-TO-DO CHECKLIST

- ☐ On the board or overhead, draw a Venn diagram (see Activity 66) and explain the purpose of the comparison.

- ☐ Identify two popular singers and label each circle. Ask the class to brainstorm how each singer sounds when performing a musical piece. Enter unique characteristics in the appropriate circle and the shared characteristics in the intersection of the circles.

- ☐ Select a sample song by each soloist. Play the songs and invite the class to list the different musical characteristics.

- ☐ Invite the class to suggest placement of these characteristics on the Venn diagram.

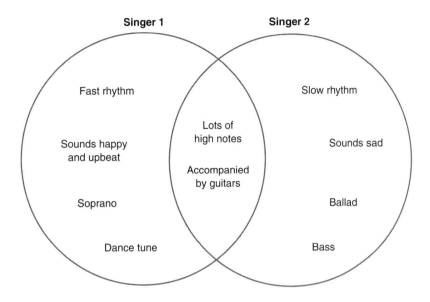

VARIATIONS

1. Tailor the complexity of the musical selections to the background of the students. Begin with simple comparisons and popular soloists.

2. Change from popular voice soloists to classical opera singers or orchestras.

Other Intelligences

- Interpersonal

ACTIVITY 112

Musical Volunteers

Targeted Grades: All

ACTIVITY AT A GLANCE

Purpose

- To explore interests in music by talking with professional musicians and by experiencing a variety of music

When to Use

- At least once every six weeks in the classroom

What You'll Need

- Guest performer (musician)

WHAT-TO-DO CHECKLIST

❒ Invite a professional musician to perform for the class. Ask the performer to explain each piece being performed and to discuss how he developed his talent.

❒ After the performance, encourage students to interview the musician, asking a variety of questions.

❒ Make an all-class list of what students liked most.

VARIATIONS

1. Use different types of music selected for a single instrument or group of instruments.

2. Use a variety of different types of instruments.

3. Before the musician arrives, brainstorm a list of interview questions that students might want to ask.

Other Intelligences

- Interpersonal

ACTIVITY 113

Magic in Music

Targeted Grades: Elementary and Middle

ACTIVITY AT A GLANCE

Purpose

- To share songs from films and stage productions

When to Use

- To tie music to a study of poetry, rhyme and rhythm, character study, drama, or scenery design

What You'll Need

- No materials necessary

WHAT-TO-DO CHECKLIST

❏ Ask students to recall the names of musical productions they have seen as a stage production or on television. List these on the board or overhead.

❏ Form mixed-ability groups (see Activity 145) of three to five students each.

❏ Allow each group to pick a production it favors and to make a question web or list of the songs it remembers.

❏ Have groups select a number of songs from the production that they will sing to an audience. Let the groups practice their songs. Encourage out-of-class practice and for students to re-create the musical scenes as they remember them.

❏ Invite parents to a class production or have students perform for an elementary classroom.

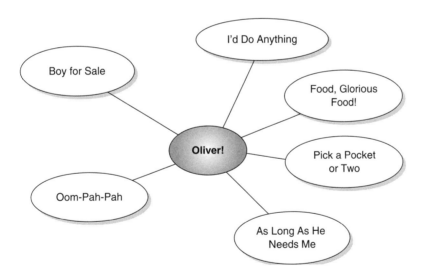

VARIATIONS

1. Select one musical production. View the film version and assign different songs to different groups of students in the class.

2. Take a field trip (see Activity 45) to see a live stage production. Before the trip, listen to a recording so students can learn the music and the melodies.

Other Intelligences

- Verbal/linguistic
- Interpersonal

ACTIVITY 114

Group Song

Targeted Grades: Elementary and Middle

ACTIVITY AT A GLANCE

Purpose

- To build team cohesion through music

When to Use

- To build team cohesion
- To increase group energy
- To celebrate student accomplishments

What You'll Need

- Music cassettes or CDs
- Cassette tape or CD player
- Chart paper

WHAT-TO-DO CHECKLIST

- ❏ Play a recording of the theme song for a state university or the local high school. Ask students why they think schools have theme songs (such as to develop or increase unity and school spirit).

- ❏ Divide the class into groups of three and have each group write a "spirit" song. Suggest that students use a popular song or commercial jingle for their melody.

- ❏ Encourage groups to use an **attribute web** (see Activity 6) to determine positive traits shared by group members. They can use these commonalities to write the lyrics to their songs.

- ❏ Give groups chart paper to use to write out their lyrics.

- ❏ Invite each group to perform its song for the class.

VARIATIONS

1. Post each group's lyrics. Have the class sing various groups' songs.

2. Use group interviews (see Activity 22) so that each group can add verses about each member.

3. Record each performance and create an audiocassette of all the songs. Accompany it with a sheet for each student that lists the words to each song.

Other Intelligences

- Verbal/linguistic
- Interpersonal

ACTIVITY 115

Group Cheer

Targeted Grades: Elementary and Middle

ACTIVITY AT A GLANCE

Purpose

- To build group cohesion

When to Use

- To energize the class
- To celebrate group accomplishments
- To encourage group unity before a challenging test or project
- To build group unity

What You'll Need

- Chart paper

WHAT-TO-DO CHECKLIST

- ❑ Move students into base groups (see Activity 141) or set up special "cheer groups" of three students each.

- ❑ Ask each group to select and practice a school cheer with words and movements. Allow each group to model its cheer. Discuss the effects of cheers on the class (such as team spirit, energy, fun).

- ❑ Provide groups with chart paper. Invite each group to create a cheer about its members' best characteristics. Use a matrix (see Activity 179) to identify these characteristics.

- ❑ Have groups present their cheers to the class. Use these cheers to celebrate accomplishments throughout the year.

Our Best Features

	What is something special about this person?	What are two words that describe this person?	What is his or her favorite subject?
Hannah	She makes me laugh.	funny imaginative	gym
Jeremy	He always helps out.	thoughtful kind	science
Cari	She's always willing to share.	generous considerate	math

VARIATIONS

1. Tailor verses to individual or specific group accomplishments.

2. Encourage addition of cheerleading moves to each cheer.

Other Intelligences

- Verbal/linguistic
- Visual/spatial
- Interpersonal
- Intrapersonal

ACTIVITY 116

Song of the Week

Targeted Grades: Elementary and Middle

ACTIVITY AT A GLANCE

Purpose

- To integrate music appreciation as a regular part of the curriculum

When to Use

- Once a week between lessons

What You'll Need

- Three-by-five-inch index cards
- Music cassettes or CDs
- Cassette tape or CD player

WHAT-TO-DO CHECKLIST

❏ When possible, fit this activity thematically with key content.

❏ Ask each student to write the name of a favorite song on an index card. Collect these.

❏ As a class, brainstorm a list of specific criteria for the favorites. Post the list.

❏ Schedule one song to play each week.

❏ Ask students to bring recordings of their favorite songs to play for the class on the scheduled day.

❏ Before playing a song, invite the student to use the posted criteria to explain her choice. Remind the class of the **DOVE guidelines** (see Activity 152).

VARIATIONS

1. Have base groups (see Activity 141) vote on the "song of the month."

2. After a song is played, ask other members of the class to use the criteria to assess the song's quality.

Other Intelligences

- Interpersonal

ACTIVITY 117

Musical Review

Targeted Grades: Elementary and Middle

ACTIVITY AT A GLANCE

Purpose

- To articulate an assessment of music based on a set of criteria for excellence

When to Use

- Once middle school students understand the basic concepts of musical composition
- As part of class study of American history, world history, or a specific culture

What You'll Need

- Chart paper
- Music cassettes or CDs

- Cassette tape or CD player
- Journals

WHAT-TO-DO CHECKLIST

☐ On the board or overhead, show standards for good music. Use vocabulary appropriate to the students' reading levels (such as melody, tonality, variations, progressions, and so on). If you are not a music buff, do an Internet search on "musical terms" for helpful information.

☐ Develop three to five criteria of excellence. Add a **Likert scale** for each criterion.

☐ Play and assess a TV jingle, popular song, and classical composition. Ask students to use the scales to evaluate each musical selection.

☐ Discuss how each genre can have its own criteria. Help students adjust the criteria so they have a set for each genre.

☐ Assign various musical pieces, one to each group, and ask students to apply the appropriate criteria.

☐ Distribute chart paper and instruct each group to scale its assessments and prepare an explanation of its members' thinking.

☐ Each group member should report on one criterion, but each group's explanations must include the ideas from all group members.

☐ Have each group play samples of the music for the class to hear.

☐ Schedule the reports over three or four days, by genre.

☐ After all reports have been presented, call for individual entries in their journals (see Activity 153) and invite students to share what they've written.

VARIATIONS

1. Use only one genre.

2. For advanced students, assign students individual pieces to assess.

3. As a concluding activity, compare three genres by constructing an all-class, triple Venn diagram (see Activity 66. With a triple Venn, you add one more overlapping circle to form a triangle of circles.).

Other Intelligences

- Verbal/linguistic
- Interpersonal

ACTIVITY 118

Rap It Up

A Summarizing Task

Targeted Grades: Middle

ACTIVITY AT A GLANCE

Purpose

- To use a familiar musical style as the medium for summarizing content learned in a lesson or unit

When to Use

- As a review
- To add interest to a lesson or unit
- To create a final product in which students demonstrate their grasp of the covered material

What You'll Need

- Music cassettes or CDs
- Cassette tape or CD player
- Journals (optional)

WHAT-TO-DO CHECKLIST

- ❏ After concluding a lesson or unit of study, invite students, individually or in groups, to write a rap song with lyrics that summarize the ideas and facts learned.

- ❏ Review the rap style with several examples. Students must select their own rap rhythm pattern.

- ❏ Coach (see Introduction, p. 25) students as they select and match ideas to the selected rhythm.

- ❏ Review the finished products. Distribute copies to each student and invite volunteers to perform for the class.

- ❏ After the last performance, make an all-class list that captures the important ideas and details of the finished unit.

- ❏ Review the format and criteria for strong summary statements (see Activity 157).

❐ Invite each student to use an "I learned . . ." lead-in (see Activity 9) to start a summary statement. Have each student supply at least three examples.

❐ Collect and give feedback according to the criteria developed.

VARIATIONS

1. Provide a single rap rhythm for all students to use.
2. Assign the rap composition as a homework task.
3. Invite parents or other classes to a performance.
4. As a final task, substitute an individual essay that communicates what was learned.
5. As a final task, provide time for an "I learned . . ." summary of the lesson or unit in their journals (see Activities 9 and 153).

Other Intelligences

- Verbal/linguistic
- Interpersonal

ACTIVITY 119

Sounds of Culture

ACTIVITY AT A GLANCE

Purpose

- To explore music from many different cultures

When to Use

- At the end of a unit that explores different cultures in order to bring students closer to their roots and to enrich their understanding of other cultures

What You'll Need

- Music cassettes or CDs
- Cassette tape or CD player
- World map or globe, markers

WHAT-TO-DO CHECKLIST

❐ Identify the cultural heritage of each student in the classroom. On a map or globe, mark the countries of origin or ancestry for each student in the room.

❐ Ask each student to investigate the types of music for which his heritage is recognized.

❏ Invite two students per week to share samples of music associated with their ethnic or cultural backgrounds.

❏ Ask students to research and share interesting information about different cultures' musical traditions. For younger students, invite parents or other relatives to share this information with their children. If there is a musician in the family, invite that person to play for the class.

❏ After each presentation, discuss what is special or unique about the music and how it relates to its cultural roots.

Non-Western Music

Country/region	Instrument used	When used	Unique feature
Native America (South & North)	flutes, drums, rattles	tribal rituals, religious ceremonies, social situations	five-note scale
Japan	flutes, gongs, drums, and plucked stringed instruments	theater, court festivities	no harmony
China	guqin and pipa (stringed instruments)	court festivities, religious ceremonies	no harmony
India	drums, tamburas, and stringed instruments such as vinas and sitars	temple and court activities	scales (called ragas) with special meanings
Africa	drums, flutes, xylophones, and stringed instruments	religious ceremonies, social rituals, festivals	complex rhythms

❏ After each demonstration, discuss the unique features of the musical traditions as well as how the music is similar to or different from music of other cultures.

VARIATIONS

1. Make this a library assignment.
2. For younger students, take a field trip (see Activity 45) to a local library's music room or to a local university's music department.
3. Create a matrix (see Activity 179) classifying music-related topics by cultures or countries.
4. Make a bulletin board that shows the music and dance of each culture.
5. Ask students who are not from the weekly culture what they appreciate about the music of the week and its culture.

Other Intelligences
- Verbal/linguistic
- Visual/spatial
- Interpersonal
- Intrapersonal

ACTIVITY 120

Rhyme Words

Targeted Grades: Elementary

ACTIVITY AT A GLANCE

Purpose

- To explore rhyme and write a rhyming poem

When to Use

- As an introduction to rhyme
- As a language tool
- To help students construct memory rhymes

What You'll Need

- Sample poem

WHAT-TO-DO CHECKLIST

❒ On the board or overhead, write "cat." Ask for a volunteer to name as many rhyming words as possible in one minute. Count these, and repeat the process with two other volunteers using the words "hot" and "roll."

❒ Ask students to explain different meanings for any of the listed words that are homophones or homonyms. List these on the board.

❒ Note that rhyming words help memory by providing key sounds to associate.

❒ Arrange students in pairs. Have pairs write a four- to eight-line poem that uses six to twelve rhymes for a single word. Share a self-created or previous student's sample.

❒ Coach the pairs as they create their rhymes (see Introduction, p. 11).

The cat sat
and watched the rat.
The rat was chasing
a big, fat gnat.
The gnat flew up
and perched on the cat.
The rat decided
that that was that!

❐ Call for volunteers to share their completed poems.

❐ Celebrate with pair-selected hurrahs (see Activity 95).

VARIATIONS

1. Invite each student to create her own poem.
2. Ask students to write poems related to a theme in a lesson or unit.
3. Go to the school library with the students and find books of poetry with lots of rhyme. Select students to read to the class or in pairs and highlight the rhymes.
4. Make a word rhyme display on the bulletin board. How many words can students find for each rhyme sound?

Other Intelligences

- Verbal/linguistic
- Visual/spatial
- Interpersonal

ACTIVITY 121

Name Poem

Targeted Grades: Middle

ACTIVITY AT A GLANCE

Purpose

- To write a poem based on a person's name

When to Use

- To review rhyming words
- To reflect on one's personal characteristics

What You'll Need

- Sample name poem
- Chart paper

WHAT-TO-DO CHECKLIST

❐ Share a name poem with the class. Point out the use of double rhymes. (See example.)

❐ Arrange students in pairs. Each person will interview the other (see Activity 22) to identify personal traits for use in the poem.

❐ Have partners construct double-rhyme name poems about each other.

❐ Post the finished poems and use a carousel (see Activity 10) so that all can read the finished work.

MATTHEW

M   is for magical, an imaginative boy

A   is for amiable, full of loving joy

T   is for talented and smart

T   is for thoughtful, with a big heart

H   is for happy, having lots of fun

E   is for expressive, a poetic one

W   is for wonderful, shining like the sun

VARIATIONS

1. Use groups of four or five students to brainstorm positive traits of each member.

2. Ask students to bring a baby photo. Attach these to the poems for a display on Parents' Night.

3. Write name poems about literary or historical figures, cartoon characters, or other imaginary or real persons.

Other Intelligences

- Verbal/linguistic
- Interpersonal
- Intrapersonal

ACTIVITY 122

Haiku

Targeted Grades: Middle and Secondary

ACTIVITY AT A GLANCE

Purpose

- To understand the haiku format and write a haiku

When to Use

- To introduce students to a new type of poem with musical rhythms

What You'll Need

- Sample haiku

WHAT-TO-DO CHECKLIST

- ❏ On the board or overhead, share a sample haiku.
- ❏ Discuss and list the characteristics of haiku. Use these as criteria for the students to write their own haiku.
- ❏ Arrange students in trios, and give each group a haiku sample. Instruct each group to analyze its poem using the criteria listed.
- ❏ Discuss each group's analysis. Invite students to read the sample haiku and point out their qualities.
- ❏ After all haiku are shared, ask students to select and discuss the haiku that best meets each characteristic.
- ❏ Invite each student to write a haiku. Coach as needed (see Introduction, p. 11).
- ❏ Display the completed haiku on the bulletin board.

**A gently swaying
Pine tree waves good morning to
The fresh fallen snow**

VARIATIONS

1. Use pairs or trios to construct the final haiku.
2. Allow individuals to analyze the sample haiku.
3. Center the haiku content around a specific unit or lesson.
4. Invite students to illustrate their haiku.

Other Intelligences

- Verbal/linguistic
- Logical/mathematical
- Visual/spatial
- Interpersonal
- Intrapersonal
- Naturalist

ACTIVITY 123

Sonnets

Targeted Grades: Secondary

ACTIVITY AT A GLANCE

Purpose

- To appreciate the sonnet form of poetry with its unique rhythm and rhyme patterns

When to Use

- To emphasize the criteria of excellence for a sonnet, especially with regard to rhyme and rhythm

What You'll Need

- Sample sonnets by Elizabeth Browning, William Shakespeare, and other poets

WHAT-TO-DO CHECKLIST

- ❐ Ask students to identify popular songs that center on the theme of love. What do these poems say or suggest?
- ❐ Show a sonnet sample by Browning or Shakespeare.
- ❐ Discuss with the class what it says and suggests.
- ❐ Introduce the sonnet form used by the poet. Contrast it with sonnet forms used by other famous poets. Highlight both rhyme and rhythm.
- ❐ Ask students to hypothesize (see Activity 50) about the effects caused by the rhyme, scheme, and meter.
- ❐ Show samples of other meters and read aloud.
- ❐ Invite students to create two- to four-rhymed lines in one of the meters. They may want to take words from a popular love song and adjust them to sonnet form. Ask questions to elicit student reactions.

❐ Select three sonnets for students to read aloud. Allow them to practice in pairs so that they can assist each other with the use of rhyme and meter.

❐ With the class, set criteria for reading the sonnets. Explain that before each reading the student will present in writing an analysis of the rhyme and meter as well as an explanation of these elements' contribution to the reading.

❐ Give feedback based on the established criteria.

VARIATIONS

1. Encourage volunteers to write a modern sonnet.

2. Select sonnets by other poets to read and analyze.

3. Write summary paragraphs on the musical quality of sonnets.

Other Intelligences

- All

ACTIVITY 124

Rhyme Stories

Targeted Grades: Elementary

ACTIVITY AT A GLANCE

Purpose

- To write a rhyming children's story

When to Use

- When teaching story structure
- When sharpening students' precise use of vocabulary sounds

What You'll Need

- Dr. Seuss stories
- Cardboard
- Construction paper
- Paper (eight inch by fourteen inch)
- Cellophane tape

WHAT-TO-DO CHECKLIST

❒ Read a Dr. Seuss story to the class. Ask students to identify the common sound-alike words or rhyming patterns. What do they think the patterns add to the story? What other Dr. Seuss stories do they remember?

❒ Brainstorm with the class a list of topics for a rhyming story. Choose one and create a storyboard or sequence chart.

❒ Add words that emphasize a rhyming pattern.

❒ Discuss with students the criteria for a rhyming story.

❒ Arrange students into groups of three and explain that they will be working together to write a rhyming story. Each group needs to have an illustrator, a rhyme maker, and a storyteller.

❒ Provide the materials to construct an eight- to ten-page, illustrated, rhyming storybook, preferably in "big book" size (at least sixteen inches by twenty-eight inches). This can be made by attaching two eight-inch by fourteen-inch sheets of paper per page.

❒ Invite students to read their completed stories to younger children.

❒ Match each group with another and ask groups to compare the finished stories with the previously established criteria.

VARIATIONS

1. Invite parents to school for a story-reading night.

2. Invite older students to your classroom to teach students in small groups.

Other Intelligences

- Verbal/linguistic
- Interpersonal
- Intrapersonal

ACTIVITY 125

Humdinger

Targeted Grades: All

ACTIVITY AT A GLANCE

Purpose

- To use music as a means to form randomly mixed cooperative groups

When to Use

- When helping students with their music listening skills

What You'll Need

- Three-by-five-inch index cards

WHAT-TO-DO CHECKLIST

- ❏ Select enough song titles so there is one for every two students. On index cards, write the titles of familiar songs, one title per card. Use each song title twice so that there are two cards for every song, and one card for every student.

- ❏ Review all the melodies with the class, but do not reveal the titles.

- ❏ Allow each student to pick one card.

- ❏ At a signal, each student will hum his melody and search for the other person who is humming the same melody.

- ❏ When all have found their partners, invite pairs to hum their melodies for the class.

- ❏ If some students can't find their partners, ask the class to stop and be quiet and allow those students to hum alone.

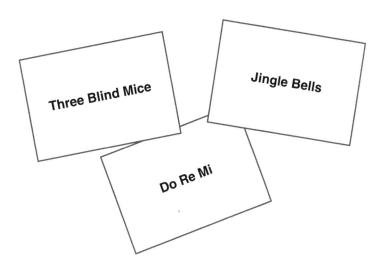

VARIATIONS

1. Invite students to submit popular melodies.

2. Make three or four cards with each song's title.

Other Intelligences

- Interpersonal

ACTIVITY 126

The Sounds in Words

Targeted Grades: Elementary

ACTIVITY AT A GLANCE

Purpose

- To help young students set up sound patterns in a sentence

When to Use

- When introducing students to sound patterns
- When coaching struggling students on how to emphasize sound patterns

What you will need

- Sheets of cardboard (nine inch by twelve inch)
- Crayons or colored markers
- Rhymed tales or short poems

WHAT-TO-DO CHECKLIST

- ❏ Using one piece of cardboard for each tale or poem, show students examples of similar sounds. Highlight similar sounds in the tale (// Jack and *Jill* went up the *hill* and *Jill* came tumbling down, etc. //).

- ❏ Read each of the sentences at least two times with accentuation of the rhyme sounds. After you have read, ask students to pick out the rhyming sounds.

- ❏ Ask the students to give a choral copy of your reading with the same accentuation.

- ❏ Repeat the same sentence with a different accentuation that does not hammer the rhymes.

- ❏ Divide the class into pairs. Present a short poem (such as "Little Bo Peep" or "Jack Sprat"). Demonstrate the reading of the rhymes.

- ❏ Coach students in reading to each other to practice the accentuation of the rhymes (see Introduction, p. 25).

- ❏ Select pairs to perform for the class. After they have given their interpretations ask them to explain why they selected the words to accentuate. (One answer might be, "Because they sound alike.")

- ❏ After the last pair reads, ask the students to tell you what they learned about rhymes. If there is time, have them give you other words that rhyme.

VARIATIONS

1. Write the sentences on the board. Ask students to break down the sentences.

2. Have each pair practice the second time with another pair.

3. Save rhyming words the students present and post a list.

Other Intelligences

- Verbal/linguistic
- Visual/spatial
- Interpersonal

PART VI

Interpersonal Intelligence

ACTIVITY 127

Our Common Goal

Targeted Grades: All

ACTIVITY AT A GLANCE

Purpose

- To teach the importance of a common or shared goal as the essential characteristic of teamwork

When to Use

- When introducing the concept of teamwork to the class
- When restoring team focus if cooperative groups lose focus of their common or shared goal

What You'll Need

- Picture of a team sports goal (a basket for basketball, soccer goal, football goalposts, and so on)
- Journals

WHAT-TO-DO CHECKLIST

- ❏ Show a picture of a team sports goal. Discuss the importance of team play and teamwork in winning a game.
- ❏ Brainstorm a class list that shows the benefits of focusing on a common goal to gain team advantage or complete team tasks. Post the list for referral.
- ❏ Have students make a list of the benefits in their journals (see Activity 153).

VARIATIONS

1. Play videotaped vignettes that show groups working together for a common purpose. Include a variety of types of groups (such as sports teams, marching bands, or children at play). After each vignette, ask students to identify the common goal of the team or group and discuss characteristics that contributed to reaching the group's goal.

2. Invite a sports coach or player to talk to the class about the importance of teamwork.

3. Brainstorm a list of non-sports-related teams (such as orchestras, police officers, or a medical team). Ask students to identify what these teams are able to accomplish that individuals working alone would not be able to accomplish.

Other Intelligences

- Verbal/linguistic
- Logical/mathematical
- Visual/spatial

ACTIVITY 128

Forming Cooperative Groups

Targeted Grades: All

ACTIVITY AT A GLANCE

Purpose

- To teach students how to participate in a cooperative mixed-ability, mixed-gender, mixed-racial, or mixed-ethnic group

When to Use

- Throughout a lesson when you wish to remix students into cooperative groups

What You'll Need

- No materials necessary

WHAT-TO-DO CHECKLIST

❒ Select a characteristic for grouping students (such as participation style) and iden-tify three attributes of that characteristic (such as "actively participates," "moder-ately participates," needs "extensive encouragement to participate"). Using observation data from the first few weeks of the school year, form a master list that identifies each student based on the selected attributes. You can then use the attrib-utes as criteria for making judgments.

❒ Form cooperative groups by selecting members with differing attributes.

❒ Identify groups that you want to stay together over time (such as a unit, a project, or a quarter) as base groups. Identify groups that change with every lesson as tac-tical groups.

   a. **Base groups**
- Build teamwork and social skills for working together.
- Stay together long term.
- Use bonding activities such as team name, team cheer, team logo, team song, team colors, and so on (see Activity 95).
- Assess cooperation.

b. **Tactical Groups**
- Change membership with each lesson.
- Apply cooperative skills.
- Focus on shared academic goal and learning tasks.
- Can be informal (such as think-pair-share) or formal (guidelines, roles).
- Assess academic work (see Activity 8).
- Develop individual accountability with each doing a part to achieve the goal.
- Use DOVE guidelines (see Activity 152).
- Use many tactics (such as jigsaw [Activity 135], three questions plus one [Activity 134], and so on).

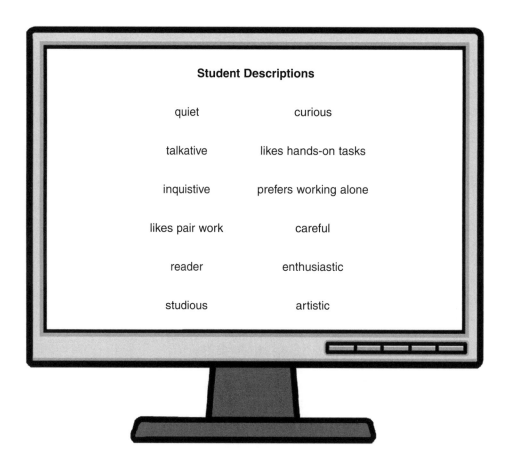

Student Descriptions

quiet	curious
talkative	likes hands-on tasks
inquistive	prefers working alone
likes pair work	careful
reader	enthusiastic
studious	artistic

VARIATIONS

1. Form the first base group from a random draw. Put each student's name in a hat and draw a whole team's name at one time. When a team is drawn, read students' names as a unit. After the first quarter, redraw to form a new base group.

2. As a class, brainstorm a list of adjectives or short phrases that describe types of students, working styles, and learning preferences. Ask students to select three adjectives or phrases that best describe themselves and write a short paragraph explaining their choices. Use students' self-descriptions as a tool for future grouping.

3. Teach roles and procedures for cooperation before beginning serious academic tasks. Develop the language of cooperation among the students.

Other Intelligences

- Verbal/linguistic

ACTIVITY 129

Group Goal

Targeted Grades: All

ACTIVITY AT A GLANCE

Purpose

- To teach how a single share group goal builds teamwork
- To teach students to write a summary

When to Use

- When introducing students to cooperative learning tasks
- When groups are not bonding
- When groups need to reevaluate how well they are working toward a goal
- At the beginning of the year to ensure all students know how to write a summary

What You'll Need

- Journals

WHAT-TO-DO CHECKLIST

❏ Form cooperative groups (see Activity 128) of three to five students each.

❏ Discuss the concept of a "goal." Invite students to give examples of both individual and team goals. Guide the discussion to differentiate individual goals from team goals.

❏ Assign a simple task or activity for the groups to complete (such as "Answer three questions about a school rule familiar to all"). Identify the team goal that each of the groups will pursue. After the task is complete, invite each team to assess its teamwork by sharing how all contributed (see Activity 127).

❏ Brainstorm a class list of what elements, behaviors, and attitudes help teams accomplish a common goal. Conclude with a discussion of the benefits of a group goal.

❏ Introduce the strategy of "making a summary." Using the list of behaviors and attitudes generated above, write a summary paragraph with a topic sentence that captures the common element in the list, and supporting sentences that capture the specifics.

❏ Check for understanding (see Activity 43).

❏ Ask each group to write a summary (see Activity 129) of what they have learned about the importance of a single, shared goal in a cooperative group. Remind them to first generate a list of specific "I learned . . ." statements (see Activity 9) before they create the topic and supporting sentences.

❏ Ask one student to read the group's completed summary. Provide feedback on the organization and logic of the summary.

❏ Invite other groups to share their summaries and have the class provide the feedback on the positive elements of a summary.

❏ Instruct each student to make two entries in their journals (see Activity 153): (1) "Why is a group goal important?" and (2) "What I learned about making a summary."

Making Teams Work

Everyone works together.

Everyone has a turn.

People help each other.

Teach someone how to do something.

Can't be selfish.

Everyone has to participate.

VARIATIONS

1. Appeal to a variety of different intelligences by selecting one of the goal-directed tasks. Cooperative games, writing assignments, visual arts, and science experiments are useful when blended with "group goals."

2. Invite students to keep a double list of goals: individual and team.

Other Intelligences

- Verbal/linguistic
- Logical/mathematical

ACTIVITY 130

Team Banner Ad

Targeted Grades: Middle

ACTIVITY AT A GLANCE

Purpose

- To teach students to participate in group work as an active participant encouraging each other to contribute to the making of a banner ad

When to Use

- When one or two students are taking over a group and doing all the work
- When single students are not contributing to the group work
- When it is necessary to emphasize individual accountability when contributing to the group goal

What You'll Need

- Internet access
- Newsprint and markers
- Journals

WHAT-TO-DO CHECKLIST

❏ Form mixed-ability groups (see Activity 145) of three students each. Assign a number from one to three to each student in each small group. The numbers indicate the students' sequence of response in the group.

❏ Assign roles by giving the recorder role to the oldest student in the group, the reporter role to the youngest and the materials manager role to the third member. As a class, brainstorm a list of responsibilities for each role and have students write the responsibilities agreed upon in their journals (see Activity 153).

❏ Assign a task with a shared goal (see Activity 129). Write on the board or overhead the three questions that will guide each group's study of the goal: what, how, why. These questions will guide each group member in preparing her own responses. The goal is for the group to further its understanding of a concept or topic they are studying in your class (such as a quadratic equation, Maya Angelo's literary style, the Constitutional Convention, or Robert Frost's poem "Stopping by Woods on a Snowy Evening").

❏ After all answers are prepared, ask students to share their answers in turn (see Activity 24) and to coach the other group members in turn. Remind students to follow their sharing order. The recorder in the group will write the answers to each question on the newsprint.

❏ Hold a discussion of the benefits of sharing in turn and of cocoaching other students in the group. Put a question web (see Activity 6) on the board for all to see. Have a student volunteer record the unduplicated responses from a round-robin questioning pattern (see Activity 24) among students in the class.

❏ Change the roles in the groups and introduce the students to banner ads on Internet sites.

❏ Show some examples of banner ads and point out their characteristics. Have students list the characteristics in their journals.

❏ Invite each group to make a banner ad about teamwork (see Activity 57). They should use ideas from this lesson that they have already recorded in their journals. Provide additional newsprint and markers. Allow ten to fifteen minutes.

❏ When all groups are finished, have each group member sign the group's banner ad, then post them around the classroom.

❏ Use a round-robin questioning pattern once more so students can respond to the question, "What I did to contribute to my team's goal achievement was . . ." (see Activity 9).

Sharing in Turn		Coaching Others	
Benefits	**Drawbacks**	**Benefits**	**Drawbacks**
I get a chance to talk.	Sometimes I want to comment on something out of turn.	It's fun to encourage others.	It's frustrating when the other person doesn't care or doesn't understand.
I get to hear everybody else's ideas.	I plan what I'm going to say and miss hearing some things.	I like thinking of ways to get someone thinking in the right directions.	Sometimes I just want to give the answer.

VARIATIONS

1. Use an all-class "in turn" by asking a sequence of groups to share and discuss one question. Use the student with the corresponding number in the group to share his or her answer.

2. Ask each group to select one person to be a coach. Rather than members taking turns to coach, the designated coach encourages students as needed and does not answer any questions. Alternate coach assignments so that all students have the opportunity to be a coach.

3. Have the students create their ads at computer stations. Print out the results and post them.

Other Intelligences

- Verbal/linguistic
- Logical/mathematical
- Visual/spatial
- Intrapersonal

ACTIVITY 131

Group Logo

Targeted Grades: Middle

ACTIVITY AT A GLANCE

Purpose

- To bond students into a cooperative group

When to Use

- When base groups need a "bonding" boost or when students need to assess their inner motivation

What You'll Need

- Newsprint
- Markers
- Sample logos
- Overhead projector

WHAT-TO-DO CHECKLIST

❑ Form students into their base groups (see Activity 141) and assign appropriate roles (such as leader, checker, encourager, recorder, reader, and so on) (see Activity 130).

❑ Review DOVE guidelines with the class (see Activity 152).

❑ Invite each base group to review its accomplishments as a team and discuss what the members think are the reasons for its success.

❑ Review familiar logos (such as Nike, Pepsi, Ford) and show samples of available logos. Ask the groups to generate ideas about what the logos communicate about the companies.

❑ Sample ideas from several groups. Encourage students to "explain why."

❑ Ask each group to create a group logo based on its own "reasons for success." Provide groups with chart paper and markers.

❑ Post the logos with accompanying signatures of group members. Invite one group a day to explain its logo to the class.

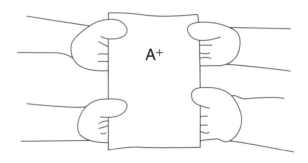

VARIATIONS

1. Design a class logo and display it on the class door.

2. Create individual logos and ask each student to explain his logo to the class.

3. Ask each group to select a historic, scientific, artistic, or literary figure of note and to design a logo that expresses that person's achievements, vision, or standards. Have students present their group's logo to the class without identifying the person on which it is based; ask other groups to guess the identity behind the logo.

4. Use the carousel (see Activity 10) to display the logos.

Other Intelligences

- Verbal/linguistic
- Logical/mathematical
- Visual/spatial
- Intrapersonal

ACTIVITY 132

Group Cheers and Songs

Targeted Grades: Middle

ACTIVITY AT A GLANCE

Purpose

- To bond students in a cooperative group

When to Use

- When celebrating base group accomplishments
- When energizing students

What You'll Need

- Newsprint
- Markers

WHAT-TO-DO CHECKLIST

- ❏ Form base groups (see Activity 141) of three to five students. Assign roles to each student in a group (see Activity 130). Review DOVE guidelines (see Activity 152) for cooperation.

- ❏ Explain the group goal: to create a song or cheer about the group.

- ❏ Talk about "cheers" the students know. Ask students for examples.

- ❏ Invite each group to create a group cheer that the group will use to cheer its own accomplishments.

- ❏ Invite each group to lead the class in its cheer.

VARIATIONS

1. After teaching a unit on poetry, assign groups to compose a poem or song about themselves or their accomplishments.

2. After completing a unit on a historic period, review popular songs from that time and have students write their own songs copying the samples.

3. Ask groups to compose a song based on the unit's content or a specific topic by adapting or modifying the words to a contemporary popular song.

Other Intelligences

- Verbal/linguistic
- Logical/mathematical
- Visual/spatial
- Musical/rhythmic
- Intrapersonal

ACTIVITY 133

Group Ad

Targeted Grades: Middle and Secondary

ACTIVITY AT A GLANCE

Purpose

- To increase bonding among group members

When to Use

- When groups are starting to work and need to initiate sharing in a safe way
- When groups need to improve cohesion among members
- When an entire class needs to understand its shared "best attributes"
- When positive communication is needed to decrease conflict in a classroom

What You'll Need

- Magazines
- Magazine and newspaper ads
- Poster boards
- Glue

WHAT-TO-DO CHECKLIST

❏ Form cooperative groups (see Activity 128) of three students each. Assign each member a role (see Activity 130).

❏ Identify the group goal: to create a visual advertisement about the group. Highlight that the best ads are cohesive representations of shared characteristics of the group.

❏ Discuss additional criteria so that each ad makes a powerful statement and is the group's best work.

❏ Share samples from magazines or newspapers. Distribute poster boards and magazines to each group.

❏ Ask groups to create their ads using pictures and words cut out from magazines.

❏ Have each member of the group sign the group's ad. Display the completed ads.

❏ Lead an all-class assessment of the ads. Highlight those that meet the criteria (see Activity 8).

❏ Instruct each group to make a list showing what each member contributed to the making of the ad. Collect lists and assess individual participation and group work.

❏ Do a round-robin questioning pattern (see Activity 24) sharing with one of the following lead-in statements (see Activity 9): "A contribution I made is _____," or "I am proud of myself because _____."

VARIATIONS

1. Ask each group to use a PMI assessment (see Activity 158) or **Mrs. Potter's questions** (see Activity 176) to assess how well students worked together as a group.

2. Incorporate the ads into a language arts unit studying mass media.

3. Make a group flag.

Other Intelligences

- Verbal/linguistic
- Logical/mathematical
- Visual/spatial
- Intrapersonal

ACTIVITY 134

Three Questions Plus One

Targeted Grades: All

ACTIVITY AT A GLANCE

Purpose

- To increase participation when working in a cooperative group on a task that requires complex thinking

When to Use

- When promoting individual contribution and participation within cooperative groups

What You'll Need

- Copies of short essays, poems, and so on
- Prepared list of three questions related to reading material

WHAT-TO-DO CHECKLIST

❒ Form mixed-ability groups (see Activity 145) of three to four students and distribute copies of a poem, short essay, short story, or newspaper editorial to each group.

❒ Request that one student in each group read the text aloud while the other group members listen.

❒ Prepare a list of four questions that each student is to answer.
  - The first question will probe for the facts learned from the reading material. Ideally, the question will require students to summarize the key ideas in their own words (see Activity 129).

Story: Cinderella

1. *Describe* the people that lived in the household with Cinderella.

2. *Tell* what happened when the clock struck midnight on the night of the ball.

3. *Select* your favorite part of the story and explain why you liked it.

4. *Explain* what the author is communicating in this story.

  - The second question will challenge each student to explain one important element of the text and tell why it is important
  - The third question will challenge each student to tell why she likes or dislikes the text's ideas.

- The fourth question will require group members to reach a consensus on the "moral" or primary message of the piece.

VARIATIONS

1. Use textbook material from social studies or science as the basis of the series of questions.

2. Use questions that promote a specific type of thinking skill. For example, use the Three-Story Intellect verbs (see Activity 22) to construct questions that require gathering, processing, or application skills.

3. Give the groups the four questions so they may work together to create the answers before selecting which member will answer each question.

Other Intelligences

- Verbal/linguistic

ACTIVITY 135

Jigsaw

Targeted Grades: Middle and Secondary

ACTIVITY AT A GLANCE

Purpose

- To review large quantities of reading material through the use of a collaborative strategy

When to Use

- When checking for students' understanding, particularly those who most need to improve comprehension

What You'll Need

- Copies of nonfiction and nonsequential material
- Copies of a graphic organizer

WHAT-TO-DO CHECKLIST

❑ Form mixed-ability groups (see Activity 145) of three students. Provide each group with one copy of a nonfiction text. Be sure the material is nonsequential so that each group can read its text without reliance on a previous part.

❑ Divide the text into sections based on logical breaks in the material. Assign each student one section of the text to read aloud while the other group members listen and take notes.

❑ Provide a graphic organizer, such as the question web (see Activity 6) or the question concept map (see Activity 53), or a set of three-level questions (see Activity 134), and ask students to list the main ideas (or other selected focus) presented in the text.

❑ Instruct group members to share responses and information entered on their graphic organizers once the entire selection has been read. Using this information create a single organizer that captures all the most important information.

❑ After the jigsaw is formed, conduct an all-class discussion of the material. Highlight the connections among the parts.

VARIATIONS

1. Use with a group matrix (see Activity 179) to compare biographical information on three to five different persons.

2. For current events, jigsaw the same event by providing different newspaper and magazine articles.

3. For secondary students, jigsaw research articles from the Internet, different points of view on a current world problem, different short stories by the same author, poems on a common topic by different poets, mathematics problems using like skills, or variations in science techniques or samples.

Other Intelligences

- Verbal/linguistic
- Logical/mathematical
- Visual/spatial

ACTIVITY 136

Expert Jigsaw

Targeted Grades: Secondary

ACTIVITY AT A GLANCE

Purpose

- To review a large amount of material that requires a deep understanding of a topic through the use of a collaborative strategy

When to Use

- When the class has a wide range of reading abilities and needs more checking for accuracy
- When there is a large amount of material to cover

Note: Use only after students have experience with the simple jigsaw (see Activity 135).

What You'll Need

- Copies of nonfiction and nonsequential text
- Copies of a graphic organizer (such as a web, matrix, and so on)

WHAT-TO-DO CHECKLIST

☐ Form cooperative groups (see Activity 128) of three students each. Provide each group with one copy of the same nonfiction text. Be sure the material is nonsequential so that each group can read its text without reliance on a previous part.

☐ Divide the text into sections based on logical breaks in the material. Ask students to take turns reading a section of the text while the other group members listen and take notes. Provide a specific focus, such as identifying main ideas, for the reading assignment.

☐ When each group has finished its reading assignment, ask students who have read the same sections to form into new groups with others who read the same material so they can check each other for accuracy. Ask these new groups to complete graphic organizers that detail the main ideas (or other selected focus). Collect graphic organizers (see Activity 47) and check for accuracy and depth of detail.

☐ Return students to their original groups so that they can construct a jigsaw for the entire reading selection. Post completed jigsaw graphics and ask each group in turn to explain its graphic. Have all students take notes from all presentations. Discuss any variations.

VARIATIONS

1. With a large amount of reading material, divide the material among the groups so that no two groups have the same material. After each group has its assignment, instruct the groups to jigsaw a graphic for the material. Provide a handout or graphic organizer so groups can select key material to share with the class. Post the graphics around the classroom and instruct each group to lead the discussion on its section of the material.

2. Have final groups make a poster (see Activity 61), collage (see Activity 68), or PowerPoint (see Activity 70). Use a gallery walk (see Activity 51) to display the posters and collages. Allow each team that selected a PowerPoint to show it to the class.

Other Intelligences

- Verbal/linguistic
- Visual/spatial
- Logical/mathematical

ACTIVITY 137

Coach a Partner

Targeted Grades: Middle and Secondary

ACTIVITY AT A GLANCE

Purpose

- To review material and coach a partner by working in pairs

When to Use

- Throughout a lesson or unit
- As a review of anchor material
- As a way to teach a collaborative review process
- At the end as an open-book test

What You'll Need

- Three-story intellect overhead or PowerPoint
- Overhead projector and screen

WHAT-TO-DO CHECKLIST

- ❏ Copy the Three-Story Intellect to an overhead or PowerPoint.

- ❏ Show the Three-Story Intellect and point out to the class that these are questions that they can ask as coaches. They should start with one from the first floor (facts) and proceed up the stairs to the top story. Model a question formed from a key verb.

- ❏ Form mixed-ability pairs (see Activity 145) of students.

- ❏ Review the goals of the unit just completed and provide each pair with a list of questions that each student will answer either orally or in writing.

- ❏ Request that students take turns asking and answering each question. Demonstrate how students are to alternate who answers each question first.

- ❏ After all pairs have finished the questions, check for understanding (see Activity 43) by asking a random selection of questions from the list of the entire class.

- ❏ Correct, clarify, or add to the responses as needed.

VARIATIONS

1. Use mixed-ability trios (see Activity 145). Have the third person ask questions as the others respond and record answers in turn.

2. Assign students to compile a list of five questions in advance of the review. Use these student-generated questions to create the master list of questions that each pair receives for the review.

Other Intelligences

- Verbal/linguistic

The Three-Story Intellect

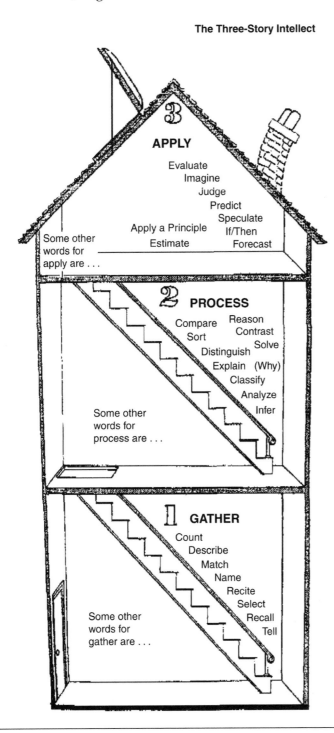

There are one-story intellects, two-story intellects, and three-story intellects with skylights. All fact collectors, who have no aim above their facts, are one-story men. Two-story men compare, reason, generalize, using the labors of the fact collectors as well as their own. Three-story men idealize, imagine, predict—their best Illumination comes from above, through the skylight.

–Oliver Wendell Holmes

3 APPLY
Evaluate
Imagine
Judge
Predict
Speculate
Apply a Principle   If/Then
Estimate   Forecast

Some other words for apply are . . .

2 PROCESS
Compare   Reason
Sort   Contrast
Distinguish   Solve
Explain   (Why)
Classify
Analyze
Infer

Some other words for process are . . .

1 GATHER
Count
Describe
Match
Name
Recite
Select
Recall
Tell

Some other words for gather are . . .

SOURCE: Bellanca, J., & Fogarty, R. (2003). *Blueprints for Achievement in the Cooperative Classroom*, (3rd ed.). Thousand Oaks, CA: Corwin Press.

ACTIVITY 138

Cooperative Guidelines

Targeted Grades: All

ACTIVITY AT A GLANCE

Purpose

- To learn guidelines for positive interaction in a cooperative group

When to Use

- At the start of all cooperative tasks until students demonstrate the ability to use the expected behaviors without review

What You'll Need

- Sample acronym

WHAT-TO-DO CHECKLIST

☐ On the board or overhead, write an acronym that describes expectations for behaviors that promote positive interaction. Ask students to give examples for each letter of the acronym or to demonstrate the behavior.

☐ Review the guidelines before each new cooperative task. On occasion, use an observation checklist to reinforce accountability.

VARIATIONS

1. Form base groups (see Activity 141) and ask each group to create an acronym with accompanying phrases for each letter to use as a team motto for positive group behavior. Create banners or posters that display the acronym and hang in highly visible areas of the room.

Primary Grade Example

Middle Grade Example

Talk with six-inch voices (small voices).

Encourage each other.

Ask teammates for help.

Make everyone a part of the team.

Watch team goal.

Organize and plan task.

Review individual responsibilities.

Keep the team on task.

2. Form base groups and create an acronym to use as a team motto. Play charades by having each base group take turns writing the acronym (letters only) on the board and acting out each letter's corresponding phrase (or initial word of phrase) while other groups guess the word or phrase.

Other Intelligences

- Verbal/linguistic
- Visual/spatial

ACTIVITY 139

Social Skill T-Chart

Targeted Grades: All

ACTIVITY AT A GLANCE

Purpose

- To identify concrete behaviors that lead to development of the social skill of cooperation

When to Use

- Once every eight to ten weeks by integrating the skill practice into a lesson

What You'll Need

- T-chart visual

WHAT-TO-DO CHECKLIST

❒ Identify the cooperative social skill students need to develop: trust, leadership, encouragement, active listening, or teamwork. Select an age-appropriate medium such as a short story, video, role-play (see Activity 92), or simulation in which the targeted social skill is displayed, modeled, or discarded (such as *Little Red Riding Hood* or *To Kill a Mockingbird*).

❒ After the students have discussed the example, show a T-chart (see Activity 47) on the overhead or chalkboard. Label the columns. Encourage students to brainstorm the behaviors that show what the skill looks like and sounds like.

Encouragement	
Looks like	**Sounds like**
Smiles	Good job!
Nods	Way to go!
Thumbs up	Attagirl! Attaboy!

❒ Post the T-chart in the room. Periodically refer to it and encourage students to practice the listed behaviors.

VARIATIONS

1. Do a triple T-chart. Add a third column, "feels like."

2. Have students create individual T-charts for different skills as the school year progresses or to reinforce a specific skill.

3. Use an observation checklist to reinforce the targeted social skill.

Other Intelligences

- Verbal/linguistic
- Visual/spatial
- Intrapersonal

ACTIVITY 140

Cooperative Roles

Targeted Grades: All

ACTIVITY AT A GLANCE

Purpose

- To demonstrate shared leadership and individual accountability and responsibility in a group

When to Use

- During each cooperative learning lesson or unit to teach students how to share responsibility on a team
- Early in the school year or a course to teach responsibilities
- As a review on a regular basis

What You'll Need

- Three-by-five-inch index cards, place markers, or cardboard figures

WHAT-TO-DO CHECKLIST

1. Form small groups and identify a job responsibility for each group member. Give the job an appropriate title (such as leader, checker, materials manager, reader, encourager, calculator, and so on).

2. Write each job title on an index card, place marker, or cardboard figure. On the back of the card, list the corresponding responsibilities.

3. Each time a group forms, dispense the cards at random in each group and review the responsibilities. Each student should keep the card visible so job performance can be acknowledged.

VARIATIONS

1. Post students' names and their job responsibilities on a bulletin board. Assign a number to each job. Each time groups are formed, rotate job numbers or have a random number draw so students have multiple opportunities to perform each job.

2. Conduct a spot check of responsibilities during a group task by asking randomly selected students to describe their responsibilities in the group.

Other Intelligences

- Verbal/linguistic
- Logical/mathematical

ACTIVITY 141

Base Groups

Targeted Grades: Middle and Secondary

ACTIVITY AT A GLANCE

Purpose

- To participate in a high-functioning cooperative group that works collaboratively over a long period of time (such as a quarter or semester) or on an intensive multi-week project

When to Use

- Throughout a long project or unit so students can work together in base groups
- When the course of instruction calls for an extensive project
- When the planned project requires multiple talents

What You'll Need

- No materials necessary

WHAT-TO-DO CHECKLIST

❒ Form cooperative groups (see Activity 128) of three students each. Review group guidelines and assign individual roles.

❒ Select a cooperative activity familiar to the class.

❒ Explain base groups.
  - What are they? ("A group that will work together for ____ weeks on a certain task.")
  - Why use them? ("To develop cooperative skills; to help each other on a challenging task.")
  - When do we use them? (Describe the schedule when base groups will work together. For example, in an elementary classroom the base group might meet every day from 11:00 to 11:45. In the upper grades, base groups might meet every day until the project is done or on specific days such as Tuesday and Thursday.)

❒ Provide a handout that describes group requirements:
  - Group and individual products expected
  - Instructions for project completion
  - Schedule
  - Criteria for success
  - Assessment of group cooperation

❏ In addition to checkups and scheduled class discussions during the project, conclude with a final assessment of how well the group worked together and met its overall objectives.

VARIATIONS

1. Change the schedule and amount of time students work together in groups.

2. Use up to five students per base group.

3. Intersperse task work with bonding activities.

Other Intelligences

- Verbal/linguistic
- Visual/spatial

ACTIVITY 142

Internet Friends

Targeted Grades: Middle

ACTIVITY AT A GLANCE

Purpose

- To bond with base group members while meeting new friends at other schools via the Internet

When to Use

- As a long-term project for base groups

What You'll Need

- Internet access

WHAT-TO-DO CHECKLIST

❏ Go to eduhound.org, thinkquest.org, global school network.org or national school network.org to identify schools that "talk together." Make contact with several regarding your project.

❏ Identify the rules for working online safely and post for all to see.

❏ Outline the project goals and activities.

❏ Obtain formal parent permission for students to work on this Internet project.

❏ Activate students' prior knowledge (see Activity 54) of social networks on the Internet such as MySpace, Facebook, Classmates On-line, and so on. Ask students what they know and make a list for all to see.

❏ Do a PMI assessment (see Activity 158) about the use of these sites.

❏ Explain to students that they are going to do a project that connects them with students at other schools.

❏ Coach students in how they will best talk with the students from the partner schools. What do they want to ask the other students?

❏ Form base groups (see Activity 141) for the project. Have each group select a partner school.

❏ Allot thirty minutes a week for the students to go online with their schools. Have them select from the questions that will guide the interactions.

❏ Teams will store the information they gather from their new acquaintances in an electronic folder.

❏ After three months of conversation, teams will create a PowerPoint about their friends.

❏ Provide a rubric (see Activity 8) to guide the creation of the PowerPoint presentations.

❏ Use the rubric to coach the students as they work on the PowerPoint presentations.

❏ Have students share completed PowerPoint presentations with their partner school and with your class.

❏ In the electronic folder, complete "I learned . . . " stems (see Activity 9).

VARIATIONS

1. Use one school only as the partner.

2. Have parents come to school and see their students' presentations.

3. Have students maintain contact with their Internet friends after the project is over.

4. Use concepts from the curriculum for the Internet discussions.

Other Intelligences

- Verbal/linguistic
- Logical/mathematical
- Visual/spatial

ACTIVITY 143

Three-to-One Synthesis

Targeted Grades: Middle and Secondary

ACTIVITY AT A GLANCE

Purpose

- To compose a synthesis of the group's responses by working in a small group

When to Use

- When individual accountability is an issue, to structure each student's contribution
- When students need to help each other with reading comprehension

What You'll Need

- Copies of reading selections

WHAT-TO-DO CHECKLIST

☐ Form cooperative groups (see Activity 128) of three students. Assign each student one of the following roles: reader, checker, or task guide (see Activity 140).

☐ Explain that this task requires students to work together as a team to create a single product. Group success is dependent on how well each individual performs his role.

☐ Give students copies of a reading selection such as a poem, essay, short story, section of a textbook, or articles from a magazine.

☐ Write the key comprehension questions on the board or overhead. Use the Three-Story Intellect (see Activity 22) so that you have one question per level.

☐ Instruct the readers to read the material aloud softly to their groups. Instruct each group member to write a response to the posted question. In turn, have students share their written answers.

☐ After all students have shared their answers, each group selects its best answer or composes a synthesis of all the answers. Task guides encourage their teammates and facilitate the group process. The checkers check that all members agree on the final answer and that each member can explain it.

☐ Select several checkers at random to share and explain group responses. Discuss, clarify, and correct.

☐ Have each group make a poster advertising the author's work (see Activity 61).

VARIATIONS

1. Give each group a set of questions so that each student will answer a different question. Vary types of questions. For example, provide a question that requires a factual response, one that requires an explanatory answer, and one that requires a hypothetical conclusion.

2. Ask each group to construct questions that can be used to review the studied material. Each group should write as many questions as there are group members, writing each question and its answer on a single piece of paper. Collect all the questions and answers, place them in a paper bag or box, and have each student select a question. Students take turns asking questions and checking answers against the supplied answer.

3. Use Mrs. Potter's Questions (see Activity 176) to help students assess their products.

Other Intelligences

- Verbal/linguistic
- Logical/mathematical
- Visual/spatial

ACTIVITY 144

Internet Investigations

Targeted Grades: Middle and Secondary

ACTIVITY AT A GLANCE

Purpose

- To learn to use the Internet as a research tool

When to Use

- After students demonstrate they can work together in groups and are ready for a collaborative project-based learning experience

What You'll Need

- Internet access for student pairs
- Three-by-five-inch index cards
- PowerPoint

WHAT-TO-DO CHECKLIST

❐ Set mixed-ability pairs (see Activity 145). Assign roles (see Activity 140) and review cooperative guidelines (see Activity 138). Explain the group activity and identify a sample mobile each group will make at the end of the project.

❐ Distribute sets of index cards to each group. Show them how to use the cards to record data and to identify Internet sources. (If students have sufficient computer experience, substitute "notes" for the index cards by using Microsoft Notes.)

❐ Identify a standard in your curriculum and change it into a hypothetical launch question (see Activity 50).

❐ Brainstorm with the class where and how they might use key words in the question to begin the research process.

❐ Coach the students as they follow leads and generate information on the cards or notes.

❐ After students have completed the information search, guide them in a categorization of the information with a concept map (see Activity 53) or other organizer (see Activity 47).

❐ Show a rubric (see Activity 8) you have made for an essay. Have the pairs use the computers to compose the essays, including footnotes and bibliography.

❐ Show students how to use PowerPoint (see Activity 70) to make a presentation of their research and connect it to the standard.

❐ Allow each pair to show its PowerPoint to the class.

❐ Conclude the project by asking students to do a round-robin questioning pattern (see Activity 24) completing the lead-in (see Activity 9) "In this project, I have learned . . ."

VARIATIONS

1. Construct a collage on the PowerPoint that shows examples of the key concepts related to the standard.

2. Brainstorm different subtopics that relate to the standard. Have different groups work on different topics.

Other Intelligences

- Verbal/linguistic
- Logical/mathematical
- Visual/spatial

ACTIVITY 145

Forming Mixed- Ability Groups

Targeted Grades: All

ACTIVITY AT A GLANCE

Purpose

- To create a new cooperative group for cooperative work

When to Use

- Any time a new cooperative group is needed

What You'll Need

- No materials needed

WHAT-TO-DO CHECKLIST

❐ Determine group size. Three students per group provides a good mix of diversity and allows opportunities for each student to participate.

❐ Select a mixing criterion:

- Learning modality. Identify students' primary learning modality—kinesthetic, visual, or auditory. Form groups to include students representing each of the learning modalities.
- Academic performances. After observing students for several weeks, rank order (see Activity 15) the class from high achievers to low achievers. Divide the list into three columns. Assign one student from each column to each group.
- Social skills. Over several weeks, observe how students interact with peers and rank order the class from those who interact well to those who interact with difficulty. Make group assignments based on a mixture of students with varying social skills.
- Race, gender, national origin. Use in combination with another grouping method to create groups that are more diverse.

VARIATIONS

1. Identify students' strengths and demonstrated abilities based on the different multiple intelligences. Group students to provide a mixture within each group. For example, a group may include a student with high logical/mathematical ability, a student with strong visual/spatial skills, and a student with well-developed musical/rhythmic skills.

2. Change task groups daily for upper grades or several times a day for elementary students. This allows a constant remix that promotes classroom cohesion.

Other Intelligences

- Verbal/linguistic
- Logical/mathematical
- Visual/spatial

ACTIVITY 146

Group Motto

Targeted Grades: Elementary and Middle

ACTIVITY AT A GLANCE

Purpose

- To increase social bonding with teammates and to improve sharing behavior when working in a group

When to Use

- At the beginning of a lesson or unit to initiate bonding in base groups or long-term task groups
- When conflict arises in groups

What You'll Need

- Chart paper

WHAT-TO-DO CHECKLIST

- ❏ Form cooperative groups (see Activity 128) that will stay together for two or more weeks.

- ❏ Give each group two sheets of chart paper. Assign roles (see Activity 140).

- ❏ On the overhead or board, show samples of well-known mottos such as "All for one, one for all" (from Alexandre Dumas' book *The Three Musketeers*). Brainstorm a list of other familiar mottos.

- ❏ Discuss with students the purpose behind mottos, or why they think individuals and teams use them. Clarify in the discussion the difference between a motto and a slogan. (Companies often use slogans, such as "You deserve a break today," as promotional devices to capture attention or present an image for advertising purposes. Such slogans differ from mottos, which are phrases that express a guiding principle or purpose.)

> *Be Creative!*
>
> *1. Think up new ideas.*
>
> *2. Come up with lots of ideas.*
>
> *3. Try something new
>   every day.*

❏ Ask each group to create a list of positive characteristics of groups (such as everyone can participate, members encourage each other).

❏ From this list, invite students to select one characteristic as an objective to focus on during a specified time. Have each group use this goal to invent their motto.

❏ Have students create a poster (see Activity 61) or banner (see Activity 130) with the group's motto, inviting students to illustrate or decorate their creations and sign their names. Display posters or banners in the classroom (see Activity 51). As a class, discuss the benefits of creating a group motto.

VARIATIONS

1. Invite students to write a one to two paragraph essay describing what the motto means to them and how they intend to work toward the goal expressed in the motto. At the completion of the group work, follow up by asking students to reread their essays and write a paragraph explaining whether they met their goals and why or why not.

2. Ask students to complete lead-in statements that describe how they individually plan to support the group's motto.

Other Intelligences
- Verbal/linguistic
- Visual/spatial

ACTIVITY 147

2-4-8 Classroom Learning Community

Targeted Grades: Middle and Elementary

ACTIVITY AT A GLANCE

Purpose

- To develop a feeling of community within the classroom

When to Use

- At the beginning of the school year to build community in the classroom
- While starting to study course content
- When encouraging reluctant students to join in on group work
- During lessons to ensure students mix in the class
- When building positive interactions among base groups

What You'll Need

- List of content-related questions

WHAT-TO-DO CHECKLIST

❏ Match students in mixed-ability pairs (see Activity 145). Provide all pairs with a list of identical questions on a topic the class will study in the year's first unit. Be sure to vary the questions' levels of difficulty. Highlight hypothetical, comparing, summarizing, and assessing questions.
  - What if Romeo had not heard Juliet utter the words, "Wherefore art thou Romeo?"
  - How are Romeo and Juliet different in the ways they express love?
  - What were Romeo's reasons for falling in love?
  - Do you think the fight between the two families was justified?

❏ After pairs have answered every question, form quartets by joining two pairs. Have the quartet compare the pairs' answers and compile a chart that lists the question number and shows whether the pairs agree or disagree on their answers for that question.

❏ After the quartets have reviewed each question and charted their responses, pair up quartets to complete the agree-disagree chart in a group of eight.

❏ Select a recorder for each group to report on agreements and disagreements. Discuss the similarities and differences.

❏ Ask each group of eight to assess its cooperative teamwork (see Activity 8).

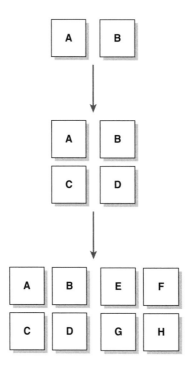

VARIATIONS

1. Select a graphic organizer to start the pair work.

2. Post the completed charts and do a carousel (see Activity 10) or gallery walk (see Activity 51).

3. Use different pairs to start each time. Encourage pairs to select other pairs with whom they have not yet worked in a four.

Other Intelligences

- Verbal/linguistics
- Logical/mathematical
- Visual/spatial

ACTIVITY 148

Pair-Shares

Targeted Grades: All

ACTIVITY AT A GLANCE

Purpose

- To encourage working together informally

When to Use

- At any time in a lesson, unit or project to engage students in a discussion

What You'll Need

- Three-by-five-inch index cards with symbols: one with a light bulb, one with two heads talking, and one with a circle of many heads
- Journals (optional)

WHAT-TO-DO CHECKLIST

☐ On the first day of class, teach the first pair-share tactic: think-pair-share.
  - Hold up the card and tell the class that you are going to ask a question.
  - No one is to answer. Tell them to just think of the response they want to make.
  - Start with a very easy and obvious question that most will know (such as, "What is the name of this school?").
  - After ten to fifteen seconds, tell the students to turn to another student across the aisle or at the next desk and tell each other the answer.
  - After each pair has listened across the aisle, call on several students to share their answers.
  - Label the three steps as think-pair-share.

☐ Repeat the process using the signal cards. Tell students what you are going to do.
  - Ask a more difficult lead-in question (see Activity 9) (such as "Why are you attending this school?").
  - Encourage all students to listen to each groups' "share" without comment.

☐ Repeat the process a third time with the cards and a more difficult question (such as "How do you think this school could become better?").

☐ Review the process so that students know how to respond when you use it during lessons.

VARIATIONS

1. Use lead-in statements to start the process.
2. Use the round-robin questioning pattern (see Activity 24) to hear responses.
3. Use the question web to record responses.
4. Use a write-pair-share with journals (see Activity 153). Allow students time to respond in the journal before working with the partner.
5. Use a draw-pair-share with journals and symbols for ideas or graphic organizers the students know.
6. Vary how students partner.
7. Use at the start of a lesson, in the middle, or at the end.

Other Intelligences

- Verbal/linguistic
- Visual/spatial

ACTIVITY 149

High Jump

Targeted Grades: Middle and Secondary

ACTIVITY AT A GLANCE

Purpose

- To identify group performance standards

When to Use

- Throughout the year to help students understand the importance of quality work

What You'll Need

- No materials necessary

WHAT-TO-DO CHECKLIST

- ❏ Show a picture of a high jumper. Ask students to explain what the jumper has to do when the bar is raised or lowered.

- ❏ Explain how the bar stands for a standard. When a standard is raised, it is harder for more people to meet it; if it is lowered, it's easier for more people to meet it.

- ❏ After the discussion, ask students to suggest fair standards for homework, spelling quizzes, projects, and so on. Vote on these standards and develop the criteria and indicators of success for each item in a rubric (see Activity 8).

- ❏ Post these and use them to evaluate student work.

VARIATIONS

1. When developing the standards, use cooperative groups (see Activity 128) to develop ideas before the entire group discusses them and selects the criteria.

2. Ask students to establish standards for success for a specific group activity. Upon completion, ask students to evaluate their work against the predetermined standards.

Other Intelligences

- Verbal/linguistic
- Logical/mathematical

ACTIVITY 150

Group-Assessment Cards

Targeted Grades: Middle and Secondary

ACTIVITY AT A GLANCE

Purpose

- To use a reusable assessment tool when working in a base group

When to Use

- On a regularly scheduled basis when base groups meet
- At the end of tasks or projects with cooperative task groups

What You'll Need

- Laminated copies of a reusable assessment tool
- Watercolor markers
- Journals (optional)

WHAT-TO-DO CHECKLIST

❐ Design a group-assessment rubric (see Activity 8).

❐ Laminate copies of the group-assessment rubric and place them in an easily accessible location.

❐ Inform groups when they are to complete a group assessment. For the first use, show students how to use watercolor markers with the laminated cards.

❐ After groups have completed their assessments, collect cards and read sample responses to the class.

❐ On the reverse side, write feedback and responses to the questions students have. Return these to groups for review at the start of the next class.

❐ Give general or summative feedback to the class as needed.

<table>
<tr><td colspan="2" align="center">**Group Assessment**</td></tr>
</table>

Group Name _Magnificentos_   **Date** _Oct. 29_

Activity _Videotaped "A Day in My Life"_

Members	**Roles**
Jerome	cameraman
Laura	storyboarder & creative director
Nicky	writer & director
Paco	props person & talent headhunter
Bruce	gofer & logistics director

What we did well

We planned the story well—tried it out before we shot it. Also, we were very organized and had props and material ready on time.

What we need to improve is

We should have had the actors and actresses rehearse more.

Questions we have

1. How many times do professional actors and actresses play a scene before the final cut?

2. What equipment and skills are needed to edit videotapes?

VARIATIONS

1. Provide a variety of laminated group-assessment tools, such as Mrs. Potter's Questions (see Activity 176) or a PMI assessment (see Activity 158).

2. Use journals (see Activity 153) for students to summarize the assessments (see Activity 129).

Other Intelligences

- Verbal/linguistic
- Logical/mathematical

ACTIVITY 151

Getting It Straight

Targeted Grades: Middle and Secondary

ACTIVITY AT A GLANCE

Purpose

- To understand the need to identify and clarify requirements or evaluation criteria for a group-based task or project

When to Use

- In the beginning of the year or course to teach students the need to clearly understand the requirements for a task or project and the criteria that will be used to evaluate an assignment
- Throughout the year to reinforce assessment practices as necessary

What You'll Need

- Sets of Legos or other toy building blocks

WHAT-TO-DO CHECKLIST

☐ Form mixed-ability groups (see Activity 145) of three students. Inform groups that they will be competing in a timed contest to build the most attractive Lego truck, using a set of Legos.

☐ Distribute sets of Legos to each group, with instructions not to start building until you announce the start.

☐ Time groups (ten to fifteen minutes, based on grade level). If students ask questions, tell them that the only thing you can tell them is it must be an attractive truck. Do not give any additional details. Announce the ending time, when all groups must stop work.

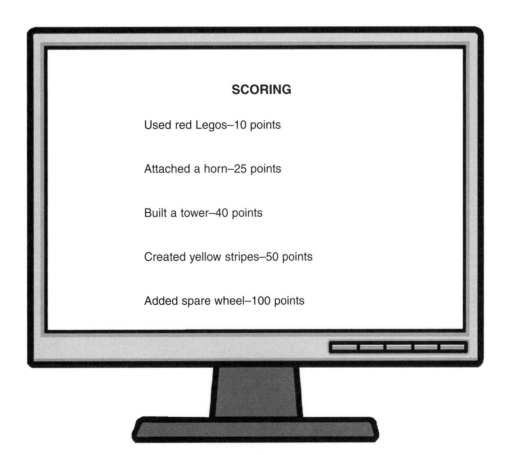

SCORING

Used red Legos–10 points

Attached a horn–25 points

Built a tower–40 points

Created yellow stripes–50 points

Added spare wheel–100 points

❏ Tell groups they will get points for certain characteristics of their models. For example, trucks that used red Legos will get ten points, trucks with yellow stripes will receive fifty points, trucks with spare wheels will receive one hundred points.

❏ Survey groups, asking each to show its model and give its score. Write each score on the board or overhead.

❏ Congratulate the group with the highest score and ask its members to explain their "winning" strategy. Lead the class in a discussion of how chance played a part in determining the "winner" for this activity.

❏ Guide the students to the recognition that knowing established criteria and the requirements for an activity at its onset is necessary in order to work toward a specific goal.

VARIATIONS

1. Ask the class what would happen if you used different scoring criteria. Assign different points to each characteristic (such as subtract ten points if red Legos were used) and have groups recalculate their scores. Use this as a lead-in (see Activity 9) to a discussion on determining evaluation criteria and specific instructions at the onset of activities.

2. Follow the truck activity with the creation of a rubric (see Activity 8) for a project or lesson that you are starting.

Other Intelligences

- Verbal/linguistic
- Logical/mathematical

PART VII

Intrapersonal Intelligence

ACTIVITY 152

Quiet Time

Targeted Grades: All

ACTIVITY AT A GLANCE

Purpose

- To reflect on goals and achievements

When to Use

- Daily at the beginning or end of a class period
- During any class to calm students down or during hectic, busy, or disruptive periods

What You'll Need

- Journals

WHAT-TO-DO CHECKLIST

- ❏ Ask students to make a list of tasks, events, and things they do during the day, both in and out of school.

- ❏ Write on the board or overhead, "This list makes me feel _____ because _____." Ask students to review their lists and complete the sentence.

- ❏ Invite students to share their completed sentences. Put DOVE guidelines in place. (Note: DOVE guidelines are used to promote a nonjudgmental, open environment for group sharing.) If students are not familiar with DOVE guidelines, introduce them:

    Defer Judgments.

    Opt for original ideas.

    Vast number is needed.

    Expand by piggybacking on others' ideas.

- ❏ Explain purpose of spending time each day to reflect. Discuss how this is helpful and why it is important. As a class, brainstorm a list of ideas for reflection such as personal goals, recent achievements, daily priorities, and so on.

- ❏ Provide several minutes for private reflection. Allow students to spend time thinking prior to writing in their journals (see Activity 153).

VARIATIONS

1. Periodically invite students to assess "quiet time." Ask them, "What makes it work or why is it helpful? Is it necessary to change anything to make it more useful?" (Suggestions: spend more time, do it at a different time, resolve problems of noise or distraction.)

2. Ask students to focus on a content-related topic and to share reflections as a class. For example, use to review material at the end of a lesson or prior to a test. Ask students to list everything they know about the topic. Reflection will help students realize how well they know the material and if they need additional review.

3. Use in conjunction with conflict-resolution or peer-mediation groups to reflect on specific areas of concern. Use guidelines prior to the group meeting to discuss these concerns.

4. Use with a cognitive function or thinking operation by making a goal statement that begins "To improve . . . ."

Other Intelligences

- Verbal/linguistic
- Interpersonal

ACTIVITY 153

Daily Journal Lead-In Statements

Targeted Grades: All

ACTIVITY AT A GLANCE

Purpose

- As a tool for reflecting on issues and concerns related to a specific class or for personal development
- To provide students opportunities to reflect on what they are learning

When to Use

- Throughout the year in any class on a scheduled or unscheduled basis

What You'll Need

- Journals

WHAT-TO-DO CHECKLIST

❏ Ask each student to bring a journal to class. This can be a simple notebook, or one the students make (see Variations).

❏ Introduce the idea of a daily reflection journal or **log**—a personal journal in which students make periodic entries (daily, every other day, weekly) that reflect what they are learning in class, their personal goals related to the class, and difficulties or problems they encounter throughout the course.

❏ For the first entry of the year or quarter, provide one of the following lead-in statements (see Activity 9):
  • "In this class, I want to learn . . ."
  • "In this class, I intend to improve . . ."
  • "In this class, I hope to . . ."
  • "My goal for this class is . . ."

❏ Invite students to select a lead-in statement, quietly reflect on and complete it, and write their reflections in their daily journals. Allow three to five minutes for students to complete and date the entries.

❏ For subsequent entries, offer students a lead-in or cue to encourage a specific focus. You may wish to repeat cues randomly or according to a set schedule. Possible lead-in statements follow:
  • "Today (this week) in this class, I learned . . ."
  • "Today (this week) in this class I improved _____ by . . ."
  • "In this class, I am pleased that I . . ."
  • "A difficulty I am having with this class is . . ."
  • "I wish that this class . . ."

❏ Periodically collect and read students' entries. Respond to students' entries with supporting comments, questions, and suggestions. Respect students' privacy by allowing them to mark some entries as private if they so choose.

VARIATIONS

1. Students can make their own journals by stapling together sheets of paper with a construction paper cover, or they can customize standard notebooks by decorating the cover.

2. Meet individually with students after reading their entries. Use this conference time to review students' concerns, needs, and progress.

3. Invite students to brainstorm a list of lead-in statements to use for daily writing. Post list in classroom or give copies to students to keep in their journals. Provide students the option to select their own lead-in or one that you offer the class.

4. Use the journal as the way to start or conclude each class period. Combine the lead-in statements with write-pair-share (see Activity 148).

Other Intelligences

• Verbal/linguistic

ACTIVITY 154

Target

Targeted Grades: Middle and Secondary

ACTIVITY AT A GLANCE

Purpose

- To set priorities for academic and personal challenges by using a target graphic

When to Use

- During a project, longer-term activity, or in conjunction with an advisor-advisee or peer-mediation program when students lack focus in their thinking, have difficulty making choices, or need help in setting a new direction.

What You'll Need

- No materials necessary

WHAT-TO-DO CHECKLIST

- ❒ Use a think-pair-share (see Activity 148) to ask students how they decide what to do first when faced with multiple choices (such as study, talk on the phone, watch TV).
- ❒ During the "share" phase, list responses on the board or overhead.
- ❒ Explain the purpose of the "target" strategy and draw the graphic on the board or overhead.
- ❒ Ask each student to copy the target graphic and select a "deciding" issue such as "doing homework," "getting good grades," or "participating in class."
- ❒ Have students list three to five options for resolving the issue (such as avoid it, do it at once, do it piece by piece, or do it with a friend).

Issue: Getting a Part-Time Job

Check help wanted ads in paper

Apply at companies in town that hire high schoolers

Check the job information board at school

❏ Have students put their first choice in the center of the target, second in the next ring, and third choice in the outer ring.

❏ Pair up students and have them explain and defend their priorities.

❏ Invite students to share their priorities and rationale with the class.

❏ Build all-class lists of the
  • benefits of a target, and
  • drawbacks of a target.

VARIATIONS

1. Pair students with similar topics or issues.

2. Have students rearrange priorities, pair up, and discuss how this would help or hinder efforts to attain a goal.

3. Use the target strategy to examine historic or literary characters' priorities and decisions.

Other Intelligences

• Verbal/linguistic
• Visual/spatial

ACTIVITY 155

One-Minute Mirror

Targeted Grades: Elementary and Middle

ACTIVITY AT A GLANCE

Purpose

• To prompt self-reflection by using a visual tool

When to Use

• At the start or end of a day, class period, or advance period
• As a break after a discussion or difficult task
• As a bridge between subjects

What You'll Need

• Mirror
• Copies of One-Minute Mirror
• Journals (optional)

WHAT-TO-DO CHECKLIST

❑ Bring a mirror to class and set it up on a wall. Activate students' prior knowledge of mirrors by asking questions such as, "What is a mirror?" "Why do you use a mirror?" Using the word "reflection," springboard into the concept of self-reflection as a way of assessing one's goals, objectives, values, successes, failures, and so on.

❑ Give each student a copy of the One-Minute Mirror. Explain that there are four variations of the mirror. Review each variation: Goals, A Concern of the Day, A Success for Today, My #1 Responsibility. Select a topic (such as this school year, homework, or hobbies) and invite students to provide examples for each mirror or variation.

❑ Assign a new topic. Ask students to select one mirror and reflect for thirty seconds on that aspect of the topic. Invite students to write key words or sketch a drawing related to their reflections.

❑ Each day select a different topic for the reflection.

One-Minute Mirror

Goals for Today

1. Prepare new spelling words.
2. Create activity cards.
3. Review my science homework.

Concern of the Day

My science quiz

A Success for Today

Got to school on time and had conference

MY #1 Responsibility

Getting enough sleep to fight this oncoming cold

VARIATIONS

1. Allow each student to pick her reflection topic for the day.

2. Pair up students and have them discuss their reflections.

3. Extend the time and space to do the reflections. A full page in a journal (see Activity 153) is adequate once students are comfortable with the process.

Other Intelligences

- Verbal/linguistic

ACTIVITY 156

Self-Progress Chart

Targeted Grades: Middle and Secondary

ACTIVITY AT A GLANCE

Purpose

- To track progress toward goals by using a visual organizer

When to Use

- To introduce the concepts of setting and assessing goals (with elementary students)
- To reinforce goal setting and assessment and to focus students on goals, social skills, or academic performance (with middle school and secondary students)

What You'll Need

- Copies of Self-Progress Chart
- Journals (optional)

WHAT-TO-DO CHECKLIST

❏ Review characteristics of effective or helpful goals. Select a goal and describe each characteristic by giving examples of those that meet and don't meet the following criteria:
  - Important to me
  - A stretch or challenge
  - Specific and measurable
  - Possible to achieve

❐ Display the Self-Progress Chart. Either give each student a copy or have students copy it down.

Self-Progress Chart		
Name _Joseph Mendrick_		
Check Date _Feb. 10_		
Goal	**Progress check**	**End date**
1. Complete term paper.	First draft done.	Feb. 28
2. Find part-time job.	Applied at grocery store.	March 30
3. Learn how to do stained glass.	Signed up for class.	May 30

❐ Invite students to complete Columns 1 and 3 by listing three goals and setting a date to complete each goal. Students leave the Progress Check column blank: this will be the column that they focus on as they check their progress against their goals on a daily or regularly scheduled basis.

❐ Each day (or per schedule), allow two to three minutes for students to check progress. Invite them to complete the Progress Check column by showing steps they have taken to achieve each goal and their outcomes.

❐ At the end of the week, pair students to discuss their progress, assess where they are, and revise goals as needed (five to seven minutes).

VARIATIONS

1. Use a single goal per week. Revise the chart so that Column 1 lists individual steps to take to complete the goal.

2. Invite students to enter the charts in their journals (see Activity 153).

3. Once a week, use a lead-in statement (see Activity 9) such as "I'm pleased that I . . ." in reference to their goal progress. Invite students to complete the statement and enter responses in journals or discuss in pairs.

4. Use the chart to identify and track goals when working in a cooperative group (see Activity 128) or as a team.

Other Intelligences

• Verbal/linguistic

ACTIVITY 157

Strong Summary Statement

Targeted Grades: Middle and Secondary

ACTIVITY AT A GLANCE

Purpose

- To learn to write strong summary statements

When to Use

- As a bridge at the start of a new lesson
- Between a completed lesson or unit and a new lesson
- At the end of a lesson or unit to capture key thoughts learned
- At the end of a group or class discussion to capture the key concepts discussed

What You'll Need

- Rubric for summaries
- Three-by-five-inch index cards
- Journals (optional)

WHAT-TO-DO CHECKLIST

❏ As an advanced organizer, ask the class to brainstorm what they think are the characteristics of a strong summary statement. List these on the board or use a web for all to see (see Activity 6).

❏ Encourage students to explain why each characteristic is important.

❏ Select the most important characteristics and put them into a rubric (see Activity 8): strong summary statements (such as a topic or keynote sentence, numbered reasons or examples, connecting words, and so on).

❏ With the class, create an example from a past lesson's key ideas.

❏ Start with a lead-in (see Activity 9) such as, "In Toni Morrison's novel *Beloved*, the theme was _____."

❏ Add the subthemes. "The major subthemes of *Beloved* were_____."

❏ Add connecting words between the subthemes.

❏ Smooth out the outline by writing the summary statement.

❏ Match it against the rubric.

❏ With the class, outline how they would summarize this lesson on how to make a summary.

❏ Have all students write a summary on a note card of the above discussion and then grade their own work with the rubric.

VARIATIONS

1. Create the example from a current event. Answer the questions who, what, where, when, how, and why.

2. Create an example after a group discussion: "In this discussion, I learned. . . .," then have students add the three most important contributing ideas.

3. Have students put entries of different summaries into their journals (see Activity 153).

4. Use a newspaper graphic (see Activity 19) to lead in to a summary.

5. Have individual students write summaries in a write-pair-share sequence (see Activity 148).

Other Intelligences

- Verbal/linguistic
- Interpersonal
- Intrapersonal

ACTIVITY 158
Plus/Minus/Interesting (PMI) Assessment

Targeted Grades: All

ACTIVITY AT A GLANCE

Purpose

- To assess attitudes, academic performance, social skills, and behavior by using a graphic tool

When to Use

- On a regularly scheduled basis, such as at the end of the day for elementary students or end of the week for middle school or secondary students
- At the completion of a major individual or cooperative group project, or at the end of a completed task such as an essay or story, lab report, test, and so on

What You'll Need

- PMI chart
- Journals (optional)

WHAT-TO-DO CHECKLIST

❏ Show students the PMI chart and explain the headings: P+ (Pluses), M– (Minuses), and I? (Interesting questions).

❏ Select a topic familiar to the students such as "attending (school name)." As a class, brainstorm lists or use a round-robin questioning pattern (see Activity 24) structure to complete each column. Do one column at a time. After all three columns are filled, select two or three ideas for class discussion.

Topic: Sharing my first draft–"When My Dog Died"–with a group	
P+ Pluses	(1) Neat how some people said they liked it. (2) Got a great idea how to change the ending.
M– Minuses	(1) One person was way too critical. (2) Kind of hard to talk about.
I? Interesting Questions	(1) Would it improve my essay if I included other people's experiences of losing a pet? (2) Do I want to include more about my feelings?

VARIATIONS

1. Assess class projects such as field trips (see Activity 45), class speakers, or major projects.

2. Assign PMI reflection for journal (see Activity 153) writing.

3. Assess affective responses to lessons that introduce new concepts or learning strategies.

Other Intelligences

• Verbal/linguistic

ACTIVITY 159

My Goals

Targeted Grades: All

ACTIVITY AT A GLANCE

Purpose

• To establish the habit of setting and assessing personal goals

When to Use

- Throughout a lesson or unit to focus students on final goals and on achieving those goals

What You'll Need

- No materials necessary

WHAT-TO-DO CHECKLIST

- ❏ Brainstorm with the class the sports that use the word "goal." List the responses on the board or an overhead in a column.

- ❏ Brainstorm areas of life (such as work, hobbies, or sports) for which students can have goals. List these in a second column.

- ❏ Invite students to explain how Column 1 and Column 2 are alike. List responses in a third column.

- ❏ Ask each student to select one goal area from Column 2 and write out a personal goal for that area. Give an example.

- ❏ Ask students to review and modify the goal according to the "ABC" criteria:
  - Is it **A**chievable? (Is it specific enough that the student can tell steps to success?)
  - Is it **B**elievable? (Can the student list and describe the talents he has that will help?)
  - Is it **C**ontrollable? (Is it a goal for which the student needs only to depend on self?)

- ❏ Pair up students. Each student will explain her goal and tell how it matches the **ABC criteria**.

- ❏ After the pair review, invite each student to write a paragraph that summarizes the goal:
  - details steps to be taken to achieve the goal,
  - identifies ways to increase achievement of the goal,
  - identifies benefits for achieving the goal, and
  - modifies the goal.

VARIATIONS

1. For elementary and middle school students, make the final step an oral activity.

2. Preselect the topic area (such as sports or homework assignments) that all students will use.

Other Intelligences

- Verbal/linguistic

ACTIVITY 160

Self-Talk

Targeted Grades: All

ACTIVITY AT A GLANCE

Purpose

- To reflect on goals, aspirations, abilities, and performance through self-talk

When to Use

- Throughout a lesson or unit to teach students a simple reflection technique
- At key spots during the school year to help students self-review

What You'll Need

- No materials necessary
- Journals (optional)

WHAT-TO-DO CHECKLIST

- ❑ Ask students, "What do you think if you hear someone talking to himself out loud?" and "Why do you think that?" Ask students if they ever talk to themselves.

- ❑ Point out that self-talk doesn't have to be public. Every time a student thinks, he is talking to himself. This quiet self-talk doesn't need to be heard by anyone but the person who is thinking.

- ❑ List the following categories on the board or overhead: goals, aspirations, abilities, and performance. Select a category and give an example of positive self-talk. Following are sample responses:
  - Goals: "This week I want to visit my grandparents. What do I need to do to get ready for the trip? Let me see. I need to . . ."
  - Aspirations: "Someday, I want to be a doctor in a developing country. Why do I want to do that? I guess because . . ."
  - Abilities: "It's time to think about high school. What courses do I want to take? If I want to be a salesperson, what will I need to know? I know I'm a good talker. I can convince my friends to do anything. I'm also great at math. . . ."
  - Performance: "How have I done this week? Well, I completed all my homework. I did a really great job on the social studies test. I think it helped that I . . ."

- ❑ Invite students to select a category and engage in self-talk (that is, have a private conversation with themselves). Allow two to three minutes.

- ❑ Invite students to share with the class what they "talked" about. Ask students for feedback on the experience. For example, "Was it easy to do? Hard? Was it beneficial? When would it be good to practice self-talk?"

❑ Summarize by identifying and describing the characteristics of self-talk:
  • Inner dialogue with questions and answers
  • Inner dialogue that is focused on a topic
  • Inner dialogue that is extensive and intensive

❑ Do a PMI assessment (see Activity 158) on perceived benefits. Chart the PMI on the board and discuss the "I" responses.

VARIATIONS

1. Replace the all-class PMI with a journal (see Activity 153) entry.

2. Demonstrate a dialogue out loud.

Other Intelligences

  • Verbal/linguistic
  • Visual/spatial

ACTIVITY 161

Self-Review

Targeted Grades: All

ACTIVITY AT A GLANCE

Purpose

  • To review goal-based academic accomplishments by using a structured format

When to Use

  • Whenever practice and a format are needed to help students review accomplishments
  • Once a week to review weekly goals
  • At the end of a grading period

What You'll Need

  • Journals or copies of Self-Review Questions

WHAT-TO-DO CHECKLIST

❑ Ask students to write one of their academic goals.

❑ Introduce or review checking a goal against the "achievable and believable" criteria. (Is it possible to achieve the goal? Does the student have the skills or talents necessary to achieve the goal?)

❑ Model the "achievable and believable" criteria with a sample goal.

❑ After modeling, invite pairs to share and review their goals using the "achievable and believable" criteria.

❑ Provide students with copies of Self-Review Questions or a model to copy in journals (see Activity 153), and invite students to write a response to each question.
  • "How far have I progressed toward my goal?"
  • "What are the barriers I have overcome?"
  • "What barriers yet remain?"
  • "What help do I need?"

❑ After completing all four questions, have students meet in pairs to share and review their responses.

❑ Following the pair-sharing, ask students to select one of the following lead-in (see Activity 9) statements and write a response in their journals:
  • "From this review, I learned . . ."
  • "From this review, I am pleased . . ."
  • "I intend . . ."

VARIATIONS

1. Use a think-pair-share strategy to start this activity.

2. Conclude with a round-robin questioning pattern (see Activity 24) and a sharing of responses to lead-in statements.

Other Intelligences

• Verbal/linguistic

ACTIVITY 162

My Problem

Targeted Grades: Middle and Secondary

ACTIVITY AT A GLANCE

Purpose

• To become familiar with solving problems through a process
• To learn how to use the **problem-solving model** as a framework to structure a personal problem-solving process

When to Use

- When introducing a thematic unit on personal responsibility (in elementary grades)
- Periodically (once a month or more frequently) during an advisor-advisee program or in conjunction with a peer-mediation or conflict-resolution program in middle grades)
- As a tool to help students solve course-related problems (in secondary grades)

What You'll Need

- Copies of Problem-Solving Model

WHAT-TO-DO CHECKLIST

☐ Activate students' prior knowledge (see Activity 54) of problem-solving processes by inviting students to brainstorm a list of approaches or strategies that they use to solve problems. Ask students to identify successful strategies and briefly discuss characteristics that successful strategies have in common.

☐ Introduce the concept of solving problems through a multistep process. Draw comparisons to student-generated strategies where appropriate.

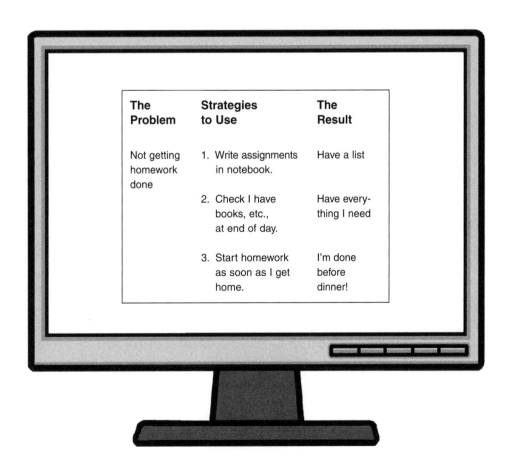

The Problem	Strategies to Use	The Result
Not getting homework done	1. Write assignments in notebook.	Have a list
	2. Check I have books, etc., at end of day.	Have everything I need
	3. Start homework as soon as I get home.	I'm done before dinner!

❒ Show the visual format of the Problem-Solving Model on the board or overhead.

❒ Guide the class through the process, asking for a random selection of ideas at each step.

❒ Use an all-class round-robin questioning pattern (see Activity 24) to discuss:
  • "What was easy to do? Why?"
  • "What was difficult?"
  • "Where can this process be used?"

❒ Distribute copies of the Problem-Solving Model or ask students to copy the format. Ask students to select a hypothetical problem and complete the model.

❒ Collect, review, and give feedback on the completed charts. Select two to three strong examples to show to the class.

VARIATIONS

1. After your review of the charts, have students work in pairs or trios and write group responses on the charts.

2. Display student work at different locations in the room and provide students with an opportunity to observe and read their classmates' work.

3. Assign a sample topic for everyone to use.

4. Use the Problem-Solving Model to study content-based problems of individuals or groups in history, social studies, fine arts, and so on.

Other Intelligences

• Verbal/linguistic

Ideas

ACTIVITY 163

It's My Call

Targeted Grades: Middle and Secondary

ACTIVITY AT A GLANCE

Purpose

- To structure the decision-making process by using a visual organizer as a framework

When to Use

- When introducing a thematic unit on personal responsibility or decision making (in elementary grades)
- Periodically during an advisor-advisee program or in conjunction with a peer-mediation or conflict-resolution program (in middle grades)
- As a tool to help students solve course-related problems (in secondary grades)

What You'll Need

- No materials necessary

WHAT-TO-DO CHECKLIST

- ❐ Activate students' prior knowledge of the decision-making process (see Activity 54).

- ❐ Share the purpose of using a visual organizer as a tool to facilitate the decision-making process. Clarify the words "decisions," "making," and "process."

- ❐ On the overhead or board, show the **mind map** visual format and invite students to volunteer topics related to decision making. Select a topic (such as working in groups) and guide the class through the process of creating a mind map. Be sure to map several choices one can make in deciding how to approach expected outcomes.

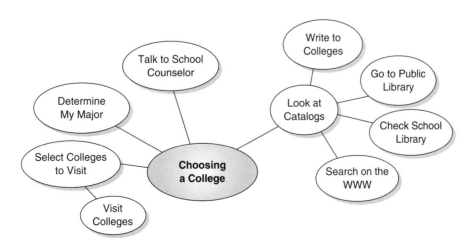

❑ Use an all-class round-robin questioning pattern (see Activity 24) structure to discuss these questions:
  • "What was easy to do with this process?"
  • "What was difficult?"
  • "What are other topics students could use with this format?"

❑ Use a triple T-chart to list the responses.

Triple T-Chart

Easy	Difficult	Other topics
Easy to come up with lots of ideas	Thinking of outcomes	Selecting a term paper topic

❑ Invite students to select a topic and use the mind map format to generate ideas and choices related to the topic. Stress the importance of mapping a variety of choices and the possible outcomes of each. Monitor and coach as needed.

❑ Ask students to write a paragraph summarizing the different options they considered in relation to their topic and to select and describe the option they most prefer. Collect, review, and provide feedback.

VARIATION

1. Work in pairs or trios (see Activities 128 and 145) to create a mind map on chart paper.

Other Intelligences

• Verbal/linguistic
• Visual/spatial

ACTIVITY 164

Standards of Excellence

Targeted Grades: Middle and Secondary

ACTIVITY AT A GLANCE

Purpose

• To identify individual standards of excellence that can be used to assess academic performance

When to Use

- At the beginning of a lesson or unit to introduce the concept of standards or to help students identify their own standards of excellence

What You'll Need

- Coin
- Chart paper or poster boards

WHAT-TO-DO CHECKLIST

- ❏ Place a coin on the overhead. Ask students to explain or guess how the government knows that this is an acceptable coin. (There is a weight standard in the National Bureau of Weights and Standards.)
- ❏ Define the word "standard" based on the phrase "flag that rallies troops."
- ❏ Distribute a sheet of chart paper or poster board to each student.
- ❏ Invite each student to construct a banner that describes her own marks of excellence.
- ❏ Allow thirty minutes to complete the banners. Hang banners across the room.
- ❏ Each day, encourage at least one student to explain his banner to the class.
- ❏ Conclude with a class discussion of the following questions:
  - "What are personal standards?"
  - "Why are personal standards of excellence important?"

VARIATIONS

1. Replace the final step above with a discussion on identifying characteristics that determine standards. For example, an acceptable coin can be identified by its weight, material, size, and shape.

2. Use trios to identify standards shared by the students in each group.

3. Invite a speaker to share her standards of excellence with the class.

4. As a class, compile a list of common shared standards.

5. Hypothesize about personal standards of excellence for historical or literary figures, people in the news, or about standards in terms of requirements for specific careers.

Other Intelligences

- Verbal/linguistic
- Visual/spatial
- Interpersonal

ACTIVITY 165

Portfolio

Targeted Grades: All

ACTIVITY AT A GLANCE

Purpose

- To collect and assess work completed during a course, subject, or over time through the use of a portfolio

When to Use

- When there is an intent to build student responsibility
- As an alternative or supplement to grades as a way of tracking student development

What You'll Need

- Construction paper
- Glue
- Tape
- Scissors
- Sample portfolio
- Criteria rubric
- Journals

WHAT-TO-DO CHECKLIST

- ❏ Share with the class what a portfolio is (a collection of someone's work over time), why it is important (to show progress over time), and how students will use a portfolio (selecting, reflecting on, and assessing the quality of their schoolwork).

- ❏ Show a sample portfolio or the work of a student from a prior year. Discuss how the sample artifacts (such as tests, essays, individual and group projects, journals [see Activity 153], charts, graphs, and other evidences of the student's work) were selected, and why each was selected (such as best, shows improvement, or "before" and "after" samples).

- ❏ Share with the class a rubric (see Activity 8) with the criteria of success that will be used to evaluate the final portfolio (such as selection, improvement, and organization).

- ❏ Provide the guidelines and a model for construction of the physical portfolio (such as size, shape, decorations, and material), which students can create either at home or as an in-class assignment. After the first artifact has been put in the portfolio, provide students with the opportunity to do a formal self-assessment using lead-in statements (see Activity 9), targeted assessment questions, or a visual organizer.

Each time a product is entered, require students to complete and attach an evaluation or self-assessment.

☐ At the end of each six- to eight-week period, instruct students to review the artifacts in the portfolio and select three to five entries that meet the established criteria of success. Ask students to write a paragraph describing their selections and why they were chosen. Collect the selected entries and paragraphs, review students' work, and provide written feedback. Invite students to take their portfolios home to share with family members and to invite family members to provide written or oral feedback.

VARIATIONS

1. Use portfolios in structured conferences to assess performance and growth over a specified period of time. Use as a springboard for students to establish goals for a new quarter or for future work.

2. Use portfolios for group projects.

3. Keep an all-class portfolio. Select the most representative artifact created by individuals or groups from each task, unit, or semester or the best artifact from each student.

4. Use the computer and a CD-ROM to create an electronic portfolio.

Other Intelligences

- Verbal/linguistic
- Visual/spatial

ACTIVITY 166

Life Timeline

Targeted Grades: Elementary and Middle

ACTIVITY AT A GLANCE

Purpose

- To reflect on past, present, and future events of importance in one's life through the use of a timeline

When to Use

- Throughout a lesson or unit to help students identify shared celebrations and to help students develop goals based on desired life events (such as college graduation)
- As an icebreaker at the beginning of a school year or quarter

What You'll Need

- Clotheslines
- Clothespins
- Three-by-five-inch index cards
- Journals (optional)

WHAT-TO-DO CHECKLIST

☐ Brainstorm with the class a list of significant events in a person's life (such as birthdays, high school graduation, and so on).

☐ Give each student a clothesline, clothespins, and index cards. Invite students to select ten to fifteen events that were or that they anticipate will be important in their lives. Have them write each one on an index card and attach cards to the clothesline in some order.

☐ Crisscross the timelines across the room, high enough so it will not be a hazard or distraction.

☐ Each day, ask students to mill under the timelines in search of events shared with other persons. Spend five minutes to discuss the similarities and differences of past and anticipated events.

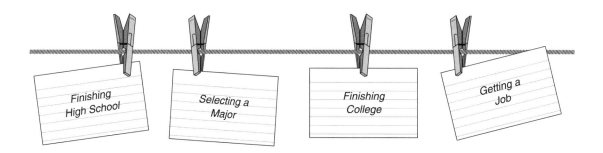

Finishing High School   Selecting a Major   Finishing College   Getting a Job

VARIATIONS

1. Stretch yarn or heavy string across a bulletin board or wall in place of hanging clotheslines across the room.

2. Enter individual timelines in a journal (see Activity 153).

3. Create timelines on chart paper or two pieces of ledger-sized paper taped together. Students can draw in a timeline and paste index cards or attach sticky notes to it. Invite students to mill around the room and find three persons with similar events and three persons with different events and ask these persons to sign their timelines. Conclude activity with a round-robin questioning pattern (see Activity 24) structure in which students tell something new they learned about one of their classmates.

4. Ask students to prioritize the events of most significance and write a paragraph explaining their choices.

5. Make a homework assignment for students to create a family timeline with their parents and other family members.

6. Use in conjunction with a goal-setting lesson to identify necessary steps to achieve future goals (such as getting a driver's license or passing a test).

Other Intelligences

- Verbal/linguistic
- Visual/spatial
- Interpersonal

ACTIVITY 167

People Influences

Targeted Grades: Middle and Secondary

ACTIVITY AT A GLANCE

Purpose

- To reflect on the influences of an important or significant person in one's life

When to Use

- As an introduction to a unit or lesson on how significant people affect our lives
- As a writing topic in a unit or lesson that teaches paragraph construction and usage

What You'll Need

- Copies of Influence Chart

WHAT-TO-DO CHECKLIST

- ❏ Use a KWL chart (see Activity 54) to activate prior knowledge of people who have influenced students or are important to them.

- ❏ Form pairs or trios and distribute a copy of the Influence Chart to each group.

- ❏ Explain each column heading. In Column 1, students list people important in their lives. In Column 2, they describe the relationship with the person (such as brother, aunt, or friend). In Column 3, students list the reason the person was selected. In Column 4, they tell how the person influenced them (such as to get good grades, the importance of humor, or risk taking). In Column 5, students tell what resulted from the influence (such as straight-A average, appreciation of humor, or joined an extracurricular activity).

Influence Chart				
Group Members _Mark, Todd_				
Date _Nov. 7_				

Important person	How related	Why important	Influence	Result
1. Aunt Rose	Mark's aunt	She's special.	Taught me to appreciate all people.	I'm more accepting.
2. Frank Lane	Todd's teacher	Believed in me.	Challenged me to learn more.	Good grades.
3. Mike Guzman	Mark's coach	Taught me a lot.	Showed me the importance of teamwork.	I play with the team—not like a solo star.

❐ Invite students to work together as a group to complete the chart. Allow ten to fifteen minutes for each team to finish its chart. Ask each student to select his most significant influence and write a summary paragraph describing this influence.

❐ Have students work in groups to share and peer edit the paragraphs.

❐ Collect and assess the completed paragraphs.

VARIATIONS

1. Do as an individual activity.

2. Instead of a paragraph, ask each group to draw two to three valid conclusions from its chart and present these to the whole class.

3. For middle school and secondary students, assign a three- to five-paragraph essay describing the people who are now or who have been the major influences in their lives.

Other Intelligences

- Verbal/linguistic
- Visual/spatial
- Interpersonal

ACTIVITY 168

Career Ladder

Targeted Grades: Middle and Secondary

ACTIVITY AT A GLANCE

Purpose

- To explore and prioritize career decisions

When to Use

- When encouraging students to explore career options
- When encouraging students to think in terms of priorities

What You'll Need

- Journals

WHAT-TO-DO CHECKLIST

1. Draw a ladder on an overhead or board. Ask students to identify possible uses of a ladder. Explain using a ladder graphic as a visual tool to identify and set priorities.

2. Brainstorm a list of careers with the students.

3. Ask a volunteer to select three careers and enter her choices on the ladder graphic. Ask the student to explain or defend her priorities.

4. Have each student repeat these steps in his journal (see Activity 153).

5. After the ranking step is done, invite each student to write a letter to his parents explaining the choices.

6. Have pairs edit and proofread the letters before the students take them home.

Dear Mom,

Someday I would love to be a famous potter. I know, though, that it will take many years to become skilled at this craft and I don't want to starve in the meantime. I've been considering possible careers and have decided that I want to become a graphic artist.

VARIATIONS

1. Substitute "goals for continuous improvement," "goals for this school year," or "goals for lifelong learning" in place of possible careers.

2. Review, select, and post a variety of examples.

Other Intelligences

- Visual/spatial
- Interpersonal

ACTIVITY 169

Seasonal Letter

Targeted Grades: Middle and Secondary

ACTIVITY AT A GLANCE

Purpose

- To write a letter to a grandparent, relative, or older person about an interesting personal experience related to a particular season of the year

When to Use

- Throughout a lesson or unit to encourage students to write from personal experience
- As the culmination of a unit on letter writing
- When promoting dialogue and sharing across generations and with family members

What You'll Need

- A copy of "A Boy's Thanksgiving Day" by Lydia Maria Child ("Over the river and through the wood")

WHAT-TO-DO CHECKLIST

- ❏ Play the song or read the words to "A Boy's Thanksgiving Day."

- ❏ Ask students how many have gone to visit a grandparent. What was the experience like? What do they remember about their grandparents?

- ❏ Review the task: students are to write a letter to a grandparent (who may or may not be living) or to an older relative or adult in their neighborhood. In the letter, students are to describe an interesting personal experience that happened in a particular season of the year.

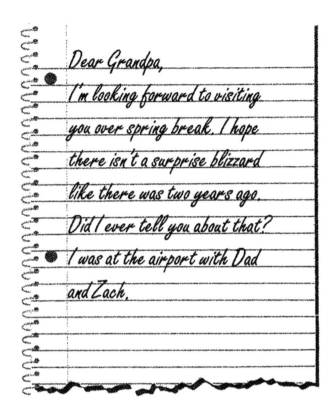

Dear Grandpa,

I'm looking forward to visiting you over spring break. I hope there isn't a surprise blizzard like there was two years ago. Did I ever tell you about that? I was at the airport with Dad and Zach.

❏ As a class, brainstorm ideas. Share a personal example or solicit student examples.

❏ Ask students to select an experience and then form pairs for a prewriting activity. In pairs, students take turns describing to whom they will be writing, the experience and seasonal connection they will write about, and why they chose it.

❏ Students work individually to write letters. Upon completion, use pairs to proof-read letters, check proper form, punctuation, spelling, and so on.

❏ If the grandparent, relative, or older person is living, help students send a copy of the letter.

VARIATIONS

1. After the topic brainstorm, list age-appropriate criteria for a well-written letter.

2. Invite students to read the poem to their parents and ask them to tell a personal experience about a family trip to a relative or a seasonal-related experience they had when they were children. Provide an opportunity for students to share their family stories in small groups or with the whole class.

Other Intelligences

- Verbal/linguistic
- Interpersonal

ACTIVITY 170

Goal Chart

Targeted Grades: All

ACTIVITY AT A GLANCE

Purpose

- To set goals and align tasks using a chart format

When to Use

- When students need to establish a regular, systematic goal process at regular times each day or week
- When students need to have a structure for thinking through and assessing their goals

What You'll Need

- Copies of Goal Chart

WHAT-TO-DO CHECKLIST

❑ Do a prior knowledge check (see Activity 54) about goals. After the check, highlight the concept that goals are targets that one wants to achieve. Personal goals can relate to family, friends, schoolwork, sports, interests, and so on.

❑ On the board or overhead, display the Goal Chart.

❑ Demonstrate the process of selecting and ranking goals by filling in the chart with examples.

❑ Group students in pairs and give each student a copy of the Goal Chart. Instruct students to spend three to five minutes talking about their goals and their plans to achieve those goals, or listening to their partner, and then to reverse roles.

Goal Chart					
Goal	Rank	Why important	How to achieve	Checkup	By when
1. Pass keyboarding	3	I need to know how to use a computer.	Practice more.	Every Friday	End of semester
2. Participate in all track meets	2	Running makes me feel great.	Rearrange job schedule; get all homework done early.	Every Friday	Ongoing until June
3. Save $3,000 for a car	4	Would make getting around easier.	Save 50% of every paycheck.	In a month	By June 1
4. Make dean's list	1	Want to do my best, plus it'll help me get in to a good college.	Study, work hard, do all assignments.	Every Friday	End of semester
5. Select two to three colleges to visit	5	Need to learn more about colleges.	Review catalogs, talk to guidance counselor.	In a month	By June 1

❐ After both partners have discussed their goals, have them list identified goals in Column 1 and, working together, complete the rest of their individual charts. Remind pairs to share in confidence and to maintain confidentiality.

❐ At the end of each week (or designated period), use pairs to review progress, adjust or add goals, and adjust "how" and timelines.

VARIATIONS

1. Make this an individual reflective task instead of a task in pairs.

2. Invite students to share goals and plans with the class.

3. Limit the chart's focus (such as academic goals for this course).

Other Intelligences

- Verbal/linguistic
- Visual/spatial
- Interpersonal

ACTIVITY 171

Plus or Minus

Targeted Grades: All

ACTIVITY AT A GLANCE

Purpose

- To assess progress and achievements by using a visual organizer as a tool

When to Use

- After students have learned to set goals to structure goal or task assessment
- When doing a task such as a project, essay, or lab report
- Throughout a lesson or unit to track progress

What You'll Need

- Journals

WHAT-TO-DO CHECKLIST

- ❏ On the board or overhead, display the Plus or Minus T-Chart.

- ❏ Model completing the chart with a goal or task related to teaching responsibilities (such as preparing a bulletin board). What were the pluses and minuses of how this task was done?

- ❏ Ask students to copy the Plus or Minus T-Chart in their journals (see Activity 153) or on paper. Invite students to select a goal or task they are working on and to complete the chart. Review goal criteria.

- ❏ Collect completed charts and provide feedback.

Plus or Minus	
Goal or Task _____ _Having students create bulletin board display_ _____	
Pluses	**Minuses**
1. Stimulates students' interest in topic.	1. Have to do after class.
2. Engages students as partners in learning.	2. May not be as comprehensive as desired.
3. Provides fresh perspective.	3. Requires me to supervise students.

VARIATIONS

1. Use the chart to assess the pluses and minuses of the goal or task itself.

2. Share charts in pairs.

3. Use the chart with team goals.

Other Intelligences

- Verbal/linguistic
- Visual/spatial
- Interpersonal

ACTIVITY 172

Autobiography

Targeted Grades: Middle and Secondary

ACTIVITY AT A GLANCE

Purpose

- To write an autobiography or autobiographical pieces

When to Use

- Throughout a lesson or unit to expand students' writing abilities

What You'll Need

- Sample autobiography
- Sticky notes or three-by-five-inch index cards

WHAT-TO-DO CHECKLIST

❏ Begin with a study of an appropriate autobiography.

❏ Using the studied example, identify the characteristics of a successful autobiography:
  - Personal story
  - Incidents reveal character
  - Connected incidents
  - Influence of background

❏ Use a sequence chart or timeline to model an arrangement of important life events. Use examples from the sample autobiography or from your own life history.

❐ Invite students to write and sequence their life stories. Ask them to write individual events on sticky notes or index cards. Demonstrate to students how to expand the events. (Elementary students may write one or two descriptive sentences for each event. Middle school students may write a paragraph. Secondary students may write several paragraphs or pages on each event.)

❐ Explain sequencing events by using a chart or timeline format.

❐ Expand the sequence chart or timeline to include a sketch or drawing for each selected event.

❐ Bend or staple the completed work and have each student title her autobiography.

❐ Assess each student's finished work according to the selected criteria.

VARIATIONS

1. Introduce a peer-editing step before the final draft.

2. Focus on a specific aspect of a student's life such as an academic autobiography or talent autobiography.

Other Intelligences

• Verbal/linguistic

ACTIVITY 173

Decision Letter

Targeted Grades: Middle and Secondary

ACTIVITY AT A GLANCE

Purpose

• To practice letter-writing skills by using an incident revolving around an important decision

When to Use

• During a lesson or unit to encourage students to establish their own criteria for success

What You'll Need

• Sample letter

WHAT-TO-DO CHECKLIST

❏ Show a model letter on the overhead or give each student a copy of a selected letter. Review the formal parts and structure of a letter (such as address, date, salutation, and so on) and the criteria for success (such as grammar, structure, punctuation, spelling, interest, and clarity). Ask students to evaluate the sample letter based on the established criteria.

❏ Assign students to write a two-page letter to a friend about an important decision they've made. Review how they will do this.

❏ As a class or in small groups, brainstorm a list of ideas for the students' decisions and topics. Following this activity, have students write their first drafts.

❏ In pairs, have students peer edit first drafts then write a second draft. Monitor and coach students as necessary. If possible, arrange to meet with students for a short conference either on completion of the first draft or at any time during the writing process.

❏ Collect final copies and review. Select examples that match the criteria and read several to the class.

VARIATIONS

1. Change the letter's topic to decisions made by historic or literary figures, school or community issues, or positions held on current events issues.

2. Pair students and invite students to write a letter to their classroom partner. Exchange letters and write a letter in response. Post sets of letters or have students meet in small groups to share them.

Other Intelligences

- Verbal/linguistic
- Interpersonal

ACTIVITY 174
School Support Letter

Targeted Grades: Middle and Secondary

ACTIVITY AT A GLANCE

Purpose

- To reflect on the benefits of school and assess individual progress

When to Use

- Throughout the school year to help improve students' assessment skills

What You'll Need

- Model persuasive essay
- Copies of an assessment tool such as the PMI assessment or Mrs. Potter's Questions
- Questions

WHAT-TO-DO CHECKLIST

- ❏ Ask students to use a PMI assessment (see Activity 158), Mrs. Potter's Questions (see Activity 176), or other assessment tool to evaluate the benefits of attending their school or participating in a particular school program.

- ❏ Assign students to write an essay that argues a supportive position for the school or a special program in which they participate. The essay must communicate the benefits from personal experience.

- ❏ Establish expectations for the completed essay. Show students a model persuasive essay and ask them to identify examples that illustrate the established criteria for success on this task.

- ❏ Use base groups (see Activity 141) or pairs to develop ideas for the topics. After ten minutes, use a round-robin questioning pattern (see Activity 24) structure to create a list of ideas.

- ❏ In class, coach students in the selection and development of their essays. Assign the first draft for homework.

- ❏ Use base groups or pairs to peer edit the first draft and develop a PMI assessment (see Activity 158) of each essay.

- ❏ Collect and review the drafts and assessments. Provide individual or all-class feedback prior to students writing final drafts.

- ❏ Require students to attach an individual PMI assessment or other self-assessment to their final copies.

VARIATIONS

1. Use to assist students in the creation of a persuasive essay. Vary the length from one paragraph to a full-blown, multiparagraph essay appropriate to the students' ages and writing expertise.

2. Change the topic to one where students have very strong feelings (such as wearing school uniforms, abolishing or expanding amount of homework, lengthening the school year). Assign students to write an essay on the benefits or drawbacks of a

particular position by drawing on their own personal experiences. Upon completion, students pair with a classmate with the opposite perspective and share essays.

3. Use Variation 2 to prepare for a class debate.

Other Intelligences

- Verbal/linguistic
- Interpersonal

ACTIVITY 175

Internet Hobby Search

Targeted Grades: Middle and Secondary

ACTIVITY AT A GLANCE

Purpose

- To deepen personal interest and knowledge of a hobby by using the Internet

When to Use

- Throughout a lesson or unit to encourage students to expand their range of interests and talents

What You'll Need

- Computers
- Internet access
- Copies of Internet Hobby Search

WHAT-TO-DO CHECKLIST

- ❏ Create a question web (see Activity 6) with the word "hobby." Ask students to describe what a hobby is. Select the most critical attributes.
- ❏ Pair students to discuss what their hobbies are and what they like about their hobbies. After a three- to five-minute discussion, call for volunteers to contribute to a class list of hobbies.
- ❏ Provide each student with a copy of Internet Hobby Search. Review rules for Internet use.
- ❏ Obtain formal parent permission for students to work on this Internet project.
- ❏ Collect copies and review students' work. Provide feedback and assist students in preparing presentations.

Internet Hobby Search

1. What are your special interests?
   art, crafts, design

2. What are your special talents?
   freeform drawing, eye for color

3. What hobbies do you have that match your interests or talents?
   batiking, sewing, tie-dyeing

4. What hobbies would you like to learn more about?
   batiking

5. Pick one hobby and use the Internet to identify resources for learning about this hobby.

   1. Custom Colors Company   *2. Creative Clothes*   *3. Batik-It*

Select two to five resources. Study them and prepare a three- to five-minute talk that describes the hobby, explains talents and skills needed for this hobby, and tells what your personal interest in this hobby is and how it might benefit you.

❏ Conduct student talks or presentations. Before the talks start, provide evaluation criteria.

VARIATIONS

1. If students don't have Internet access, use the school or local library for resource identification and to access resource materials.

2. After students have completed their research, have students form groups of three to five. Ask students to discuss what they have learned about their hobbies and brainstorm a list of questions that would apply to all of the group's hobbies (such as, "What materials are used?"). Using these questions and each student's hobby, have students create a group matrix.

3. In place of a class talk, give students the option either to write a multiparagraph essay or share information out loud in pairs or trios.

Other Intelligences

- Verbal/linguistic
- Visual/spatial
- Interpersonal

ACTIVITY 176

Mrs. Potter's Questions

Targeted Grades: All

ACTIVITY AT A GLANCE

Purpose

- To assess academic performance or the effects of personal decisions by using a critiquing process

When to Use

- As a conclusion to any assignment, lesson, or unit to focus on the process of the task to encourage self-assessment
- On a scheduled basis each week or month in conjunction with a journal and course-specific skills
- Quarterly, when assessing the portfolio-selection process

What You'll Need

- List of Mrs. Potter's Questions

WHAT-TO-DO CHECKLIST

☐ On the board, overhead, or a bulletin board, display Mrs. Potter's Questions. (Note: Mrs. Potter is a teacher who uses these questions to help her students assess their performance. For additional information on Mrs. Potter's Questions, see Bellanca and Fogarty, 1993.)

☐ Introduce questions as a tool that students can use on a regular basis to assess their performance. Describe the different ways this can be done (such as journal [see Activity 153], post-task writing activity, pair discussion, and so on).

Mrs. Potter's Questions

- What was I expected to do?

- What did I do well?

- If I did the same task again, what would I do differently?

- What help do I need?

❏ Using an example from personal experience (such as how I prepare for class or how I grade student portfolios), demonstrate answering each question.

❏ Use the example to highlight "indicators of excellence," or overall standards that you have previously identified and communicated to students such as these:
  • Uses at least three specific examples for each question.
  • Shows insight into personal strengths and sees areas to improve.
  • Spells correctly.
  • Uses complete and grammatically correct sentences.

❏ Provide an age-appropriate topic for a whole-class demonstration, such as these:
  • Elementary school—doing my homework
  • Middle school—cleaning my room
  • Secondary school—saying no to alcohol or drug pressures

❏ Set discussion guidelines to ensure receptive climate.

❏ Invite student responses to each question. Record the responses on the board or overhead.

❏ Review the process with a four-column T-chart on the board or overhead. Encourage multiple responses.

Expected to do	Did well	Do differently	Help
Clean my room	Put stuff away	Clean out closet and drawers first	How to organize things better—ask my mom

❏ Use the "Help" column to list specific concerns. Encourage students to respond to each item in the "Help" column before adding additional items (such as, "How can you get the help you need? Who can you ask for help?").

❏ Check for understanding. Assign a homework or in-class assignment that will conclude with students responding to Mrs. Potter's Questions.

VARIATIONS

1. Use as a process introduction. Instead of teaching all four steps together, do one step at a time until all students grasp the concept.

2. Invite students to use this prior to midterm (or other checkpoint) student-teacher conferences to assess progress and performance.

Other Intelligences

  • Verbal/linguistic
  • Interpersonal

PART VIII

Naturalist Intelligence

ACTIVITY 177

Green Garden Classroom

A Project

Targeted Grades: Elementary and Middle

ACTIVITY AT A GLANCE

Purpose

- To create and care for a garden

When to Use

- As a botany unit integrated with mathematics and language arts (in elementary grades)
- As an investigative unit of the growing cycle (in middle grades)

What You'll Need

- Garden plots
- Seeds or seedlings (several different types)
- Gardening tools
- String
- Fertilizer
- Yardsticks or tape measures
- Journals

WHAT-TO-DO CHECKLIST

- ❐ Use a prior knowledge identifier (see Activity 54) to determine what students know about gardens.

- ❐ Introduce the project—creating a class garden—and brainstorm what students might learn from the experience (such as mathematics, geometry, counting, measurement, and so on).

- ❐ Form mixed-ability groups (see Activity 145) of three students each. Preview the tasks each group will do: one group will measure the plot, one will lay out the plot by rows or quarters, one will till the plot, and one will augment the soil (using the correct organic soil amendment or fertilizer for soil type). Identify the land to be used (ideally, a five- by five-foot plot for each group). The space needs easy access, good protection, good sun exposure, nearby water source, and relative ease of use.

- ❐ Provide planning time for students to select what they will plant (review catalogs online) and how.

❑ Have students identify appropriate roles or tasks (such as recorder, leader, tools manager) and select roles and tasks for each group member (see Activity 140).

❑ Provide students with a selection of seeds or transplants (four types per group) with planting and watering instructions. Start gardening by preparing the soil and designing the plots.

❑ Encourage students to keep a gardening journal (see Activity 153) in which they record information about their gardening activities (such as type of soil, effects of mixing, annual life of the soil, weather conditions, and the effects of fertilizing).

❑ Provide students opportunities to share and discuss their observations, both in their groups and as a class.

❑ Make weekly (or more frequent) visits to the plots for thinning plants, tending the soil, weeding, watering, and fertilizing. Students should continue recording observations of the growing cycle and factors affecting growth (such as weather and fertilizer).

❑ Hold weekly discussions about their observations.

❑ Harvest the crops and send samples home.

❑ Revisit the goals of the project and complete the KWL class list of what was learned (see Activity 54).

VARIATIONS

1. Record weather conditions and observed stages of growth in a comparison or relational chart.

2. Draw observed stages of growth for each plant and chart growth rates.

Other Intelligences

- Verbal/linguistic
- Logical/mathematical
- Visual/spatial
- Interpersonal

ACTIVITY 178

Observation Sketches

ACTIVITY AT A GLANCE

Purpose

- To enhance observation skills

When to Use

- When introducing students to scientific observations

- At the beginning of lab units when starting botany or zoology projects
- As closure to a biology unit

What You'll Need

- Sketch paper
- Colored pencils
- Erasers
- Dried flowers, leaves, or plants
- Journals

WHAT-TO-DO CHECKLIST

❑ Ensure that each student has a box of colored pencils, eraser, sketch paper, and a single dried flower, leaf, or plant.

❑ Using the overhead or board, demonstrate how to observe a sample flower. Have students look at the flower's colors, shape, lines, angles, size, patterns, and so on. Have them list their observations in their journals (see Activity 153). Demonstrate the replication process by drawing and labeling the sample as accurately as possible.

❑ Invite students to study their specimens and list the features they observe. Ask them to sketch their flower, leaf, or plant as completely and accurately as possible.

❑ Display completed sketches in a gallery (see Activity 51).

❑ As a class, discuss what was challenging and what was easy to do in this activity. Use a T-chart to record responses (see Activity 139) gathered in round-robin questioning pattern (see Activity 24).

❑ Conclude activity by asking students to write a paragraph using a lead-in statement (see Activity 9) such as "When I observe, I . . ." or "When I draw what I observe, I . . ."

VARIATIONS

1. Use a single plant, flower, or leaf for all to observe and sketch.

2. Use pairs for the observation step. Each pair will make a single list.

3. Ask students to draw an object using a list of observations created by another person. Once the drawing is complete, compare it to the actual object. Pair students so that the observer and the sketcher can review the list of observations and drawings. Have each pair identify the accuracy of sketched features. In addition, have each pair determine what additional information would have helped the sketcher to draw a more accurate representation of the object.

4. Have middle school students observe collected specimens of small plants and insects with a magnifying glass and sketch what they see.

Other Intelligences

- Verbal/linguistic
- Logical/mathematical
- Visual/spatial
- Interpersonal

ACTIVITY 179

Classification Matrix

Targeted Grades: Middle and Secondary

ACTIVITY AT A GLANCE

Purpose

- To classify items using a visual organizer

When to Use

- During a lesson or unit to teach students how to distinguish characteristics of items
- When teaching the meaning of classification
- When teaching how to make generalizations based on shared attributes of items

What You'll Need

- Copies of a matrix

WHAT-TO-DO CHECKLIST

- ❑ Display a matrix on the board or overhead. Select a family or group of items related to a specific unit being studied (such as trees or planets). Label each column with a characteristic or category that can be used to describe, or classify, the items. List individual items in the far-left column.

- ❑ Explain the meaning and value of the term "classification" and demonstrate how to enter identified features for each item onto the matrix.

- ❑ Ask students to complete individual matrixes as they study the topic. Provide opportunities throughout the unit to add items to the matrixes.

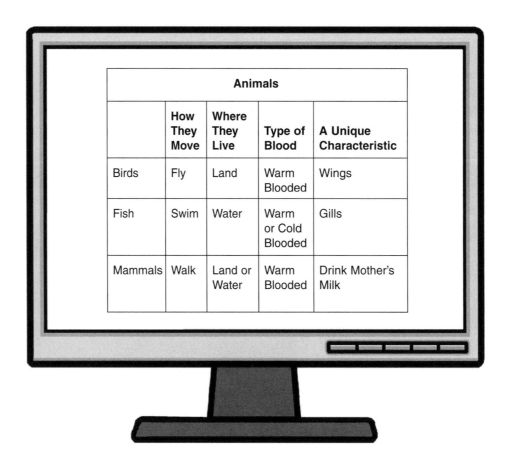

Animals				
	How They Move	Where They Live	Type of Blood	A Unique Characteristic
Birds	Fly	Land	Warm Blooded	Wings
Fish	Swim	Water	Warm or Cold Blooded	Gills
Mammals	Walk	Land or Water	Warm Blooded	Drink Mother's Milk

❏ As a class, discuss what thinking steps students used as they completed the matrixes.

VARIATIONS

1. Use cooperative groups (see Activity 128) to complete the matrixes.

2. Provide several related items (such as leaves, books, buttons) to several groups of students. Ask students to identify characteristics that can be used to categorize the items (such as shape, type of book, or number of buttonholes) and to label the matrix columns accordingly. Next, list each item in the far left column and, working as a group, complete the matrix.

3. Follow up with items that are more complex and require higher-level classification skills.

Other Intelligences

- Verbal/linguistic
- Logical/mathematical
- Visual/spatial

ACTIVITY 180

Plant Observation Project

Targeted Grades: Elementary and Middle

ACTIVITY AT A GLANCE

Purpose

- To deepen or develop observation skills in conjunction with growing plants

When to Use

- When introducing younger students to the importance of observation in the science field
- When helping older students learn care and precision in making observations
- When introducing the topic of the growth cycle of plants

What You'll Need

- Poster boards or chart paper
- Variety of seeds, pots, potting soil
- Journals

WHAT-TO-DO CHECKLIST

❏ Provide each student with seeds from three different plants: a flower, a weed, and a legume. Give each student three pots and enough potting soil to put in the pots.

❏ Ask students to make charts in their journals (see Activity 153) that they will use to show the growth cycle of each plant. To start, have students sketch each seed, using actual size and dimension, and label each drawing. Tell students that they can chart each plant either horizontally or vertically, but that they need to allow space for numerous other entries (both sketches and written descriptions) to be made during the growth cycle of the plants.

❏ Discuss what must happen for the seeds to grow (they need to be planted and watered, and they need access to sunlight). Ask students to create a list of growing instructions for each plant.

❏ Ask students to examine their plants on alternate days for signs of growth and to record their observations on their charts. Students may record their observations by sketching what they see or through short written descriptions.

❏ After the plants are six to seven weeks old, have students create an all-class chart or matrix (see Activity 179) listing common features they observe for each plant.

❏ Follow up with additional matrixes or charts at different stages of the growing cycle.

❏ Have students create charts that show how each plant is similar to the others and how it is different. Emphasize accuracy and completeness of observations.

❏ Once plants have reached a fairly mature stage, ask students to write summaries (see Activity 129) that describe the characteristics of each plant at various stages of the growing cycle.

VARIATIONS

1. Use pairs or trios for this task. Designate roles such as observer, recorder, and encourager (see Activity 140). For each chart activity, have students alternate roles so that each one has a chance to observe, record, and encourage. (Role variations also can include artist and writer.)

2. Upon completion of all charts, students select one plant and create posters (see Activity 61) that describe the growth cycle of that plant. Students can incorporate existing drawings, charts, and written notations, or they can create new ones. Have a carousel (see Activity 10).

3. Create a class people search (see Activity 27).

Other Intelligences

- Verbal/linguistic
- Logical/mathematical
- Visual/spatial
- Interpersonal

ACTIVITY 181

What Is The Problem?

Targeted Grades: Middle and Secondary

ACTIVITY AT A GLANCE

Purpose

- To sharpen the ability to identify a scientific problem

When to Use

- In a lesson or unit to introduce students to scientific problem-solving methods

What You'll Need

- Copies of letters to the editor from a newspaper that represent different points of view on a specific issue such as global warming

WHAT-TO-DO CHECKLIST

☐ Form mixed-ability groups (see Activity 145) of five students each.

☐ Give each group a letter or memo about a current issue (such as the presence of harmful chemicals in the drinking water or the causes of global warming). Each letter should represent a unique point of view.

☐ Ask students to imagine that they are on a committee that will advise a local commissioner on how to resolve the problem. However, before they can recommend any solutions, they need to agree on the nature of the problem.

☐ Ask groups to read their letters, discuss the issue, and form a consensus on what the problem is and how best to solve it. Request that groups present this information to the class and explain their reasoning.

☐ After all presentations are complete, mediate a discussion on which methods and reasons were appropriate for identifying and solving the problem.

☐ List problem-identification criteria on the board or overhead.

☐ Select a second problem and have groups use the criteria to develop the solution.

VARIATIONS

1. Provide copies of all letters to each group.

2. Do this activity in conjunction with a lesson on persuasive writing.

3. Provide the class with a set of "problem" criteria to contrast with their ideas.

Other Intelligences

- Verbal/linguistic
- Logical/mathematical
- Interpersonal

ACTIVITY 182

Science Interview

Targeted Grades: Middle and Secondary

ACTIVITY AT A GLANCE

Purpose

- To develop interviewing skills as a means of gathering and organizing information

When to Use

- In conjunction with a research project that requires students to obtain first-hand, or direct, information

- During a lesson or unit on research skills
- As an introduction for an essay assignment

What You'll Need

- Copies of background information on different scientists or inventors

WHAT-TO-DO CHECKLIST

☐ Ask students to brainstorm a list of questions a television talk show host might use to interview a guest expert on a current scientific issue. Display the list on the board or overhead.

☐ Explain the activity.

☐ Assign each student one scientist or inventor.

☐ Have each student interview another student to obtain information on an assigned scientist or inventor. Once the scientist is identified, the student will research that scientist and the related issue.

---

1. What is your most significant accomplishment?

2. When did you first get interested in the science field?

3. Did you do well in science when you were in school?

☐ Pair up students and have one student interview the other to obtain information on his assigned subject, then reverse roles. Questions should focus on who, what, when, where, and why.

☐ Ask students to write individual reports using the information they obtained from their interviews.

☐ End with a discussion that examines the interviewing process and the value of using questions in an interview for collecting accurate information.

VARIATIONS

1. Use historic or literary figures as the subjects for the essays.

2. Assign a position paper on a topic related to community or global concerns or environmental issues. Ask students to interview one of their family members or a friend to obtain information and to use this information to write their essays.

Other Intelligences

- Verbal/linguistic
- Interpersonal

ACTIVITY 183

Aha! Log

Targeted Grades: Middle and Secondary

ACTIVITY AT A GLANCE

Purpose

- To learn how to make process notes during a scientific inquiry

When to Use

- During a long-term science lab experiment or one that will occur over several class periods

What You'll Need

- Videotape or DVD on Leonardo da Vinci or Marie Curie
- VCR or DVD player
- Journals

WHAT-TO-DO CHECKLIST

❐ Introduce students to the notebooks of Marie Curie or Charles Darwin. (Videotapes about their scientific accomplishments most likely will show how they kept their logs. Research this information on the Internet.)

❐ Ask students to use a journal (see Activity 153) to log information during a lab experiment. Instruct students to include the following for each log entry: date, topic of study, sketch or written description of the day's lab topic, notes on procedures used, and at least one **aha!** gained from the experiment. ("Aha!" or "Eureka!" is an exclamation made when a person discovers something or when a confusing concept or fact suddenly becomes clear.)

❐ Select the lab experiment.

❐ Select five to six logs daily to collect and read. Provide brief commentary or feedback on each student's precision and accuracy.

❐ At the end of the experiment, instruct students to review their logs and make a closing entry about the log process and their own reactions to it. (For example, "Describe the most important thing you learned during this process. Has keeping a log been an advantage or disadvantage to you? Why?")

VARIATIONS

1. Provide opportunities for informal or small group sharing of logs throughout the process.

2. Select student sketches and transfer them to overhead transparencies. As a class, discuss strengths of displayed sketches.

3. Use logs during literature or music classes to record daily "Ahas!"

4. Introduce by explaining the concept of "Ahas!," or "Eurekas!," and ask students to reflect on prior experiences and recall a significant "Eureka!" Invite students to share their experiences.

Other Intelligences

- Verbal/linguistic
- Logical/mathematical
- Visual/spatial

ACTIVITY 184
Comparing Phenomena

Targeted Grades: Middle and Secondary

ACTIVITY AT A GLANCE

Purpose

- To compare and contrast natural phenomena using a Venn diagram

When to Use

- When comparing and contrasting similar phenomena in a science unit

What You'll Need

- Objects for comparison

WHAT-TO-DO CHECKLIST

❐ Ask two students to stand in the front of the room. On the board, draw a Venn diagram with two interlinked circles and label the circles with the students' names.

❐ Ask the class to identify ways in which the students are similar and ways in which they are different.

❐ Ask one student to be the recorder. Ask her to list differences in the appropriate circle and to list similarities in the area shared by, or the intersection of, both circles.

❐ Display two versions of the same object (such as microscopes, globes, or triangles) and ask students in pairs to create Venn diagrams (see Activity 66) that show the shared and unique characteristics of each selected object.

❐ When students have finished their diagrams, create an all-class Venn diagram that incorporates all the characteristics noted by the class.

❐ Select material from the textbook that allows for visual and verbal comparison (such as African versus Asian elephants, or deciduous versus coniferous trees). Instruct students to construct a Venn diagram from this text material. Review the results.

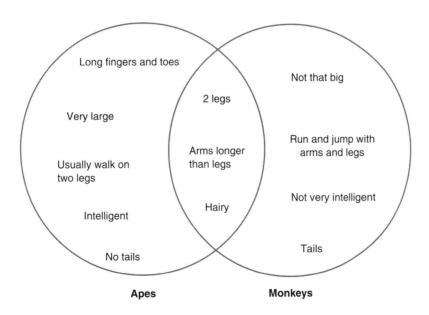

❐ Close with a discussion that identifies the criteria for a successful comparison with a Venn diagram, when it is useful to use Venn diagrams, and the value of Venn diagrams in naturalist study. Start the discussion with lead-in statements (see Activity 9) from these questions and responses in a round-robin questioning pattern (see Activity 24).

VARIATIONS

1. Use pairs or trios to construct the Venn diagrams.

2. Increase the number of objects compared.

3. Use Venn diagrams in other content areas (such as comparing literary characters or historic periods).

Other Intelligences

- Verbal/linguistic
- Logical/mathematical
- Visual/spatial
- Interpersonal

ACTIVITY 185

Science News

Targeted Grades: Middle

ACTIVITY AT A GLANCE

Purpose

- To summarize naturalist observations

When to Use

- During an interdisciplinary unit involving science and writing
- When connecting students' observations of nature with appropriate conclusions
- When developing or enhancing students' observation skills

What You'll Need

- Access to land with diverse plant life
- Clipboards
- Paper
- Pencils or pens
- Pegs or sticks
- Sample essay

WHAT-TO-DO CHECKLIST

❏ Assign students an "in-the-field" observation task: to examine a specific plot of land, identify at least three plant species growing on it, and report their findings through written descriptions and sketches.

❐ Arrange students in cooperative groups (see Activity 128) of three each. Review the group roles (see Activity 140) and guidelines (see Activity 138).

❐ Go to an outdoor area that has a variety of plants. Mark off the boundaries of specific plots by having students walk around the areas they will study. Use sticks or pegs and tape measures to identify then to show boundaries.

❐ Provide each recorder with a clipboard, paper, and pens or pencils. Review the terms (such as flora, species, and so on) appropriate to the assignment.

❐ Ask students to find three samples of the item, sketch the identifying features of each item, and label each sketch.

❐ Upon return to the classroom, present a model three- to five-paragraph essay. Review its parts: introduction, and detail paragraphs describing the key features observed and the locale of the observation. Ask students to write descriptions of their findings as if they were addressing scientific readers interested in new discoveries.

❐ Use small groups or a peer-editing process to review first drafts, to edit, and then to revise.

❐ Upon completion, form groups of six to eight students each. Distribute essays and ask each group to select reports from other students and create a newspaper with name, headlines, and so on. Post the completed newspapers on the bulletin board or select one to duplicate for all students.

VARIATIONS

1. Group students into observation teams for outside study.

2. Vary the type of site (such as prairie, forest, desert, or backyard garden).

3. Conduct observations of the same site at different times of the year. Create new editions of the newspaper to report on seasonal differences.

Other Intelligences

- Verbal/linguistic
- Logical/mathematical
- Visual/spatial
- Interpersonal

ACTIVITY 186

Prediction Check

Targeted Grades: Middle and Secondary

ACTIVITY AT A GLANCE

Purpose

- To develop and practice prediction skills in relation to scientific topics

When to Use

- When introducing the use of prediction in science experiments

What You'll Need

- Coins
- Individual-sized cereal boxes (five per pair)
- Sets of similar items with unknown quantities of contents

WHAT-TO-DO CHECKLIST

- ❒ Invite a student to take a coin and stand in front of the class. Have other students, one at a time, "call" a coin flip. Assign a student to record each "heads" or "tails" call and post the result on the board or overhead.

- ❒ After twenty-five to thirty tosses, ask several students to predict the next five tosses and explain the rationale for their choices. Test their predictions.

- ❒ Ask students to identify what it takes to make a "probable" prediction, that is, one that is likely to happen. (The answer should be sufficient, accurate data in a repeated pattern.)

- ❒ Identify when predictions are used (such as waiting for a bus or forecasting the weather). Describe probability guidelines.

- ❒ Form pairs. Give each pair five individual-sized boxes of cereal. (Each person in a pair must have the same type of cereal. Different groups may have different types of cereals.) Instruct pairs to predict the number of cereal pieces in each box.

- ❒ After the first box, test their predictions by counting out the pieces.

- ❒ Repeat for the remaining boxes using established probability guidelines.

- ❒ Review each pair's predictions. Discuss and determine which predictions were valid. Review the probability guidelines and repeat the task with another set of items.

VARIATION

1. Use musical notation from a popular song to show predictable patterning.

2. Use bags of small stones (predicting weight based on size of bag) or seedlings that sprout (predicting how long to the full sprout).

Other Intelligences

- Verbal/linguistic
- Logical/mathematical
- Interpersonal

ACTIVITY 187

Internship in Science

Targeted Grades: Secondary

ACTIVITY AT A GLANCE

Purpose

- To gain direct experience working in a science-related profession

When to Use

- After the first semester or quarter with secondary students who have taken science classes or have science-related work experience

What You'll Need

- List of available internships in community
- Journals

WHAT-TO-DO CHECKLIST

☐ Provide interested students with a list of open internships within the local science community (such as working in botanical gardens, missions, university science departments, the school's science department, or local manufacturing companies with in-house labs).

☐ Arrange interviews for the students. Ask students to prepare for interviews by writing questions to ask to identify their roles, responsibilities, job expectations, and criteria for success during the internships. Have students role-play the interviewing process.

☐ Ask students who obtain internships to keep journals (see Activity 153) of their experiences. Provide targeted questions or topics for different checkpoints of their internships (such as first impressions, description of work done in the company or department, and the most important thing learned to date).

☐ During the internship, visit the site, observe the student, and confer with the student and supervisor.

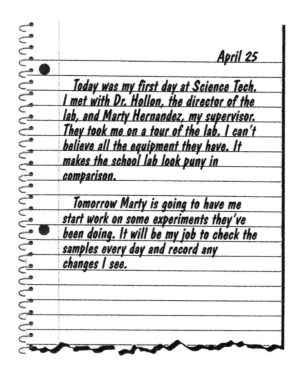

April 25

Today was my first day at Science Tech. I met with Dr. Hollon, the director of the lab, and Marty Hernandez, my supervisor. They took me on a tour of the lab. I can't believe all the equipment they have. It makes the school lab look puny in comparison.

Tomorrow Marty is going to have me start work on some experiments they've been doing. It will be my job to check the samples every day and record any changes I see.

VARIATIONS

1. Let interested students seek their own internships.

2. Assign students to research (through interviews) a person working in a science-related profession. Brainstorm a master list of interview questions related to the type of work the person does, requirements of the job (such as education, skills, and aptitude), working conditions, and satisfactions or drawbacks of the job. Allow students to present their information as a written report, in a journal or newsletter format, or on videotape.

Other Intelligences

- Verbal/linguistic
- Intrapersonal

ACTIVITY 188

Nature Directions

Targeted Grades: Elementary and Middle

ACTIVITY AT A GLANCE

Purpose

- To use physical landmarks and geographical features to provide directions to a specific location

- To focus attention on the natural environment
- To sharpen students' observation skills

When to Use

- At the beginning of the school year or course

What You'll Need

- Sketch paper

WHAT-TO-DO CHECKLIST

☐ Ask for two to three volunteers to describe the route they take from their homes to the school.

☐ After their responses, ask if they could describe the route without using any street names and using only geographical features (such as hill, trees, or rock).

☐ Ask a volunteer to draw a map using only geographical features on the board or overhead.

☐ As a class, brainstorm a list of geographical features and physical landmarks such as buildings or fences that can be used to provide directions.

☐ Ask students to draw maps that illustrate the route from their homes to the school. Instruct them to use pictures or symbols only (no words allowed) to represent geographical features and physical landmarks. Stress the need for specificity and clarity.

☐ Share maps and display them in a gallery (see Activity 51). Follow up with a group discussion to review the activity and students' reactions. Ask students when this type of map would be especially helpful.

VARIATIONS

1. Ask students to draw maps from one specific point in the schoolyard (or other outdoor area) to another using only geographical features and physical landmarks. Randomly distribute completed maps and have students use the provided directions to move from one location to another.

2. Use in conjunction with a literature selection that provides detailed setting descriptions. Ask students to draw maps that show a particular area or locality.

3. Combine with a study on topographical features of maps.

Other Intelligences

- Verbal/linguistic
- Visual/spatial

ACTIVITY 189

Cause and Effect

Targeted Grades: Middle and Secondary

ACTIVITY AT A GLANCE

Purpose

- To analyze cause-and-effect relationships by using a graphic organizer

When to Use

- During a lesson or unit with curriculum material that calls for or demonstrates the importance of cause-and-effect analysis
- When a situation arises in a lab experiment that calls for a cause-and-effect analysis

What You'll Need

- Model of fishbone diagram

WHAT-TO-DO CHECKLIST

❐ Identify prior knowledge (see Activity 54) of cause-and-effect relationships.

❐ Display the fishbone diagram (see Activity 44) on the board or overhead.

❏ Demonstrate how to use the diagram to illustrate cause and effect. For example, select an environmental-related problem or effect, such as polluted beaches, and write this in the "effect" box (fish's head).

❏ List primary causes on the diagonal bones of the fish's skeleton. Record supporting evidence or facts on the secondary (or horizontal) bones.

❏ Review the entire diagram to understand how the elements that compose the fish's skeleton contribute to or cause the effect (fish's head).

❏ Ask students to select a content-related topic (such as energy flow cutoff or photosynthesis). Explain the selected topic briefly before asking students to create a fishbone diagram to show the cause-and-effect relationship. Share completed diagrams with a carousel (see Activity 10).

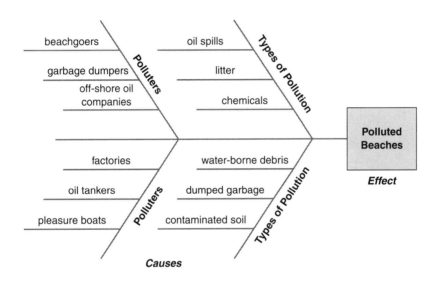

❏ Close with a discussion of what students learned about cause-and-effect relationships and when they might use this tool (see Activity 9).

VARIATIONS

1. Use cooperative groups (see Activity 128) to complete the fishbone diagrams.

2. Use in conjunction with a history or literature lesson. Have students identify a problem, effect, or outcome of a key event, and then to list the causes and contributing factors on the fish bones.

Other Intelligences

- Verbal/linguistic
- Visual/spatial
- Interpersonal

ACTIVITY 190

Science Exhibition

Targeted Grades: All

ACTIVITY AT A GLANCE

Purpose

- To create a science exhibit at the end of a unit or semester of scientific study
- To provide opportunities for students to use their cumulative knowledge to display information in a public forum

When to Use

- At the end of a major lesson, unit, or semester

What You'll Need

- Videotape or DVD on a world's fair or exhibition
- VCR or DVD player
- Books and information on science fairs
- Sample exhibits
- Journals (optional)

WHAT-TO-DO CHECKLIST

- ❏ Activate students' prior knowledge (see Activity 54) about exhibitions (such as at museums, the Epcot Center, or science fairs).

- ❏ Discuss the purpose of an exhibition. Show students a videotape about a recent world's fair or other exhibitions.

- ❏ Assign the creation of a science exhibit well in advance of its due date. Provide criteria for success (such as a single idea, data chart, visual display, and so on) (see Activity 164). Show samples of exhibits from previous classes and highlight the notable qualities.

- ❏ As a class, brainstorm a list of topics or ideas that could be used for the science exhibit (such as Tinkertoys arranged to show energy flow or a chemical reaction).

- ❏ Post the list in a visible spot for reference by students needing ideas. Provide books on science exhibitions for reference as well.

- ❏ Define expectations for time devoted to the exhibits and the time and location of the exhibition. Ask students to invite parents, relatives, and other classes.

- ❏ Create posters (see Activity 61) or signs to advertise the exhibition.

❐ Coach as needed (see Activity 137). Encourage a variety of media, visual charts, and so on.

❐ Hold the exhibition.

❐ Follow up with a discussion of the activity, what students learned, and what they would do the same or differently for future exhibitions.

VARIATIONS

1. Allow students to work in teams.

2. Visit a museum and arrange for the museum staff to explain its criteria for an exhibition.

3. Have students keep a journal (see Activity 153) of the steps taken in preparing the exhibition.

4. Brainstorm exhibition criteria with the students.

Other Intelligences

- Verbal/linguistic
- Visual/spatial
- Bodily/kinesthetic

ACTIVITY 191

Science Yearbook

Targeted Grades: Middle and Secondary

ACTIVITY AT A GLANCE

Purpose

- To create a visual and written record of class accomplishments in science

When to Use

- Throughout the year as a synthesis of the year's science curriculum

What You'll Need

- Duplication equipment and materials
- Camera

WHAT-TO-DO CHECKLIST

☐ At the start of the year, develop the criteria for a high-quality science yearbook. Post these criteria in an area designated for yearbook-related information (see Activity 8).

☐ Call for volunteers for a yearbook staff for the science class. Be sure everyone has a job (photographer, writer, artist, and editor) and knows the responsibilities and how to accomplish them (see Activity 140). Note that everyone in the class should contribute.

☐ Decide on the yearbook's format (such as sequential, thematic, and so on) and allow one day a month for students to work in class on their specific contributions.

☐ On a monthly basis, ask students to check progress with the yearbook. Use the rubric (see Activity 8).

☐ Near the end of the year, spend two weeks in class assembling the yearbook. This is a key part of the year's review and a time to help students synthesize what they have learned.

☐ Print or reproduce yearbooks and distribute at the end of the school year. Celebrate with a class dedicated to yearbook signing and reviewing students' accomplishments.

VARIATIONS

1. Allow students with like jobs to work as teams.

2. Keep a library of past yearbooks as models for the class.

Other Intelligences

- All

ACTIVITY 192

Bubble Talk

Targeted Grades: Elementary and Middle

ACTIVITY AT A GLANCE

Purpose

- To provide directions for a lab experiment

When to Use

- After teaching an important lab procedure to heighten students' recall and to increase their understanding of why the procedure is important

What You'll Need

- Chart paper and markers

WHAT-TO-DO CHECKLIST

❏ On the board or overhead, write a list of necessary steps to conduct a lab experiment. Form student pairs and assign each pair one step of the procedure.

❏ Provide each pair with chart paper and markers. Show students how to divide the paper into four to six sequenced boxes. In the boxes, the pair will illustrate two people performing a specific step of the procedure, using figures and bubbles to show dialogue and action.

❏ After the bubbles are complete, ask each pair to find other pairs who completed different steps of the procedure and to tape their drawings together in sequence to illustrate the entire procedure.

❏ Display completed procedures on the wall and encourage students to view the completed projects (see Activity 51). Close by mediating a discussion of this project's value.

VARIATIONS

1. Use bubbles to help students hypothesize (see Activity 73) about or imagine the thinking processes of famous scientists at work on a specific project (such as Thomas Edison, Marie Curie, Jonas Salk, and Jane Goodall).

2. Use bubbles to create cartoons that depict extreme positions on contemporary scientific issues.

3. Use illustrated procedures as instructions to perform an actual lab experiment.

Other Intelligences

- Verbal/linguistic
- Logical/mathematical
- Visual/spatial
- Interpersonal

ACTIVITY 193

Discovery Game

Targeted Grades: Middle

ACTIVITY AT A GLANCE

Purpose

- To examine like items using inductive reasoning skills

When to Use

- As a lesson to introduce inductive reasoning
- Prior to a lesson introducing the use of microscopes

What You'll Need

- Seven canisters
- Water
- Mud
- Food dye
- Five different colors of solidified gelatin

WHAT-TO-DO CHECKLIST

- ❏ Line up seven similar canisters. In one, put water and color with food dye. In a second, put muddy water. Put a different color of solidified gelatin in each of the remaining canisters.

- ❏ Draw a two-column T-chart (see Activity 163) on the board or overhead and label columns as "true" and "not true." Ask students to describe what they see. List student responses in the appropriate column of the chart.

- ❏ After the lists are completed, ask students to explain why specific descriptions are in each column. (Answers might be that the true statements are accurate observations or valid conclusions, the false statements are inaccurate observations or assumptions.)

- ❏ Explain that the type of thinking they used—arriving at a general conclusion from specific data—is called inductive reasoning. Identify other instances where they have used or seen inductive reasoning being used.

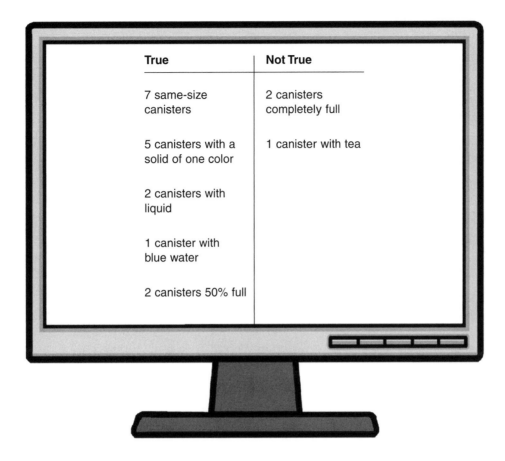

True	Not True
7 same-size canisters	2 canisters completely full
5 canisters with a solid of one color	1 canister with tea
2 canisters with liquid	
1 canister with blue water	
2 canisters 50% full	

VARIATIONS

1. Use pairs or trios. Give each group a set of samples that look alike in one way.

2. Use sample pieces of music that are alike in only one way.

Other Intelligences

- Verbal/linguistic
- Logical/mathematical

ACTIVITY 194

Futuristic Science Fair

Targeted Grades: Middle and Secondary

ACTIVITY AT A GLANCE

Purpose

- To design and build a prototype of a futuristic invention and display this invention at a class futuristic science fair

When to Use

- Throughout the year as a motivating tool to stimulate creativity, hypothetical thinking, and interest in scientific concepts

What You'll Need

- Materials to build models
- Background information on futuristic displays

WHAT-TO-DO CHECKLIST

❏ Show pictures and tell a story about a world's fair that exhibited futuristic displays, or displays containing hypothetical future inventions. Identify some of the inventions that were displayed and whether they were ever mass-produced.

❏ Tell the class that it will end the school year by creating its own futuristic science fair. After each unit in science, brainstorm a list of ideas for futuristic inventions based on what students have learned. Post lists in a designated area.

❏ Form mixed-ability invention teams (see Activity 145). Each team will take one idea from the list and adapt and improve it, making the idea more useful and beneficial.

❏ Ask each student to draw a design of the future product.

❏ Ask each team to review its members' designs and discuss the viability and feasibility of each in terms of building an actual model. Have students select one design and build a model of the new invention.

❏ Have teams build displays to exhibit their models, create advertisements promoting their products, and write invitations to the fair to other classes, parents, and community members.

❏ Set up and hold the fair.

❏ Brainstorm enough awards that all receive a ribbon of some type.

VARIATIONS

1. Engage parents and community members to judge the fair. Give a variety of awards.

2. Have students build models and compete by demonstrating their inventions.

3. Create a class newsletter that includes news about the fair and drawings, articles, cartoons, surveys, and interviews about the inventions.

4. Draw parallels to manufacturers' design-to-production cycle (such as idea conception; design and revisions; analyses of materials, production method, and labor

costs; building prototypes; production; and marketing and advertising). Ask each team to create a working portfolio that includes notes from brainstorming and planning sessions; all sketches, drawings, and doodles; and all other related materials. Upon completion of the project, ask each team to write a five- to six-paragraph essay describing its design-to-production process and to include examples from its portfolio to illustrate different stages of the process.

Other Intelligences

- Verbal/linguistic
- Logical/mathematical
- Visual/spatial
- Interpersonal
- Intrapersonal

ACTIVITY 195

Nature Rubbings

Targeted Grades: Elementary and Middle

ACTIVITY AT A GLANCE

Purpose

- To demonstrate how symmetry appears in nature

When to Use

- At the beginning of a lesson or unit that will use the concept of symmetry

What You'll Need

- A variety of leaves
- Drawing paper and crayons

WHAT-TO-DO CHECKLIST

- ❏ Take the class on a nature walk. Have each student collect several leaves of different sizes, shapes, and textures.

- ❏ Ask students to cover each leaf, vein side up, with a sheet of paper and rub over it with a crayon. Show students how to use one hand to prevent paper from moving while they rub with the other hand.

❏ Hang the completed rubbings and discuss the variations. Use different examples of rubbings to illustrate the symmetry in the leaves.

❏ Ask students in a round-robin questioning pattern (see Activity 24), "What conclusions do you draw from what you have seen in the rubbings?"

VARIATIONS

1. Select other plants to use for the rubbings. Contrast symmetry in tree leaves with other plant leaves.

2. Use clay to form impressions of leaves and stems. Have students soften the clay into patties that cover the leaves and stems so they can get a strong impression.

Other Intelligences

- Verbal/linguistic
- Logical/mathematical
- Visual/spatial
- Bodily/kinesthetic.

ACTIVITY 196

Window to the World

A Mural

Targeted Grades: All

ACTIVITY AT A GLANCE

Purpose

- To collaborate on a class mural that illustrates concepts learned over an extended period

When to Use

- Throughout the school year to motivate interest in science study and to help students communicate what they have learned through a visual medium

What You'll Need

- Paint
- Paintbrushes

- Poster boards or chart paper
- Pictures of sample murals
- A blank wall

WHAT-TO-DO CHECKLIST

❐ Inform students at the beginning of the year or course that they will create a class mural at the end of the year or course that illustrates what they have learned. Show pictures of sample murals.

❐ Identify a place for the mural (such as a blank wall in the cafeteria or hallway, or a wall in the community).

❐ During the year, brainstorm ideas for the mural after each unit, record ideas, and post the list of ideas in the room (or on a designated "Mural" bulletin board).

❐ Decide on a central unifying theme and tie ideas to this theme.

❐ Begin to plan the mural a few months before the end of the year. Use a strategy that involves the entire class in the planning and painting of the mural.

❐ Review the criteria: the content of their science study must be central to what is depicted in the mural (see Activity 8).

❐ Assemble the students in mixed-ability groups (see Activity 145) based on their sketches. Have students paint the mural.

❐ Use the rubric (see Activity 8) or Mrs. Potter's Questions (see Activity 176) to assess both individual contributions and teamwork.

VARIATIONS

1. Divide the mural into sections and identify a class theme. Have students work in groups to complete designated sections of the mural.

2. If there is no wall available, use large strips of chart paper or poster boards taped together.

3. Create a Mural Graffiti board (using chart paper) where students post ideas and key concepts during a unit. Post new chart paper for each unit or whenever a sheet becomes full, save the completed chart paper, and use them as a review of all units during the actual planning stage of the mural.

Other Intelligences

- Visual/spatial
- Interpersonal

ACTIVITY 197

Scientific Scenario

Targeted Grades: Elementary and Middle

ACTIVITY AT A GLANCE

Purpose

- To identify and research current issues and concerns presented in a case scenario

When to Use

- At the beginning of a lesson or unit to stimulate interest in a unit of study that has a connection to a current issue

What You'll Need

- Copies of a prepared scenario
- Access to library materials or the Internet, or both

WHAT-TO-DO CHECKLIST

❑ Prepare a scenario (a scenario is a short, one- or two-paragraph story that describes the case or incident) related to the key concepts in a unit (such as deer eating local flora as an introduction to the food cycle). Be sure the scenario meets the following criteria (see Activity 8):
  - Brief (two to three paragraphs)
  - Describes a simple instance of a common problem
  - Sets up a problem situation that is not easily solved
  - Illustrates the issues central to the unit of study

❑ Distribute copies of the scenario to each student.

❑ Assign students to find and read two to three articles related to the issue using library or Internet resources, or both.

❑ Conduct an all-class discussion, identifying the following:
  - The issue in the scenario
  - How the specific case ties to a larger issue or issues
  - How the issue or issues relates to the articles read

VARIATIONS

1. Use several different scenarios on the same issue. Ask students to compare the key problem in each scenario to identify the main issue.

2. Use the Problem-Solving Chart (see Activity 25) to identify the issue.

3. Assign students a three- to five-paragraph essay to report the results of their research. Request that they reference one to two facts or examples from the resource materials they used, and that they identify sources in text. (Model a demonstration if introducing this concept or if students need a review.)

Other Intelligences

- Verbal/linguistic
- Interpersonal

ACTIVITY 198

Video Record

Targeted Grades: Middle and Secondary

ACTIVITY AT A GLANCE

Purpose

- To videotape a lab experiment and to use the videotape to identify individual performance, group technique, best practices, or areas for improvement

When to Use

- During a lesson or project to assess students' abilities, to identify "model" techniques for sharing with other students in the class, and to enable students to see themselves in action

What You'll Need

- Video or DVD camera
- VCR or DVD player
- Blank videotapes or writeable DVDs
- Journals (optional)

WHAT-TO-DO CHECKLIST

- ❏ Prior to a lab experiment, set up a camera to capture one group at work. Instruct group members to narrate what they are doing as they perform the experiment.

- ❏ View the video with the group upon completion of the experiment. Ask students to identify specific instances that illustrate strong techniques or model practices. Discuss the overall group technique and ways to improve it.

- ❏ In following experiments, use other groups until all members of the class have had a review.

VARIATIONS

1. Record one group each day of the experiment and view the results with the group or entire class.

2. Edit a tape of best lab practices to share with the class.

3. Ask students to write individual assessments of both their own and the group's performance and to recommend one area for improvement.

4. Make a rubric (see Activity 8) before starting the experiment. Use this in each group's review.

5. Have students keep a record of the feedback in their journals (see Activity 153). Have them use that feedback before their next experiment.

Other Intelligences

- Verbal/linguistic
- Logical/mathematical
- Visual/spatial

ACTIVITY 199

Just Collect It

Targeted Grades: Elementary and Middle

ACTIVITY AT A GLANCE

Purpose

- To learn the techniques of collecting and classifying animate and inanimate matter

When to Use

- Throughout a lesson or unit to connect the learning of the process of classification to science units in the curriculum

What You'll Need

- Poster boards
- Glue

WHAT-TO-DO CHECKLIST

❒ Activate students' prior knowledge of collecting using the KWL (see Activity 54) or other advanced organizer. Ask students to bring in and share their collections of stamps, coins, or bottles.

❑ Invite students to make a scientific collection to learn the principles of classification. As a class, select a curriculum-related object to collect.

❑ Conduct a collection hunt and help students gather many samples.

❑ Ask students to sort the objects into at least four groups. Provide each student with a large sheet of poster board and invite students to create visual displays of their collections that show this grouping. Have students label each group and note the "critical attribute" of each object that determined its inclusion in that group. Display the collections.

❑ Create a gallery walk (see Activity 51).

VARIATIONS

1. Take students on a field trip (see Activity 45) to a museum where they can see how collections are made on a grand scale.

2. Have students work in groups to collect items and construct visual displays.

3. Conclude by inviting parents to a museum night.

4. Invite students to use these techniques to collect and classify their favorite characters from literature.

Other Intelligences

- Visual/spatial
- Verbal/linguistic
- Interpersonal

ACTIVITY 200
Agree/Disagree Issues

Targeted Grades: Middle and Secondary

ACTIVITY AT A GLANCE

Purpose

- To examine a position related to a scientific issue

When to Use

- During a lesson or unit to wrap around a topical issue related to the curriculum

What You'll Need

- Copies of Agree/Disagree Chart

WHAT-TO-DO CHECKLIST

❏ Introduce the class to a science-based current event issue in the community or state (such as laws regarding auto emissions or state wilderness preservation). Ask students to share what they know about the issue.

❏ Form mixed-ability groups (see Activity 145) of three with roles (see Activity 140), guidelines (see Activity 138), and a clear goal (see Activity 159).

❏ Distribute copies of the Agree/Disagree Chart. Using the board or overhead, list statements about the issue that show a variety of positions.

❏ Allow time for students to check their position on each statement in the "Before" column.

❏ Discuss areas where students agree and disagree. Probe and discuss reasoning on all positions. Collect charts for future use.

Agree/Disagree Chart

Topic: Overpopulation of deer

	Before		After	
Statements	Agree	Disagree	Agree	Disagree
1. Allow hunting to to reduce number of deer.		X	X	
2. Deer hunting is cruelty to animals.	X			X
3. Deer are starving to death due to lack of vegetation.	X		X	
4. Deer are nuisances that destroy shrubbery and other plants.		X		X
5. Capture deer and relocate them in undeveloped areas.	X		X	

❐ Study the topic and ask students to look for facts related to the agree/disagree statements.

❐ After studying the topic, redistribute the charts. Ask students to check their position on each statement in the "After" column. Discuss changes in students' positions and probe for rationale behind their choices.

VARIATIONS

1. After students check their "before" positions, pair students with opposing views, and hold an all-class debate.

2. Prior to studying the unit, pair students with opposing views. Ask students to write a persuasive letter to their partners in which they try to convince them to change their viewpoint. Upon completing the unit of study and reexamining their positions, ask students to respond to the original letters.

Other Intelligences

- Verbal/linguistic
- Visual/spatial
- Interpersonal

ACTIVITY 201

Issue Investigation

Targeted Grades: Middle and Secondary

ACTIVITY AT A GLANCE

Purpose

- To investigate a hypothesis about a current world problem or science-based issue

When to Use

- To develop students' problem-solving skills and provide practice in using content material to back up opinions and prove hypotheses

What You'll Need

- No materials necessary

WHAT-TO-DO CHECKLIST

❐ Select a current scientific issue and present a hypothesis (such as, "Global warming is caused primarily by human's use of fossil fuels").

❐ Divide the class into cooperative research teams (see Activity 128). Set the teams to work together with identified roles (see Activity 140), guidelines (see Activity 138), and a clear goal (see Activity 129).

❐ Ask each team to do initial research on the Internet. From the data they find, have them agree on a pro or con hypothesis about the major question.

❐ Direct each group to identify one scientist who will support their hypothesis. Have them write and e-mail a letter asking that scientist for facts that support the position.

❐ While waiting for a reply, have the groups use the Internet to find additional online support for their position.

❐ After groups have amassed their data, they are to prepare a poster (see Activity 61) that states the hypothesis and shows the supporting data. (If they cannot find sufficient data, they will show that the hypothesis failed.)

❐ Teams should then hand in their posters and participate in a carousel (see Activity 10).

❐ Conclude by holding an all-class discussion on what it takes to prove a hypothesis.

VARIATIONS

1. Use in conjunction with a unit or lesson on researching skills. Require students to use multiple reference materials to obtain additional information on their topics and to use this information to support their recommended solutions.

2. In place of class presentations with posters, ask each group to write a letter to the editor of an imaginary newspaper explaining and defending the group's position. Display letters on a large mock-up of a newspaper editorial page or compile all letters in a sample newspaper and distribute copies to students.

Other Intelligences

- Verbal/linguistic
- Logical/mathematical
- Visual/spatial

Resource A

DESIGNING ACTIVE LEARNING LESSONS AND PROJECTS

To design a lesson or project that increases the amount of student engagement is a simple task. Think about this task as you would if you were planting a garden. When planting a garden, you will have a number of jobs to do. None is difficult but all are important if you want to produce an abundance of beautiful flowers and delicious vegetables.

First, start with the soil. Prepare it well by turning it over, adding fertilizers, and breaking down the chunks of dirt. Then select what flower and vegetable plants you want, where each will grow best, the color combinations, and so forth. To follow this analogy, use this checklist.

1. Review the required STANDARD for the lesson or unit you are going to teach. Look at both the process such as "students will understand . . ." or "students will compare . . .") and at the content (such as "the concept of a fraction" or "the economic causes of World War II").

   The content element of the standard tells what might be tested; the process element tells how the students will have to think in order to answer the test question.

   The STANDARD.

   The process verb: _____

   The content: _____

2. Select the activity that you are going to use. Review it.

A. The Title
   Back to the Future

B. Targeted Grades: Elementary, Middle, and Secondary

   The targeted or recommended grades. See "Variations" below if there are recommended adjustments for use with other grades. Make whatever adjustments in the checklist that you think will make the activities more appropriate for the students you are teaching.

C. Activity at a Glance

Purpose

- To review prior knowledge and connect to a new topic by constructing a time capsule.

This describes the intention of the activity. In this case, the intention is to have students start the lesson by reviewing what they already know about the content you are going to teach and how you are going to do it (such as construct a time capsule).

When to Use

- At the beginning of a course, unit, lesson or project

This tells you where the activity fits best in the lesson or project.

What You'll Need

- Artifacts collected by students
- A container for the collected artifacts

This details the materials you will need to prepare before you start the lesson. You may add other items that you will need in the lesson. For instance, you may want to add student journals for use throughout the lesson. If you combine this activity with another at the end of the lesson such as making posters to display what the students learned, you will need to add the required additional materials.

D. What-to-Do Checklist

- ❑ Show students or ask older students to research news stories about time capsules.

- ❑ Use a question web to brainstorm what students would want to include in a time capsule from this year.

- ❑ Put students into groups of three. Each group is to find artifacts that they will put into the capsule. Have each artifact represent some idea or concept from the lesson you are introducing with this advanced organizer.

- ❑ Select a container that will last at least ten years when it is buried in the ground.

- ❑ Label the artifacts that the class selects to include in the capsule.

- ❑ Allow each group to propose how it will decorate the outside of the container. Select the winning design.

- ❑ Carefully pack the capsule container.

- ❑ Locate a place to bury the container.

- ❑ Invite each student to write a letter to the principal telling where the capsule is located and when it should be dug up.

The checklist walks you through the major procedures of the activity. Because this checklist covers only the prior knowledge element of your lesson, there are several things you will want to remember as you design the lesson. Remember, you are not using a script that you must blindly follow step by step. You are making a lesson that will best fit the needs and intelligences of the students in this class.

a. What is the standard that you selected for this lesson?
b. After you have used this activity to check student's prior knowledge, how will you connect the prior knowledge to the standard. For instance, you may decide to have items in the time capsule that are symbolic of the main ideas, concepts, or facts that you will want students to draw from the lesson. At the end of the activity, you will want the students to capture the ideas or facts. For this purpose, the letter to the principal should review these core ideas and connect to the lesson goal.
c. Does the checklist include any references to tactics that are unfamiliar to you? If so, refer to that tactic, review it, and see how you will incorporate it into the lesson. If you have not used the referenced tactic with this class, be sure that you carefully teach the class how to use it before going on. Once they are familiar with the tactic, you will only have to mention the title and quickly review the procedures. Failure to make students familiar with a tactic that you use can lead to discipline problems from confused students.
d. Design the body of the lesson or project. In some cases, you may elect to combine this advanced organizer activity with an active lesson or project design from this book.
e. If the lesson design you select from this book does not include an assessment strategy, make sure that you add an active assessment strategy at the end of the lesson.
f. Revise the checklist to fit your style with your intent to develop the multiple intelligences of the students in this class as you teach the content called for in the standard.
g. Assess the lesson or project to see how well it contributes to building a classroom that promotes shared learning and a learning community among the students.

E. Variations

In this section, you will find recommendations to make changes within an active learning experience. You may wish to make different changes based on what you know about the students in each class.

F. Other Intelligences

This element identifies other intelligences that are included in the activity or tactic.

Resource B

Blacklines

AGREE/DISAGREE CHART

Topic: _____

Statements	Before		After	
	Agree	Disagree	Agree	Disagree

GOAL CHART

Goal	Rank	Why Important	How to Achieve	Checkup	By When

GROUP ASSESSMENT

Group name _____ Date _____

Activity _____

_____

_____

_____

What we did well: _____

_____

_____

_____

What we need to improve: _____

_____

_____

_____

Questions we have: _____

_____

_____

_____

INFLUENCE CHART

Important person	How related	Why important	Influence	Results

INTERNET HOBBY SEARCH

1. What are your special interests?

2. What are your special talents?

3. What hobbies do you have that match your interests or talents?

4. What hobbies would you like to learn more about?

5. Pick one hobby and using the Internet identify resources for learning about this hobby.

Select two to five resources. Study them and prepare a three- to five-minute talk that describes the hobby, explains talents or skills needed for this hobby, and tells what your personal interest in this hobby is and how it might benefit you.

PEOPLE SEARCH

Find a person who . . .

1. _____	2. _____
3. _____	8. _____
5. _____	6. _____
7. _____	8. _____

Plus/Minus/Interesting (PMI)	
P(+) **Pluses**	
M(−) **Minuses**	
I(?) **Interesting** **questions**	

PROBLEM-SOLVING MODEL

The problem	Strategies to use	The result

SCENARIOS

"Mary is a new girl in school. She has no friends. On the playground she is standing all by herself." Your group sees her. Decide how you can help her. Make a play without words to show this.

"Juan has lost his milk for lunch." Decide what you can do to help him. Make a play without words to show this.

"Sue Ellen forgot to bring a note from home to go on the field trip." Decide what you can do to help her. Make a play without words to show this.

"Carl was in a fight on the bus with a bully. He is afraid to get on the bus again." Decide what you can do to help him. Make a play without words to show this.

"Marie was absent for a whole week. She has a lot of math to catch up." Decide what you can do to help her. Make a play without words to show this.

"Margaret's best friend was hurt. The friend fell from her bike and hit her head. The friend is in the hospital." Decide what you can do to help her. Make a play without words to show this.

"Carla's mom forgot to pick her up after school. Your sister is going to pick you and your friends up and drive you home." Decide how you can help her. Make a play without words to show this.

"Jamie lost his new team jacket. He thinks someone stole it." Decide how you can help him. Make a play without words to show this.

"Some big kids said mean things to Kate. They hurt her feelings." Decide how you can help her. Make a play without words to show this.

"Gerry just had a fight with her group. She walked away. She said she never wants to be in that group again." Decide how you can help her. Make a play without words to show this.

"Jo called Tony, her best friend, a bad name." Decide how you can help her. Make a play without words to show this.

"Tom doesn't have any lunch. He is very embarrassed." Decide how you can help him. Make a play without words to show this.

"A gang member wants Ralph to join the gang and deliver crack." Decide how you can help him. Make a play without words to show this.

SELF-PROGRESS CHART

Name _____

Check Date _____

Goal	Progress check	End date

SELF-REVIEW QUESTIONS

How far have I progressed toward my goals?

What are the barriers I have overcome?

What barriers yet remain?

What help do I need?

Resource C

Glossary

ABC criteria: Identification of goal as being achievable, believable, and controllable.

Aha!: The moment of discovery when one learns something new or a confusing concept suddenly becomes clear; also called Eureka!

Artifact: End product of student work, such as an essay, story, sketch, sculpture, mobile, writing sample, or artwork.

Attribute web: Visual diagram that illustrates attributes or characteristics of a topic or concept.

Base group: Core group of students who work together over an extended period.

Brainstorm: Group process to trigger spontaneous, fluent production of ideas.

Bridge: Connection or transition between concepts or units; often used to connect new information with familiar concepts or prior knowledge.

Carousel: Group rotation to view displayed student work at multiple locations throughout a room.

Concept map: Visual diagram that illustrates relationships in free flowing thoughts.

Cooperative group: Structured small group in which members have designated roles and responsibilities.

DOVE guidelines: Guidelines to promote an open, nonjudgmental environment for group sharing. DOVE is an acronym representing the following: Defer judgment, Opt for original ideas, Vast number is needed, and Expand by piggybacking on others' ideas.

Fishbone: A diagram used to illustrate cause-and-effect relationships.

Four corners: Each corner of the room represents a different idea. Students are asked to select an idea and move to that corner for discussion.

Graphic organizer: Visual format used to organize ideas, concepts, and information. Also called visual organizer.

Human graph: Simulation of graph with participants physically positioning themselves along a continuum to indicate degree of agreement with an idea or issue.

Hurrah: Cheer or physical movement, or both, used to celebrate people and accomplishments (such as Whirly Bird, Standing "O"vation).

Jigsaw: Cooperative learning strategy that distributes portions of a whole to each person in a group to learn and then teach to the other members of the group.

Journal: A student diary consisting of verbal and visual entries that usually include personal reflections, self-assessments, and spontaneous writing.

KWL: Visual organizer to illustrate what one knows about a topic, what one wants to know, and what was learned; oftentimes used to identify prior knowledge of a topic.

Likert scale: Measurement tool that assesses performance on a gradient scale. Also used to rate opinions, show a position on an issue, and indicate frequency of occurrence (such as 1 = never, 3 = sometimes, 5 = always).

Log: A student record consisting of verbal and visual entries reflecting personal reactions to learning, usually in relation to a specific course or topic.

Matrix: Chart that classifies items by dual categories, given in both a column and a row. Items must meet the criteria of both categories.

Mind map: Visual representation of thinking strategy that starts with a central idea and branches off to new ideas. It can include pictures, patterns, and colors.

Mrs. Potter's Questions: Mrs. Potter represents a teacher who asks students to use four questions to assess their learning and performance: "What was I expected to do?" "What did I do well?" "If I did the same task again, what would I do differently?" and "What help do I need?"

Paired think-aloud: Strategy that involves one person in a pair verbalizing her thinking as the partner listens, monitors, and then asks questions for clarification.

PMI: Graphic organizer or thinking strategy used to identify the pluses, minuses, and interesting questions related to an activity or lesson. (Developed by Edward de Bono. See de Bono, 1976.)

Portfolio: Collection of student work, usually comprising a student's best work or work that shows development. Also used to collect a group's or class's work.

Portmanteau: Strategy of combining two words to create a new word with a new meaning (such as toehole: a hole in one's sock that expands as one plays with it).

Problem solving: Specific strategies that use creative synthesis and critical analysis to generate viable alternatives to perplexing situations.

Problem-solving model: Visual organizer used to identify a problem, list strategies to use to solve the problem, and describe results of each strategy.

Question web: Visual diagram showing questions and answers branching off a central concept or idea.

Random check: Assessment of student learning at sporadic moments, not based on a pattern or schedule.

Ranking: Rating system that prioritizes choices.

Rebus: Representation of words through pictures

Round-robin questioning pattern: Response in turn around a group.

Rubric: Assessment tool that specifies criteria for different levels of performance.

Self-assessment: Any tool or strategy used by an individual to examine and evaluate one's own work.

Sequence chart: Chart that lists steps of a process or procedure in the order in which they need to occur.

Six-inch voice: Soft voice that cannot be heard beyond a six-inch radius. Also called ten-centimeter voice.

Standard: Criterion used to assess performance.

Storyboard: A series of sketches that show action and dialogue.

T-chart: Chart made by writing a "T" to form two columns.

Target: Visual aid of three concentric circles used to identify priorities.

Think-pair-share: Strategy that allows individual thinking time, discussion with a partner, and then all-class sharing.

Three-level questions: Questions aligned to the three levels of thought identified in the three-level intellect model.

Three-Story Intellect verbs: Categorization of verbs to use in formulating questions that elicit responses based on different levels of thinking; such as one-story verbs prompt factual recall; two-story verbs ask for comparisons, reasoning, and generalizations; and three-story verbs stimulate imagination, hypotheses, and syntheses. Also called three-level questions.

Triple T-chart: T-chart with three columns.

Triple Venn diagram: Venn diagram comprising three circles.

Venn diagram: Overlapping circles used to compare and contrast objects, people, ideas, and so on.

Walk through: Demonstrate or model steps in a process or activity.

Web: Visual diagram that illustrates new ideas and concepts branching off of a central topic or idea.

Wraparound: A structured answering strategy in which students respond in turn.

Bibliography

Bellanca, J. (2007). *Graphic organizers.* Thousand Oaks, CA: Corwin Press.

Bellanca, J., & Fogarty, R. (1991). *Blueprints for thinking in the cooperative classroom.* Thousand Oaks, CA: Corwin Press.

————. (1993). *Patterns for thinking, patterns for transfer.* Arlington Heights, Il: IRI/Skylight Training and Publishing.

————, eds. (1995). *Multiple intelligences: A collection.* Arlington Heights, IL: IRI/SkyLight Training and Publishing.

Bellanca, J., Chapman, C., & Swartz, E. (1997). *Multiple assessments for multiple intelligences (Course Ed.).* Arlington Heights, IL: IRI/SkyLight Training and Publishing.

Bellanca, J., & Rodriguez, E. (2006). *What is it about me that you can't teach?* Thousand Oaks, CA: Corwin Press.

Berman, S. (1995). *A multiple intelligences road to a quality classroom.* Thousand Oaks, CA: Corwin Press.

Brown, A. L., & Palincsar, A. S. (1989). "Guided, cooperative learning and individual knowledge acquisition." In L. B. Resnick (Ed.), *Knowing, learning, and instruction: Essays in honor of Robert Glaser.* Hillsdale, NJ: Lawrence Erlbaum.

Campbell, L. (1992). *Teaching and learning through multiple intelligences.* Seattle, WA: New Horizons for Learning.

Chapman, C. (1993). *If the shoe fits . . . How to develop multiple intelligences in the classroom.* Thousand Oaks, CA: Corwin Press.

Chapman, C., & Freeman, C. (1976). *Multiple intelligences centers and projects.* Thousand Oaks, CA: Corwin Press.

de Bono, E. (1976). *Teaching thinking.* New York: Penguin.

Feuerstein, R. (2001). *Mediated learning experience in teaching and counseling.* Jerusalem: ICELP Press.

Feuerstein, R., Feuerstein, R., & Rand, J. (2007). *Instrumental enrichment: An intervention program for cognitive modifiability.* Jerusalem: ICELP Press.

Fogarty, R. (1997). *Problem-based learning and other curriculum models for the multiple intelligences classroom.* Arlington Heights, IL: IRI/SkyLight Training and Publishing.

Gardner, H. (1983). *Frames of mind: The theory of multiple intelligences.* New York: Basic Books.

————. (1993). *Multiple intelligences: The theory in practice.* New York: HarperCollins.

Gregory, G. (2007). *Differentiated instructional strategies in practice.* Thousand Oaks: CA: Corwin Press.

Johnson, R., & Johnson, D. (1991). *Learning together and alone.* Interactive Book Co., Edina, MN.

Martin, H. (1996). *Multiple intelligences in the mathematics classroom.* Thousand Oaks, CA: Corwin Press.

Marzano, R., Pickering, D. J., & Pollack, J. E. (2001). *Classroom instruction that works.* ASCD, Alexandria, VA.

Murnane, R., & Levy, F. (1996). *Teaching the new basic skills: Principles for educating children to thrive in a changing economy.* New York: Free Press.

O'Connor, A. T., & Callahan-Young, S. (1994). *Seven windows to a child's world: 100 ideas for the multiple intelligences classroom.* Arlington Heights, IL: IRI/SkyLight Training and Publishing.

Perkins, D., & Salomon, G. (September, 1988). "Teaching for transfer." *Educational Leadership, 46:* 22–23.

Williams, B. (2007). *Multiple intelligences for differentiated learning.* Thousand Oaks, CA: Corwin Press.

Index

CORWIN PRESS

The Corwin Press logo—a raven striding across an open book—represents the union of courage and learning. Corwin Press is committed to improving education for all learners by publishing books and other professional development resources for those serving the field of PreK–12 education. By providing practical, hands-on materials, Corwin Press continues to carry out the promise of its motto: **"Helping Educators Do Their Work Better."**